GunDigest® PRES...

The ABCs of
RELOADING
10th Edition

Philip P. Massaro

Published by

Gun Digest® Books, an imprint of Caribou Media Group, LLC
Gun Digest Media
5600 W. Grande Market Drive, Suite 100
Appleton, WI 54913
www.gundigest.com

To order books or other products call 920.471.4522 ext. 104
or visit us online at **www.gundigeststore.com**

DISCLAIMER: Any and all loading data found in this book or previous editions is to be taken as reference material only. The publishers, editors, authors, contributors, and their entities bear no responsibility for the use by others of the data included in this book or the editions that came before it.

WARNING: For any modern firearm, it is essential that you adhere to the loading recommendations put forth in the reloading manuals of today's components manufacturers, as well as to the owners manual of the maker of your individual firearm (some of today's firearms are so specialized that they will chamber and function reliably only within a very narrow set of criteria in a given caliber range). The potential for things to go wrong is exacerbated in guns long out of production, those chambering obsolete cartridges, and those using cartridges containing black powder or cordite. As a separate caution, you must never fire any cartridge in any gun just because it looks similar to, or has a similar designation to, the cartridge the gun is chambered for. This can be extremely dangerous. Almost is not good enough, so if you are at all uncertain about the proper cartridge, have a competent gunsmith check the bullet diameter and case dimensions and firearms chamber and headspace.

ISBN-13: 978-1-951115-27-2

Design by Jong Cadelina
Edited by Corey Graff

Printed in the United States of America

10 9 8 7 6 5 4 3 2 1

TABLE OF CONTENTS

INTRODUCTION

Hello, and welcome to *The ABCs of Reloading 10th Edition*, your guide to learning how to reload your own ammunition. The act of reloading ammo, if done carefully and responsibly, is a safe, fun, and productive pastime. It will allow you to reuse spent cases and hulls and have more expendable ammunition for hunting, target practice, and plinking. It gives you the freedom and control to tune the ammo to the firearm; you can choose the projectile or shot size and weight, the velocity, and many other parameters that will affect your chosen combination's performance.

There is a special pride when you approach a target and see a tiny cluster of shots printed by loads you've assembled, or when you stand over a game animal taken with your creation. As you'll see, the process of reloading is simple. Yet, the subtleties of the methods and the results they yield can easily take one 'down the rabbit hole,' making the handloading process a lifelong pursuit of accuracy and optimum ballistic performance.

The concept is simple: Start with the used cartridge case or shotshell hull (the only reusable component of the equation). Reform it to a proper dimension, install a new primer. Add an appropriate charge of powder.

The author at the reloading bench.

And press the shot column or projectile. You may have seen eager-eyed shooters hunched over at the range, greedily picking up spent brass cases; these people are reloaders, and they intend to turn those spent cases into new ammunition. Quite obviously, you'll need a healthy supply of components (primer, powder, and projectiles), but you'll also need a specific set of specialized tools. That toolset can be minimalistic —

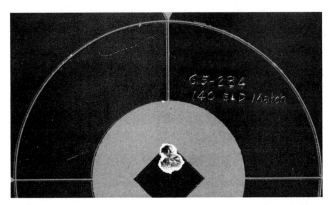

The 6.5-284 is an accurate cartridge, which can deliver pinpoint accuracy with handloaded ammunition.

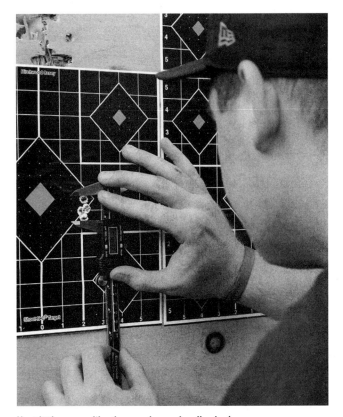

Neat little groups like these make any handloader happy.

I've made an obscene amount of ammunition with the simplest setups or those comprising the latest and greatest tools available. No matter, the goal is the same: to make the best ammo possible.

Let's be honest about a few things to keep things in perspective. Our factory ammunition is the best it has ever been and — when readily available — is more affordable than ever. If you are looking into reloading for its economic value, you may find it difficult to justify the investment unless you look at the big safari cartridges. With the expense of factory-loaded Nitro Express cartridges, you may be able to cut those costs considerably. But if you're comparing the prices of reloading the standard cartridges (say .223 Remington or 9mm Luger) vs. buying factory ammunition, you will be hard-pressed to beat the cost of factory ammo.

But cost isn't everything. Twice in the last decade, there has been a severe shortage of ammunition, to the point where the shelves are bare, and shooters began to panic. Having the means of providing your own loads is quite liberating, and it's nice to know that if the components are there, you will have the expertise to assemble them safely and reliably. Sheer availability is an excellent reason to learn how to reload ammunition.

Then there are those firearms chambered for cartridges, which are nearly impossible to obtain; you can either retire the gun or learn how to make cartridges for it. Reloading obsolete cartridges will put those guns back in the field. For example, I am very passionate about all things African safari, from the wildlife to the people to the classic rifles and cartridges associated with it. One of the more popular cartridges of the Golden Age of safari is the .318 Westley Richards, yet there are no factory-loaded ammunition sources. I turned to reloading to solve the problem, and I've had the pleasure of taking my .318 rifle and handloaded ammunition to Africa.

Lastly, there is the control and flexibility that reloading offers. There are projectiles available in component form for hunters, which aren't loaded by the ammunition manufacturers. Reloading will allow you to create

The author handloaded these 250-grain Woodleigh Weldcore bullets in his .318 Westley Richards. He recovered the bullet from a bull kudu.

custom loads, enhancing your standard cartridge's performance. The target crowd — and especially those who enjoy the extreme long-range shooting that has become so popular lately — very often rely upon handloaded ammunition to achieve the highest level of accuracy and precision.

Throughout this book, you will read the terms *reloading* and *handloading*. While often used interchangeably, I would like to differentiate between them for our purposes within this book. I use *reloading* for the processes of using spent cases or hulls and merely bringing them back to the point where they will function again. I may be attempting to replicate the original factory performance, or I could be concerned about the economic advantage. *Handloading* is more specific, in that its goal is to make ammunition as least as good as any factory stuff, if not better, often using new components. It's a slight difference, but you'll often hear shooters say, "I would never shoot reloads…" as if they are unsafe. Follow the processes outlined in this book. Your ammunition will not only be perfectly safe but in many cases, it will outperform factory loads when it comes to accuracy.

Reloading has a rich history, and many of our most revered gun writers were proficient handloaders. Philip B. Sharpe, Jack O'Connor, Elmer Keith, Col. Townsend Whelen, Finn Aagaard, Jon Sundra, Craig Boddington, and Layne Simpson all had a part in cartridge development. Each helped to keep old cartridges alive, and all are well-versed in metallic cartridges. Companies such as DuPont and Hodgdon (which began to sell surplus smokeless powder at the end of World War II), RCBS and Redding (developing reloading gear), Speer, Hornady, and Sierra (bullet manufacturers) all played a crucial role in the development of the equipment and components we use. Lyman has provided reloading data for decades, and there are many superb reloading manuals both in print and now on the Internet. Think of them as a list of recipes in a cookbook.

This book is not a compilation of load data — that is what the reloading manuals are for — but rather a detailed "how-to" book, covering the parts, nomenclature, function, and processes involved in creating ammunition. Load data will be referenced. But the intent of this book is to be used in conjunction with safe, reliable load data. I hope this book encourages you to delve deeper into the world of reloading and continually expand your horizons. While the methods and procedures covered here are a means of safely and responsibly loading ammunition, there may be other techniques that are equally safe. I can confidently say that my methods are the product of decades of experience.

At this point and again at other points throughout the book, I would warn you against data you find in Internet chatrooms, forums, and other sources that are unproven. Some people push the boundaries and post data they insist is safe in their rifle or handgun; I've seen the terrible results of using such unproven data and will advise you to stay away from it. Please use safe, proven data to keep your anatomy, and your firearm, in its proper configuration.

You have an incredible amount of power in your hands when you grab the handle of your reloading press, and I'll ask that you do not forget that statement.

Reloading ammunition is no more dangerous than driving a car, using the kitchen stove, or operating a chainsaw. Yet, like any of those examples, we can become complacent in using or implementing the tools, and the results can be catastrophic. Reloading ammunition is not to be rushed. It requires an environment of complete focus, with no distraction from phones, or children, or any other potential source. If that isn't possible, wait until it is. Reloading will require you to be on point for each session to ensure that the finished product is safe. The safety of reloaded ammunition is a large focus of this book, and I will reiterate, *ad nauseam*. However, lest I frighten you to the point of declining to participate, if you develop a routine and stick to it, avoid pushing the envelope and other silly ideas, you'll have a lifetime of enjoyment and an outstanding supply of ammo.

So, let's get the ball rolling and start your journey. You'll be reloading ammo before you know it. |||

ABOUT THE COVER

The Frankford Arsenal F1 Single Stage Press is an ergonomic design incorporating some new features with a familiar look and feel. Constructed with steel rod frame pillars for strength without bulk, the F1 uses a steel ram that rides on ball bearings for an ultra-smooth feel on every press stroke. Designed to hold standard 7/8-14 reloading die bodies and standard shellholders, Frankford's F1 also comes with a switchable LED light to illuminate your work while reloading. A roomy, quick-detach bottle takes spent primers, or you can convert to a 5/16-inch hose to deposit used primers into a bucket or can. For an affordable, effective, and convenient press, the Frankford Arsenal F1 is a solid choice.

Winchester's StaBALL 6.5 powder, which is manufactured by Hodgdon Powder Company, has proven to be an excellent choice for reloaders. It has a burn rate suitable for a multitude of rifle cartridges, from the .223 Remington and .22-250 Remington, through the 6.5 Creedmoor, 7mm-08 Remington and .270 Winchester, all the way up to the .375 H&H Magnum and .416 Remington Magnum. It is also useful in the .300 WSM and .270 WSM. Its spherical grain structure takes up less room in the case and meters very well through powder measures and dispensers.

Berger Bullets have an excellent reputation — especially among reloaders — for superb accuracy. Berger holds its highly concentric J4 bullet jackets to extremely tight tolerances, and the sleek bullet profiles make a natural choice for long-range work where consistency and accuracy are paramount. |||

01

OVERVIEW — CARTRIDGE FUNCTION

It's easy to take today's ammo for granted: you load your firearm, and with a squeeze of the trigger, the projectile or shot column speeds on its way to the target. Replace the cartridge or shotshell, and repeat the process. It wasn't always this way, as just 150 years ago or so, the second shot in anything other than a double-barreled gun took a considerable amount of time. The individual components — powder, bullet, and percussion cap for the more recent guns, or priming charge for flintlocks — needed to be loaded and carried separately. Watch any movie on the Civil War, and you'll quickly see how soldiers needed time between volleys and why a saber, bayonet, or sidearm was so crucial.

By the 1870s, the metallic cartridge and shotshell were available to the shooting public, and it was an absolute game-changer. The revolver, developed for cap-and-ball, was converted to use cartridge technology. But the metallic cartridge directly influenced the development of the repeating rifles and shotguns that would dominate the last quarter of the 19th century.

The cartridge/shotshell principle is simple: a single unit houses all the components. After trying copper, early innovators settled upon brass as the case material. It is hard enough to resist deformation yet malleable enough to be loaded into a chamber and reshaped and reused. Companies such as Winchester and Lyman offered accessory tools in the late 1800s to reload

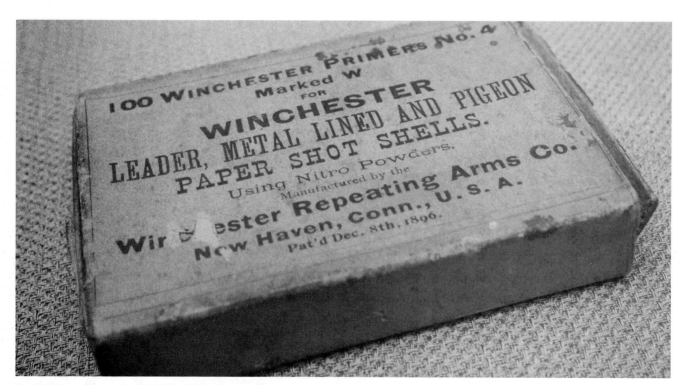

A vintage box of (now obsolete) Winchester No. 4 primers.

ammunition using fired cases. The centerfire brass case is more than just a vessel to hold the powder charge; it has a centrally located pocket at the shell's base to hold the primer, and the mouth and neck contain the projectile. Those constructing early shotshells used brass. They kept the charge inside the hull.

For this book, we'll ignore the rimfire cartridges, as reloading them is just not feasible. The actual priming compound would need to be kept on hand and applied, and those processes are beyond the scope of the recreational reloader. So, from this point forward, I'll be discussing centerfire rifle and pistol cartridges and shotgun shotshells.

The primer begins the ignition process. It initiates a chain of events that sends the bullet or shot down the barrel. Modern, non-corrosive primers use a metallic cup containing a small amount of priming compound held against an anvil. Primers get pressed into the pocket in the center of the case head. When the firing pin crushes the primer, a shower of sparks is driven through the flash hole (located centrally in the primer pocket) to ignite the powder charge. The resultant pressure from the burning powder's gases pushes the bullet or shot column in the only direction possible — out the barrel.

This violent process, sometimes generating pressures over 65,000 psi, not only launches the payload but causes the brass case to expand to the dimensions of the chamber. But, through the use of reloading tools, you can bring that cartridge or shotshell back into the proper measurements to be used again. Two organizations standardize those dimensions. Here in the United States, the governing body for cartridge and shotshell dimensions is SAAMI, the Sporting

Modern primers are cleaner and more reliable than they've ever been. These are Federal Gold Medal Large Rifle Magnums.

Modern Federal 28-gauge shotshells, with plastic hulls.

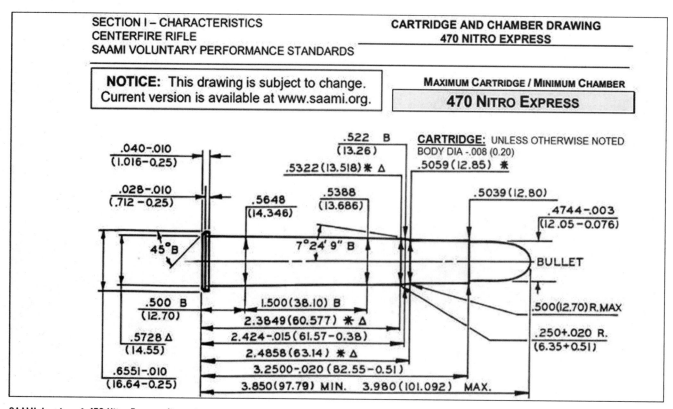

SAAMI drawing of .470 Nitro Express dimensions.

Arms & Ammunition Institute, Inc (saami.org). In Europe, the governing body is C.I.P. or *Commission internationale permanente pour l'épreuve des armes à feu portatives* (Permanent International Commission for the Proof of Small Arms). Ammunition, firearm, and reloading tool manufacturers must adhere to the published dimensions for a particular cartridge or shotshell, or the ammo wouldn't fit in guns.

Our cartridges and shotgun shells' jargon can be quite an interesting history lesson, if not downright confusing. Shotshell terminology is the easiest to grasp, as all but one are named by *gauge*, which is the number of lead balls of that particular diameter it would take to comprise one pound. So, 12 gauge means that 12 lead balls of that diameter would make a pound, 28 gauge would take 28, and so on. This rule's exception

Metallic cartridges come in all sorts of shapes and sizes.

is the .410 bore, which measures the hull diameter in decimal portions of an inch.

Metallic rifle and pistol cartridges are a whole different ball of wax. The naming system is a mix of metric and imperial dimensions, nominal bullet diameter (or possibly some number close to it), or the diameter of the lands in the barrel. Some cartridges list the powder charge, some the year of development; some contain all or portions of the name of the case from which it was developed, others bear the company's name or the person who created it. I'll give some examples.

The .308 Winchester is a cartridge developed by Winchester, which uses a bullet of .308-inch (nominal) diameter. The .300 Winchester Magnum uses the same .308-inch diameter bullet, but in a more massive case to give faster (magnum) performance. The .30-30 Winchester uses a .308-inch bullet and a powder charge of 30 grains, while the .30-06 Springfield is a .30-caliber (.308-inch) cartridge, developed in 1906, at the Springfield Armory. The .307 Winchester is a rimmed variant of the rimless .308 Winchester yet uses the same projectile. And I'm just scratching the surface. We'll cover this in greater detail later on.

There are different shapes of metallic cartridges, grouped (typically) by their headspacing method. What is headspacing? Headspace is the distance from the chamber wall stopping the cartridge's forward motion to the face of the bolt. Our earliest cartridges and shotshells used a rimmed base. The rim simplified effective extraction and made headspacing consistent. Some examples of rimmed cartridges are the .30-30 Winchester, .22 Hornet, .38 Special, .45-70 Government, .470 Nitro Express, and .44 Remington Magnum. The rimmed cartridge works wonderfully in revolvers, single shots, double rifles, and traditional lever-action guns. The cartridges are loaded one at a time, and the ejector or extractor pulls them out of the chamber. However, in the bolt action and semi-automatic rifles, they can be a problem, as the rim can get hung up in a magazine.

The rimless cartridges use a base the same diameter (or sometimes a little less) as the case body and have a built-in extractor groove. Some cartridges headspace off the shoulder where the body angles toward the neck of the case. Others headspace from the case mouth. The former group includes the .308 Winchester, .30-06 Springfield, .270 Winchester, .223 Remington, and 6.5 Creedmoor, while the latter group consists of the 9mm Luger, .40 S&W, and .45 A.C.P. The bottlenecked cartridges usually (but not always) have a considerable shoulder angle, say over 15 degrees, one exception being the .404 Jeffery, which has a slight 8-degree shoulder. These cartridges perform wonderfully in bolt actions, semi-automatics, and fully automatics and have been the cartridge-style choice for U.S. military firearms since the early 20th century.

The British firm of Holland & Holland came up with an ingenious blend of rimmed and rimless cartridges in the first decade of the 20th century (when so many of the great British safari cartridges were developed) by using a belt of brass at the base of the cartridge. This unique design gave the rimmed cartridges solid headspacing, with the ease of feeding like the rimless cartridges. The most famous were the .375 and .300 Holland & Holland Magnums, though there were others. These belted cartridges became synonymous with the word 'magnum.' They became the basis of the Weatherby cartridges of the 1940s and the series of Winchester cartridges in the 1950s. All the cartridges that wear the Holland & Holland belt use it for headspacing, though most popular belted cases can be handloaded to use the shoulder for headspacing instead of the belt.

"Magnum" is reserved for those cartridges that give a faster velocity than the standard rounds. Some magnum cartridges — such as the .375 Holland & Holland Magnum — look like magnums, while others (for example, the .338 Lapua) aren't called magnums but certainly have the performance. To the unknowing, the outward appearance of the .44 Magnum that Dirty Harry famously carried is hardly different from the .45 Colt, which dates to 1873.

Why do we need to know this seemingly useless information? Well, if a reloader confuses a cartridge

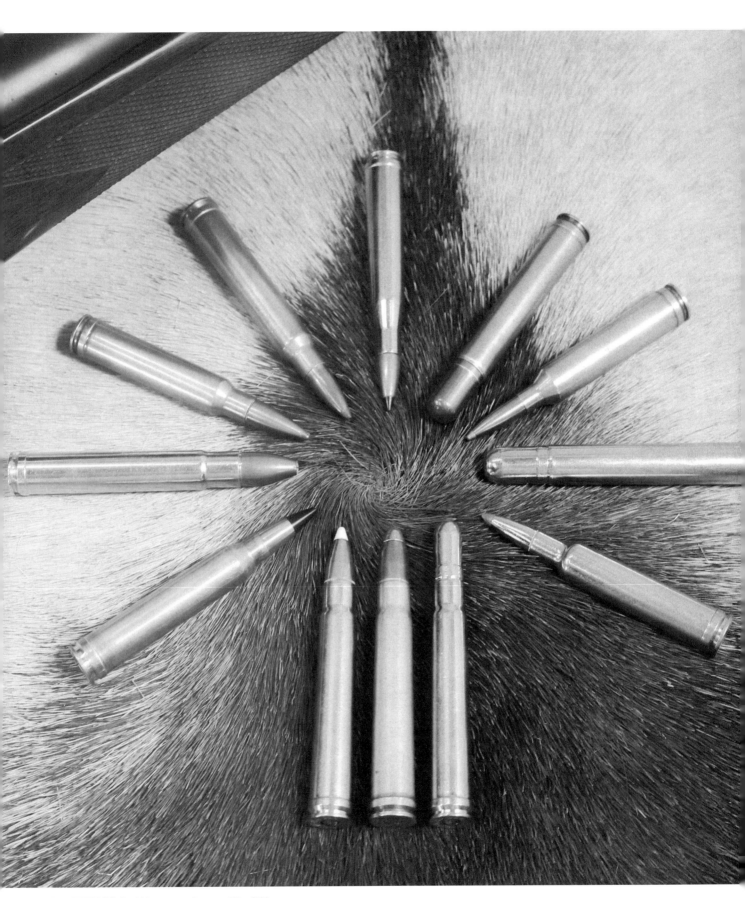

The .375 H&H Belted Magnum and many of its children.

designation, the results can be catastrophic. A .270 Winchester can look an awful lot like a .280 Remington, but firing the latter in a rifle chambered for the former will be, let's say, very bad. Likewise, you can modify a case to make ammunition for another related cartridge. For example, I routinely use cases that began life as the .30-06 Springfield to create ammo for the .338-06 A-Square, .35 Whelen, and .318 Westley Richards.

As a reloader, I need to know — either at a glance or by measuring the cartridges — that I'm not handling .30-06 ammo when I should be using something else.

Simply put, the reloader needs to be very familiar with the various families of cartridges and have both a library of reference materials with the data to ascertain the type of ammunition they are working with and tools for accurately measuring cases or shotshells.

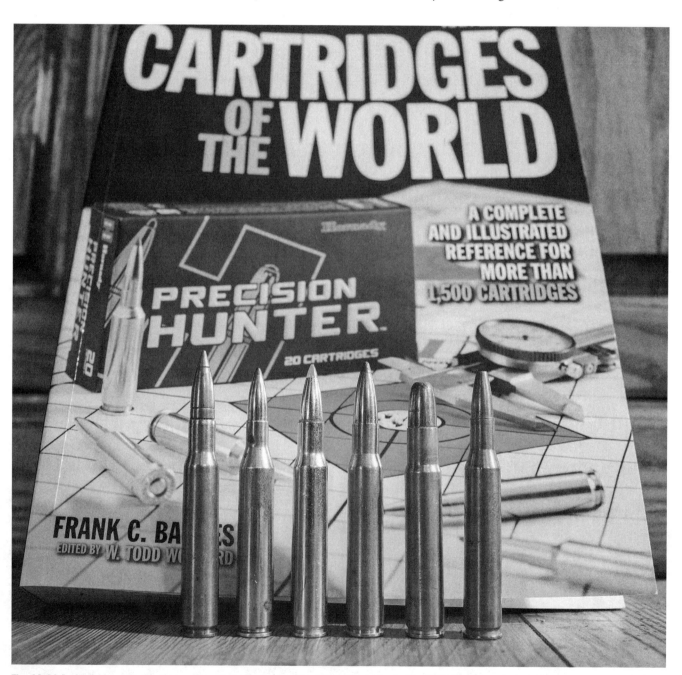

The .30-06 Springfield and its offspring — shown here ranging from the .25-06 Remington to the .35 Whelen — can look similar. A book like *Cartridges of the World* will help shed light on the wide variety of cartridges.

I said earlier that our centerfire metallic cases are made of brass, though you will invariably find nickel-plated cases. Such plating provides a harder surface and is used for corrosion resistance as well as for smoother feeding. Note that I've seen instances where the volume of a nickel-coated case may differ significantly from a standard brass case. Nickel cases have the potential to scratch the inside of your reloading dies and may require a bit more lubricant during the resizing process. Admittedly, this hasn't posed a real issue for me over the years.

As you become more particular about the subtleties of your ammunition, you may find slight, though significant, variations between brands of cartridge cases. Not all brands are created equal, and Federal, Winchester, Remington, Hornady, Norma, and Lapua cases for the same cartridge may show minor dimensional differences. For ammo used in hunting guns, for example, where reliable feeding is paramount, those differences may be insignificant. But when developing a load for precision shooting, say out past 1,000 yards, they may make all the difference in the world.

The centerfire cartridge case hasn't changed radically in design since it first saw the light of day in the 1860s and 70s. Having an intimate knowledge of the history, development, and nuances of the myriad cartridges we have will undoubtedly make you a better reloader. Though it is beyond this book's scope, I recommend one of the best references available, *Cartridges of the World* (available at GunDigestStore.com). Also, most reloading manuals give a cartridge history at the heading of each cartridge, along with a detailed, well-dimensioned drawing to best aid the reloader. |||

02

RELOADING COMPONENTS

Take a look at the website of any reloading supply shop, and you'll find a list of components that is nothing short of mystifying. Various brands and types of primers, powders, cases, hulls, shot, and bullets will comprise the lists, and to the unknowing, it can be overwhelming. Now I'm not going to say you'll need to memorize the characteristics of every single component ever devised. Still, you should have a basic working knowledge of the general groups of items to understand how they apply to your task at hand and prevent you from making unnecessary purchases.

Primer, case/hull, powder charge, shot/wad, or bullet;

that's all there is to it, but the combinations can be endless, and the varying rifle, pistol, and shotgun requirements of cartridges/cases are radically different. I've been asked quite often: "Is there one powder I can buy for all my reloading needs?" No, sadly, there isn't. So to best prepare for a lifetime of reloading, let's look at the particulars of the components of both metallic centerfire cartridges and shotshells.

PRIMERS

The primer is the first stage of the cartridge system, and there are different sizes, applications, and power levels. The most popular primer style used here in the

The primer initiates ignition, and thankfully our modern ones are very consistent.

Primer, case, powder, and bullet — a wonderfully simple yet sufficiently complex combination.

U.S. is the Boxer primer, which utilizes a centrally-located flash hole and an anvil in the primer cup. Elsewhere in the world, you'll find the Berdan primer, which uses a pair of offset flash holes and has the anvil located in the primer pocket as a part of the case itself. Note that there are Berdan-style cases. Do not use these cases for reloading, as you'll damage your resizing die in an attempt to knock the old primer out.

Boxer primers were developed by a British gentleman, Col. Edward Mounier Boxer, who received an English patent in October 1866, and a U.S. patent in June 1869. They have been the primer of choice for our ammunition in the U.S. Primers are divided into four major groups by diameter.

Small pistol and rifle: 0.175-inch diameter, the small rifle primers have a harder cup than the small pistol variety, in addition to providing a hotter spark. There are magnum variants of both small pistol and small rifle used to ignite heavier powder charges.

Shotgun/inline muzzleloader: 0.209-inch diameter (hence the popular '209' designation) inside a flanged brass cup (the cup measures between .241- and .245-inch depending on the brand). Shotshells and the modern inline muzzleloading rifles use this primer. It is usually employed both for standard and magnum loads. However, CCI offers a 209-Magnum primer.

Large pistol and rifle: 0.210-inch diameter, large rifle primers are 0.008-inch taller than large pistol primers. The rifle variants have a thicker, harder cup than the pistol primers, and there are large rifle magnum and large pistol magnum choices for igniting hefty powder charges.

.50 BMG primers: 0.315-inch diameter, these are for the behemoth .50 BMG cartridge, burning over 200 grains of powder in some instances.

Rumors swirled at one point in time that there was a medium-sized primer of 0.204-inch diameter, manufactured by the Frankford Arsenal of Pennsylvania; but I've never personally seen one. No matter, there are no cases that call for its use.

Each company has different designations for their

Boxer primer pocket, which uses a centrally located flash hole.

CCI BR-2 Large Rifle Benchrest primers.

primers, and you'll need to be aware of how they are named. Here are the most common:

Small Pistol: CCI 500, Federal 100, Winchester WSP, Remington 1 ½

Small Pistol Magnum: CCI 550, Federal 200, Winchester WSPM, Remington 5 ½

Small Rifle: CCI 400, Federal 205, Winchester WSR, Remington 6 ½

Small Rifle Magnum: CCI 450, Federal 250M, Remington 7 ½

Large Pistol: CCI 300, Federal 150, Winchester WLP, Remington 2 ½

Large Pistol Magnum: CCI 350, Federal 155, Winchester WLPM

Large Rifle: CCI 200, Federal 210, Winchester WLR, Remington 9 ½

Large Rifle Magnum: CCI 250. Federal 215, Winchester WLRM, Remington 9 ½ M

There are also match-grade primers, designed for the most consistent performance. Federal offers its Gold Medal Match line in all pistol and rifle primer designations and even has a primer specifically for the AR-15 crowd. Federal designates its Large Rifle Match primers as GM210M by adding a "G.M." prefix and an "M" suffix. Too, CCI makes a military-type primer for 5.56 NATO, 7.62x51 NATO, and .50 BMG, labeled as No. 41, No. 34, and No. 35, respectively, as well as its Benchrest primers. There are also 209 primers explicitly designed for the inline muzzleloading rifles. Winchester has recently announced its line of USA

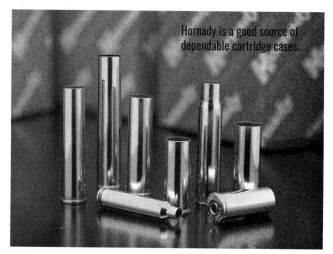

Hornady is a good source of dependable cartridge cases.

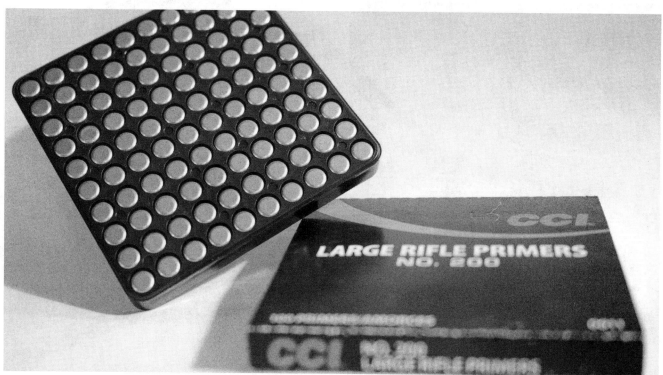

Once you find a primer that gives the performance you like, buy a bunch of them and stick with it.

Ready match-grade primers in Small and Large Pistol and Small and Large Rifle.

Consistent use of the same brand and type of primer is an essential part of creating accurate ammunition. Keep this rule of thumb in mind throughout your loading career: when changing primers, always reduce your loads to the minimum and work back up, as the variations in primer heat can have a drastic effect on the pressures. When you begin to assemble your handloaded ammo, refer to one or more of the reloading manuals (you'll probably end up with a collection of books and proven data), and pay special attention to the primer used. You may see a magnum primer used in a cartridge, which generally calls for a standard primer — perhaps it gave better results with a slower-burning powder. You may also see the load listed with a particular primer brand; I highly suggest you either obtain some of that type or brand of primer or find

Nosler might be the best choice for out-of-the-box cases but will still require some attention, as brass can become dinged during shipping.

some load data using the kind of primer you have.

You should always install primers into the primer pocket to sit either flush or slightly recessed; this applies to both factory-loaded and handloaded ammunition. If the primer sits too far out of the primer pocket, the risk of a "slamfire" drastically increases. Regularly check your primer depth. When I toured the Norma factory, I saw the employees using a gauge to check primer depth, which is a big reason for its accuracy.

Lastly, a couple of points regarding the use and storage of primers: if you plan to use several different types of primers, have only the ones you are currently using on your reloading bench at any one time; put all the others away. This way, you cannot inadvertently install the wrong type of primer into your cases.

Primers ignite by percussion — think about the firing pin slamming into the primer — thus, storing them requires forethought. Always keep your primers in their original container, even if there are just a few left, so you don't mix them up. Avoid storing them in desk drawers or other places where they could spill and wedge themselves. Don't set off yours by accidentally closing the drawer on one. And if you spill a tray of primers — and if you reload enough, you will — make sure you account for all of them. It can be rather shocking when you roll an office chair over a live primer, and it goes off; I can attest to that fact personally, and so can those in my presence, alerted by a string of obscenities that would make a sailor blush. Avoid sparks in your reloading area. Potentially igniting large amounts of powder is extremely dangerous and should be avoided at all costs.

CARTRIDGE CASES

In the last chapter, we discussed the evolution and varying shapes and sizes of cartridge cases. When it comes to reloading, make sure your cases are made of brass — some inexpensive ammunition brands use steel cases for plinking ammo. Don't attempt to reload steel cases. If you have a hard time discerning steel-cased ammunition from brass or nickel, a small magnet can be a handy tool. Brass or nickel-plated cases aren't magnetic at all, while ferrous steel cases will stick to a magnet quickly.

Keep your brass segregated by brand unless you're reloading ammo for plinking, in which case you'll be less concerned with accuracy. If using once-fired factory brass, put the cases through a rigorous visual examination. You are looking for cracks, significant deformations, bent rims, large corrosion areas, or noticeable dents you can't remove during the resizing process. If you find any of these, crush the case with a pair of pliers so it cannot find its way back into the mix.

Brass is a malleable yet strong metal, but it will tarnish and corrode. You'll need to keep your brass clean and have a means of polishing it, as dirty ammo doesn't feed well, and debris introduced into the chamber is never a good thing. Brass stretches and flows each time a cartridge fires, and a bit of brass will flow forward, increasing the cartridge case's length. Should the case stretch to the point that the length exceeds the figure specified by SAAMI, the case will need to be trimmed back down to the proper length. Consistent case length will play an essential role in the cartridges that headspace off the case mouth (.45 ACP, 9mm Luger, .40 S&W, 10mm Auto) as well as any case requiring a roll crimp (the case mouth crimps into a groove, known as the "cannelure," in the bullet).

You will need a few tools to trim and dress cases appropriately (see Chapter 3 for reloading tools). New and previously fired brass needs to be 'tuned.' Even newly manufactured brass can be dinged or dented in shipping. I'd be willing to bet that as you get the bug for reloading, you will insist on preparing each case, new or used. Some premium brands of component brass include Nosler, Norma, Lapua, and Roberson. These will require little work, but I know of no brand that will require no work at all. As a reloader, the case is the only part of the cartridge that you can trim, resize and deburr (the process we call "working" the brass). You can weigh bullets, segregate them into lots, or choose the type and amount of powder, but you can't control

...wever, you can work ...ions or give a custom ...ptions, especially for

...sure chamber holding ...all variations in case ...ect accuracy. If variances ...case walls or base, the ...er will vary. Dumping a ...two cases with disparate

internal volumes, it's not hard to envision that they would generate two different pressure levels. Now, if the differences are small, there may be no measurable effect, but if the variance is drastic — as it can be when switching between brands — you will see the results at the target.

For example, and speaking hypothetically, if I were to use a mix of cases from Federal and Remington in, say my .30-06 Springfield, they would likely have different internal dimensions. They might yield different

Remington nickel-plated cases are great for resisting corrosion from sweaty hands but can scratch your reloading dies.

velocities and group sizes. The point of impact could also shift, perhaps not enough to cause an errant shot on a deer's vitals, but it may make a significant difference to the target shooter. I'm not suggesting that one brand is better than the other. It just means that they are different, and — this won't be the last time you read these words — *reloading and accuracy is all about uniformity.*

Not all cases are created equal. Over the years, construction methods have changed. For example, wall

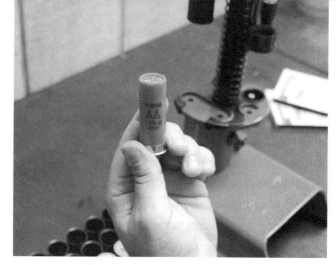

The classic Winchester AA hull is the shotshell reloader's friend. It is the gold standard in the industry.

A diversified lineup of classic and modern smokeless powders.

thickness for the .45-70 Government and the .30-30 Winchester (released in 1873 and 1895, respectively) are relatively thin compared to a .308 Winchester or even a .30-06 Springfield (1952 and 1906, respectively). There are modern rifles for the two former cartridges that can handle all sorts of pressures, but the cartridge cases themselves can only take so much. If these cartridges are overloaded (usually to obtain higher velocities), extraction can become difficult. Primers will show signs of increased pressures, and cases will stretch abnormally. What's more, case life will be cut short. I remember an adage my mother used: "Don't try to make a silk purse from a sow's ear."

Mother's phrase often runs through my head as I sit at the reloading bench, perusing a reloading manual, and looking at the data and correlative velocities. For years, my only big game rifle was a Ruger 77 in .308 Winchester, a Christmas gift from my father in 1993. Now, Dad shot .308 for years — Ol' Grumpy Pants' favorite being a Mossberg Model 800A — and I was

Alliant's Blue Dot flake powder is suitable for both shotshells and handgun applications

proud to use the same cartridge with which I'd seen him take so many whitetails. It coincided with the beginning of my reloading career, and we sat down to come up with some different recipes to try. Each time he and I would try to agree on the load, I'd end up wanting to push the envelope and grab every last bit of velocity. He would shake his head and grin as I'd come in from the backyard range with cratered primers, a bolt handle that wouldn't lift, and other easily avoidable mistakes.

What I was trying to do was turn a .308 Winchester into a cartridge closer to the .300 Winchester Magnum — a losing proposition to begin with — and it didn't work. I should have stayed within the parameters and velocity range that the .308 can produce. Once I realized what I had in that rifle and loaded for it appropriately, it all worked out just fine. 165-grain bullets at 2,650 fps toppled over a whole lot of whitetail

Ball powder such as H414 will take up less room in your case due to the grain structure.

deer, the 180-grain bullets handled black bears, and 125-grainers acquired coyotes, woodchucks, skunks, and more. Moral of the story: when you sit down to load for your chosen cartridge, be sensible about it. If your cartridge doesn't give you the results you're after (within reason), it's probably best to look for a new cartridge.

In the vast spectrum of handgun and rifle cartridges exists something for everyone. Straight-walled, belted, rebated rim, short, fat, long, thin, magnum, standard, huge, tiny, so on and so forth; the beauty of reloading is that you can create your pet loads so long as the components and reloading tools are available. We have had almost 150 years of excellent cartridge development, so I'm sure you can find something to tickle your fancy without subjecting your rifle to unnecessary torture. As you get into reloading, and as I admitted above, you'll invariably try to push the envelope. Cartridge design culminated with a performance level in mind. Looking at the reloading data for each cartridge produces a specific set of safe velocities. Those velocities will typically be slightly *lower* than factory ammunition's advertised velocities. There are reasons for this, which we will address later. Still, if you examine the velocity range for a cartridge/ bullet combination in a few reloading manuals, odds are you won't be disappointed in the results.

While most centerfire cases are brass, you will find some ammunition loaded in steel cases, and, as previously mentioned, they are not reloadable. There are also nickel-plated brass cases from Federal, Norma, Browning, and Winchester that resist corrosion, which is especially handy when cartridges are handled often throughout a hunting season or are used in your everyday carry handgun. These cases are fully reloadable, though the nickel plating is much harder than brass and can scratch your reloading dies. This cautionary note doesn't mean you shouldn't use nickel cases. I use them often for hunting ammunition. But you should be aware of the potential issues with your dies.

Extruded stick powder is the most popular design for rifle cases.

SHOTSHELLS

Much like the metallic cartridge case, a shotgun shotshell uses a primer, powder, and shot in a convenient, portable package. The original shotshells were all brass with paper wads, making a transition in the late 1870s to a brass head (the area at the base of the shell holding the primer) and a waxed paper body and overshot card. In the 1960s, they transitioned to plastic hulls and wads capable of being crimped. All the varying sizes of shotshells use the "209" primer, from the little .410 bore up to the massive 10- and 8-gauge heavyweights. A powder charge sits between the primer and the wad, which holds the shot column, slug, or ball. The end of the modern plastic shell typically employs a six- or eight-point star crimp. When I was a kid, standard shotshell loads were 'low brass,' meaning they had a smaller band of brass on the body, and magnum loads were 'high brass,' having a more considerable amount of brass down along the body. I always believed the brass case head was necessary to handle the pressures generated, but much to my chagrin, in the mid-to-late 1980s, shotshells made entirely of plastic came on the market.

There isn't a lot to say about a shotshell design; reloaders usually look for the most durable hulls to reload. The Winchester A.A. hull is the benchmark, as it is a rugged design with a thick brass head and a polyethylene body you can reload numerous times. Choosing a gauge to suit your needs used to be relatively cut and dry, but the latest advancements in shot material have begun to change the game.

There are differing wads that will change your handloaded shotshells' performance, so you can fine-tune for breaking clay birds, sorting out a big tom turkey, or loading up buckshot to defend the home.

POWDER

Friar Roger Bacon is often credited as the first European to devise a proper formula for blackpowder. However, there is strong evidence that he may have seen Chinese firecrackers before doing so. Though the Chinese far predated Bacon, the fact remains that gunpowder changed the world. It enabled tiny projectiles to be fired by a single soldier at a relatively high velocity, ruining metal armor's effectiveness, and allowed a cannon crew to launch heavy missiles, better known as cannonballs, diminishing the protection afforded by the castle.

Blackpowder was a simple blend of sulfur, saltpeter, and charcoal. Still, it would go on to change the face of warfare, fuel the exploration of the remote corners of the earth, and nearly cause the extinction of our megafauna before we tightened the leash of conservation. Muzzleloading firearms and vintage cartridges such as the .45 Colt, .45-90, and other late 19th century classics still use blackpowder. It hasn't changed that much over the centuries. It is still as corrosive as it ever was (you'll want to clean your gun with hot, soapy water as soon as possible), and its burning characteristics remain as they were. Several substitutes, such as Hogdgon's Pyrodex and Triple Se7en, offer a cleaner alternative.

There are four grades of blackpowder, graded according to the fineness of the mixture. Fg is the coarse cannon powder, FFg and FFFg are used in rifles and pistols, and the finest, FFFFg, works best for flash pan ignition in flintlocks.

The 1840s saw a quantum leap in propellant technology. Manufacturers added Nitric to cellulose to make nitrocellulose, better known in the shooting world as 'guncotton.' Five to six times as potent as blackpowder, it would be some time before the metallurgy of firearms would catch up to the power generated. In 1887, Alfred Nobel mixed nitroglycerin with nitrocellulose to create a plasticized, stable compound. Sir Frederick Abel and Sir James Dewar jointly patented a similar product two years later, resulting in a court suit. Nobel lost the lawsuit, but Cordite (the product's abbreviated name) became the smokeless powder *du jour*. They extruded the double-base propellant into long, spaghetti-like strands. Finally, they cut it to fit into the cartridge case. ("Double-base" means that it contains both nitroglycerin and nitrocellulose.) Cordite fueled many of my favorite rounds, namely the classic safari Nitro-Express cartridges. From the .375 H&H Magnum to the .416 Rigby and .404 Jeffery, they all ran on Cordite. Quite obviously, Cordite worked. The hunters and market shooters of that era put a severe dent in the game populations. However, Cordite earned a reputation for hypersensitivity to temperature changes.

Cartridge development in jolly old England, where the weather is usually gloomy albeit relatively moderate, is one thing, but switching to Africa and India's tropics where the sun scorches hotter than Hades, created problems. Extraction was sticky, with cases getting stuck in the chambers. To combat this, you saw large brass cases for cartridges such as the .416 Rigby and .470 Nitro Express, which were oversized to keep the pressures low, for use in those hot climates. Many of those classic cartridges are still in use (the .470 N.E. is my favorite cartridge for a double rifle), but newer, higher-pressure rounds do the same job in a smaller package. By the Second World War, gun powders were rapidly becoming what we know today, with many of those propellants still in everyday use 80 years later.

Modern powders take one of three primary forms:

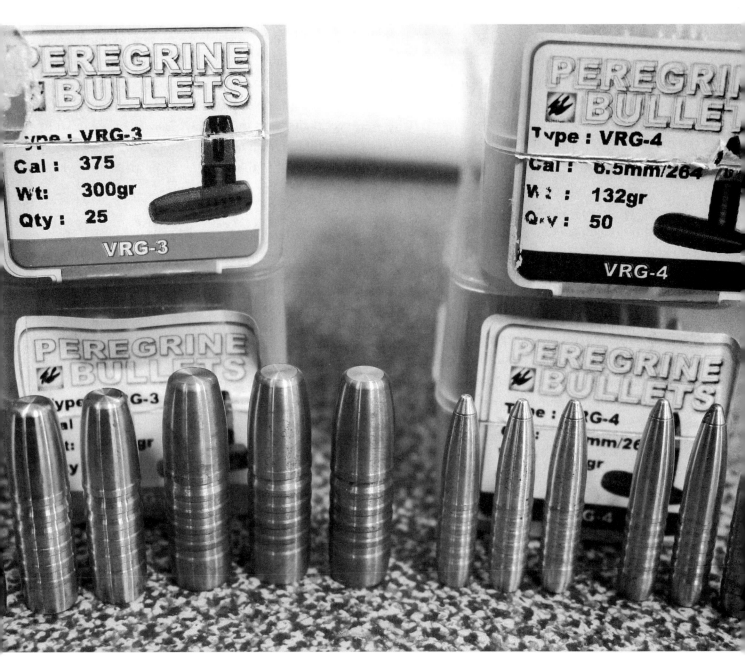

Peregrine Bullets are a fantastic monometal design, with reliable expansion and high weight retention.

flake, ball, or stick. Flake powder, with its grains resembling tiny discs, looks like little slices of pepperoni. The flake powders usually see the most duty in shotshells and pistol cartridges, as they are among the fastest-burning propellants available. Red Dot, Green Dot, and Unique are all classic flake styles. Ball powder has a grain structure — you guessed it — of little round balls. Not nearly as popular or numerous as the stick type, ball powders are an excellent choice when case capacity is compromised, as there are fewer air voids and the load takes up less space. Hodgdon's H335, H380, BL-C(2), H414, Winchester's W748, and new StaBALL 6.5 are good examples of ball powders.

Our stick powders are the most popular for the wide range of rifle cartridges; the powder is extruded into long thin strands and then cut to length. They can be fast, medium, or slow-burning and come in many different sizes for many other applications. They are coated with a retardant to manage the burn rate, from a fast burn such as IMR 3031 to a medium burn such as IMR 4064 and Hodgdon's VARGET, to a slow burn in the instance of the powders designed for the large magnum cartridges such as IMR 7977, H1000 and Retumbo.

Powder names can be just as confusing as the system used to name the cartridges. Some powders have names, others use numbers, yet more still are a blend of both, and it is not difficult to confuse them. Therefore, you must understand the various names, pay strict attention to what the recipe calls for, and keep meticulous records of the components you used for each batch of ammo.

The IMR family of powders (formerly made by DuPont) were named for "Improved Military Rifle" and carry the IMR prefix with four digits following, sometimes with letters. For example, IMR 4064 is a classic medium-burning powder suitable for rifle cases from .22-250 Remington to .308 Winchester and .30-06 Springfield, on up to the .375 H&H Magnum and the .416 Remington Magnum. Some of the IMR powders are as old as the hills, and there are some fantastic new releases. Manufacturers phase out the older ones as shooter interest wanes. For example, initially, the .308 Winchester used IMR 4320 as the factory choice of powder. Now, new developments yield better performance in that cartridge. IMR's Enduron line, released over the last eight years or so, was designed to be as insensitive to fluctuations in temperature as possible, making life easy for those who hunt in all sorts of different climates. IMR is now owned by Hodgdon, which has done an excellent job keeping the historic brand alive.

Hodgdon also has a fascinating history. It dates back to World War II when Bruce Hodgdon began selling surplus military powder. The Hodgdon brand has a fervent following, its powder named with an 'H' prefix, followed by three or four numbers, or sometimes just a name. H380 is a ball powder designated for Bruce's pet load in the .22-250 wildcat (38.0 grains under a 55-grain bullet), H4350 is the favorite choice for 6.5 Creedmoor

fans, and H1000 is a staple for those who load for the largest magnums. VARGET, TiteGroup, RETUMBO, and Clays are all examples of Hodgdon's line of powders. Hodgdon also owns Winchester Powders, named with three digits — as in 572, 231, 748, or 760 — or with an identifier such as AutoComp, WSF, WST, or 6.5 StaBALL. All of the Winchester propellants are ball powders, and I've used them in several instances where case capacity was an issue.

Alliant also offers a complete line of canister-grade powders suitable for handgun, rifle, and shotshell loads. Famous names such as Herco, Unique, Red Dot, Blue Dot, and the Reloder and Power Pro series of rifle powders are all part of the Alliant line and make an excellent choice for any of your reloading needs. Some of the newer offerings such as Reloder 16, 23, and 26 have produced very consistent results across a wide temperature range and have been a source of excellent hunting and target ammunition alike.

Western Powders, Inc. is the distributor for several excellent smokeless powders, including Ramshot, Accurate, and most recently Norma from Sweden. While often overlooked by reloaders, these brands have come to the rescue in finicky rifles. Ramshot's Hunter, TAC, and ZIP powder, as well as Accurate No. 9 and AA4350, have been superb choices in both rifles and handguns; Norma's 200 and MRP have been the go-to choice in big-bore rifles as well.

Shooter's World Powder is relatively new on the scene. It offers a full range of shotshell, handgun, and rifle powders for the reloader, from the lightest trap and target loads to the behemoth .50 BMG cartridge. Long Rifle, Match Rifle, Heavy Pistol, and Clean Shot are among the powders offered by Shooter's World. Based on the results I've seen, this company will be a welcome addition to reloaders.

Vihtavouri is a product of Finland and has a product range capable of handling shotshells, handgun rounds, and rifle cartridges, from the small-bore to the big-bore safari cartridges. Vihtavouri products typically have an 'N' prefix — such as N140, N310, or N550 — except

The Hornady InterLock is a simple cup-and-core design that remains a proven hunting bullet.

for its Tin Star powder for Cowboy Action Shooting, or some of its products using a numerical prefix such as 3N37 and 3N38. All the Vihtavouri powders now have a 'decoppering' agent added to the powder, which reduces the amount of copper fouling in the bore, from either bullet jackets or from shooting lead-free bullet designs.

The technology to develop smokeless powder has become more complex and involved in recent years. While I still rely upon standard powders (IMR 4064 and IMR 4350 come quickly to mind), some of the old faithful are being phased out in favor of the newer designs using revised grain length. IMR 4320, once the factory choice for loading the .308 Winchester, is being discontinued due to lack of demand. IMR 4064, IMR 4166, and VARGET all have similar burn rates. Hodgdon has discontinued IMR 4320 and now focuses on keeping its other supplies readily available. Hodgdon and Alliant both have added copper fouling reduction chemicals to their newer designs. (The CFE in Hodgdon's CFE223 powder stands for 'copper fouling eliminator.') I'm noticing that most newer reloaders embrace the new powders, which isn't a bad thing. I have long been a fan of Reloder 22 and 25, yet for any new load development work, I find myself reaching for Reloder 23 and 26, which are improvements on the previously mentioned powders. My .300 Winchester Magnum still loves good old IMR 4350, but it seems to like IMR 4451 from the Enduron line just as well. I feel the newer IMR 4451, which has served very well from the freezing temperatures of the Adirondack and Catskill mountains of New York to South Africa and Zimbabwe, where it can easily exceed 110-degrees Fahrenheit, is an improvement on the older IMR 4350. However, I'm not exactly willing to drop all the loads I've developed with the older powder.

As you'll see later in this book, there is an awful lot of powders to choose from when handloading your ammo. While you'll want to avoid overlap as much as possible, sometimes loading a new powder can make all the difference in the world.

BULLETS & SHOT

Whether your ammo was loaded in a factory or at your kitchen table, the only thing that touches the intended target is the projectile. It doesn't matter if it's a column of shot destined for a cackling pheasant or a sleek hollowpoint boattail bullet ready to make the long journey to a piece of steel. The projectile is what matters. Highly figured walnut or gold embossed engraving matters not if the bullet or shot doesn't go where it is supposed to.

The history of projectiles parallels that of humankind; from the first thrown rock to the intercontinental ballistic missile, man has long sought the ability to strike someone or something from afar. The earliest

The classic Nosler Partition remains a sound choice for a hunting bullet.

The Barnes TSX is a monometal hollowpoint that produces impressive penetration.

firearms used a single lead ball and a smooth bore; this lasted even into the 19th century. This combination was inaccurate compared to modern equipment, but it was better than hand-to-hand combat. The modern projectiles for both rifle and handgun, and even the conformation and construction of shot, have developed rapidly over the last few decades, and the choices are better now than they ever were. As a reloader, you have the flexibility to choose the projectile that will best serve your needs, be it based on price, availability, performance, or some combination of the three.

In addition to the cost-effective nature of reloading, there is also the opportunity to use some projectiles that are simply unavailable in factory loads. For example, there is a relatively unknown bullet company from South Africa named Peregrine Bullets, and it has a unique design. Peregrine produces a monometal hollowpoint, capped with a bronze plunger, leaving a pocket of air underneath. Using the principle that oxygen is not easily compressed, upon impact, the brass plunger at the nose is shoved rearward into the hollow cavity, compressing the air and forcing the bullet's sidewall outward, perpendicular to the long axis of the bullet. The system produces devastating expansion, and I've used this bullet in several different cartridges on game animals from reedbuck and warthog up to Cape buffalo. Had I not learned to reload, I would've missed out on this bullet and the excellent terminal ballistics it delivers.

Let's take a look at what makes our modern projectiles tick to understand what shape, style, and conformation will work best for you when it comes time to assemble your handloaded ammunition. The simple lead projectile still exists — even in round ball form used in muzzleloading rifles — and you can either purchase lead projectiles or molds to pour bullets from molten lead. While the pure lead projectiles, or even hardened lead projectiles, can be affordable to shoot and fun to create, they will foul a barrel quickly, and cleaning can become a chore. That said, they are fun to load for plinking and practice, and with a bit of antimony added to harden the mixture, you can make bullets suitable for hunting.

The lead bullet was the universal choice for handguns and rifles, for hunting and military, throughout the majority of the 19th century. While the lead projectile certainly worked, pushing the bison, elk, pronghorn antelope, and whitetail deer all to the brink, it can only handle velocities up to 1,800 or 1,900 fps before the bullet starts to 'skid' down the barrel, smearing lead throughout the rifling. Manufacturers achieved unprecedented speeds as propellant technology improved, making the transition from blackpowder to the new smokeless offerings. Velocities soared to over 2,000 fps. Simply put, the lead bullet couldn't handle the heat, and it was in 1882 that Swiss Colonel Eduard Rubin developed the jacketed bullet.

Using a jacket, or cup, of copper gilding metal over a lead core was a game-changer, and it's a formula we use to this day. Copper has a greater hardness than lead,

but not as hard as the steel of the barrel. This hardness allows the rifling to engrave the bullet, but the copper will stand up to the higher velocities. When a bit of lead is left exposed at the nose, the copper jacket controls the rapid expansion upon impact. The cup-and-core bullet remains a popular choice among hunters, target shooters, and handgunners, as it is efficient, affordable, and works as well as it did a century ago. Thickening the copper jacket can make a bullet stronger for hunting applications or optimized for magnum handguns. A precision jacket held to tight tolerances and a uniform lead core free of voids results in a match-grade bullet. The jacketed bullet made a vast difference in terminal ballistics and reduced lead fouling in the barrel. But the new magnum cartridges revealed the cup-and-core's limitations.

Then came John Nosler. Nosler was using a .300 Holland & Holland Magnum with cup-and-core bullets while hunting moose in Canada when he placed a shot at close range on a big bull's shoulder. The bullet simply couldn't handle the stress of the high impact velocity, and premature breakup left only superficial wounds on the beast's shoulder. Nosler realized the issue and placed a second killing shot. This debacle caused him to rethink the standard bullet's construction and 'build a better mousetrap,' as the saying goes. The Nosler Partition was born. It uses a partition of copper between

Federal's Trophy Bonded Bear Claw features a short lead core bonded to a thick copper jacket and base.

The Nosler Ballistic Tip Varmint uses a thin jacket and polymer tip for explosive expansion.

two lead cores. The partition expands the front half of the bullet to destroy vital tissue yet leaves the rear core intact for deep penetration. With the Nosler Partition propelled to worldwide fame, it remains a popular choice to this day. Nosler created the premium bullet industry. For years, before Federal picked the bullet for its Premium line in the 1970s, the Partition was only available in component form, to be handloaded.

Reloaders employ other methods to control the rate of a bullet's expansion. Chemically bonding the lead core to the copper jacket is a proven method of increasing a bullet's strength, slowing the rate of expansion, and increasing penetration. Many rifle bullets and handgun bullets are available that feature a 'bonded-core,' and I have relied on them for years. Randy Brooks of Barnes Bullets had the idea of removing the lead core from a bullet altogether and making it out of a copper alloy. It took a bit of experimentation, but the monometal soft-point was born. In light of California's laws prohibiting the use of lead bullets, the copper-alloy alternatives have saved the day. As I mentioned in the example of Peregrine Bullets, the monometal projectiles are a tough and accurate design, capable in nearly any hunting situation. I've recently seen excellent monometal designs in the handgun and long-range target bullets as well. Though I doubt the

Federal's lineup of proprietary bullets offers good long-range hunting performance, as their conformation creates flat trajectory and effective wind deflection values.

monometal design will replace the lead-core bullets completely, the monometals gain ground every year in the hunting fields. From the sheep mountains of British Columbia or the Zimbabwe buffalo's thick jesse bush, the monometals build a large fan base each season.

There are also some 'hybrid' bullets, which blend the attributes of different styles. The Federal Trophy Bonded Bear Claw, a slight modification from the original Jack Carter design (and its offspring, the Trophy Bonded Tip, and Terminal Ascent), uses a shortened lead core, chemically bonded to the thick copper jacket, and a long shank of copper at the rear of the bullet. This arrangement keeps the bullet's weight forward — a big help when it comes to straight-line penetration. Its rear shank allows the bullet to penetrate thick hide and bone, guaranteeing vital tissue damage.

Varmint and predator hunters will want a very frangible bullet with a thin jacket, just tough enough to withstand the high velocities that the smallbore cartridges can generate. The concept is to deliver an immediate energy transfer, causing a quick death to varmints. And to minimize pelt damage on the fur-bearing predators.

Bullet shape will influence your technique and choices as a reloader. The round-nose and flat-nose bullets, which keep their weight forward, will take up less room

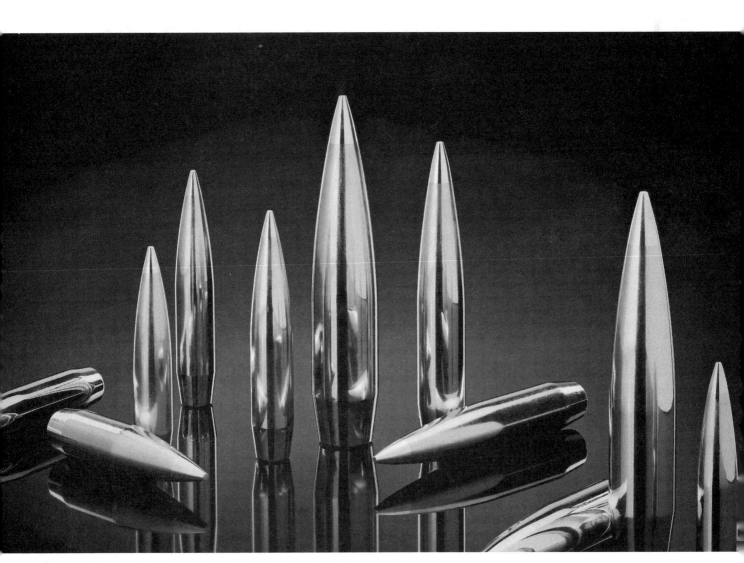

A-TIP Match is an excellent long-range bullet, available only to handloaders.

in the case compared to a long spitzer boattail bullet. (As a historical note, the term 'spitzer' is a derivative of the German word *spitzgeschoss*, which roughly translates to "pointy bullet.") Pointed bullets slice through the atmosphere easier than round- or flat-nosed projectiles, resisting the effects of atmospheric drag, and retain both velocity and energy farther downrange. Add a boattail — the angled base of a bullet — and you will further enhance the ability to resist atmospheric drag and wind deflection. The result? Making hits on distant targets becomes much more attainable. Imagine the difference between a delivery van and a sports car rolling down the highway: once the driver lets off the gas (fires the cartridge), the van will slow down faster than the sports car due to the aerodynamic shape. Further, many bullet companies have embraced the idea of a polymer tip at the nose of the bullet, set into a hollow cavity. Polymer tips not only keep the bullet's nose intact (maintaining that aerodynamic shape in the magazine box and throughout the flight), but the polymer tip acts as a wedge, and upon impact, will initiate expansion.

Extreme long-range shooting has become a market unto itself. Super high ballistic coefficient (B.C.) bullets have become the norm with their long ogive (the curve of a bullet's front end) and severe boattail angles. However, these come with unique loading requirements. The seating dies require a specialized stem, so the *meplat* [pronounced MEE-PLAH, the top area of a flat-nosed projectile] of the bullet isn't damaged. Also, there are tools for the advanced reloader to measure bullet runout and loaded ammunition concentricity. You must remove the slightest deviation, which will amplify variance at long distances. There are 'bore rider' bullets, which help align the projectile to the rifle's bore, and they have their unique requirements.

There are also boutique bullet companies – Hawk Bullets from New Jersey comes quickly to mind — to fuel those rifles chambered for obscure cartridges. As a reloader, you'll need a source of brass, whether once-fired, made from another existing cartridge, or sourced from a specialty company like Roberson Cartridge Company. Also, get reliable reloading data and bullets of proper diameter for the task at hand. With all of this and some practice, you can keep that rifle well fed.

Handgun bullets use several different shapes, depending on their application. The round-nosed bullets feed best in the autoloading pistols, wherein a revolver you can use nearly any bullet shape you want. That's because revolver shooters feed rounds into the cylinder by hand, and feeding from a magazine is of no concern. There are flat points, wadcutters (designed to cut a perfect circle in a paper target, for scoring purposes in competitive shooting), semi-wadcutters, and more.

Like rifle bullets, handgun projectiles have seen equal advances, with bonded-core and monometal offerings in addition to the more traditional cup-and-core style, some with very thick jackets to best serve the magnum handgun cartridges. Bullets such as the Federal Hydra-Shok, Speer Gold Dot and Gold Dot 2, and Hornady XTP all have a stellar reputation for defensive projectiles. And for hunting, Swift A-Frame and Barnes monometals are now used in revolvers.

Shotguns have experienced similar technological advancements, as the traditional lead shot and steel shot shares the stage with Bismuth and tungsten, and the results are eye-opening. (Bismuth and tungsten shot are non-lead, environmentally friendly alternatives that use heavy alloys to replicate the performance of lead and outperform standard "steel shot.")

Just as I started hunting, the New York State turkey seasons were becoming a real thing, with both huntable populations of birds and the welcome addition of a spring hunting season. At that time, a healthy charge of No. 4, 5, or 6 shot was the prescription for tom turkeys, with some going as big as No. 2, in either lead or copper-plated shot, to resist deformity. Like the traditional lead and cup-and-core rifle and pistol bullets, the lead shot for targets and upland game and the steel shot for waterfowl remains a viable and popular choice, but the new heavy metals are changing the game.

Where the 12 gauge was the undeniable choice for turkey hunters, we're now seeing the 28 gauge, and .410 bore in the turkey woods, making kill shots at over 50 yards, using shot sizes considered only suitable for breaking clay birds up until a few years ago. Those heavier, denser metals carry their energy farther than lead, and it's not uncommon to see those smaller guns using TSS shot in No. 7, 8, 9, and 10; this would indeed have made my grandfather cock an eyebrow. If you want to load shotshells, it's worthwhile to investigate what the varying metallic compositions can do to extend your shotgun's capabilities. |||

The Sierra GameKing hollowpoint combines match bullet accuracy with the strength of a hunting bullet.

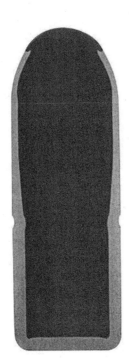

The Woodleigh Weldcore is an excellent big game bullet. It's found in very few factory loads but is readily available to reloaders.

03

RELOADING TOOLS

You can't reload ammo if you don't have the tools. Thankfully, the selection of tools available to the reloader is wide and varied; your setup can be as simple or complex as you want to make it. There are budget-minded entry-level tools, and then there are the top-of-the-line ones. I've reloaded using just about all of them, and after three decades, I have strong opinions but am always willing to learn something new.

You'll have to perform the basic functions of reloading:

resizing spent cases, removing spent primers, trimming the cases, charging them with the appropriate amount of powder, and seating a new projectile on top. On the simplest level, with a Lee Loader Kit, a hammer, and a wooden block — combined with the essential components — you can start reloading ammunition for your rifle or handgun in a matter of moments. Mind you it will be neck-sized ammo (meaning that you only size the neck portion of the case), which will only work in the firearm in which it was initially fired.

Reloading requires quality, specialized tools.

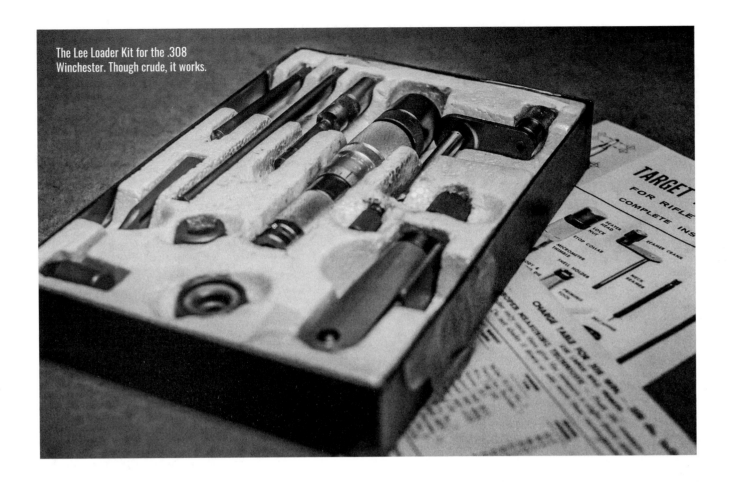
The Lee Loader Kit for the .308 Winchester. Though crude, it works.

A Lee Loader Kit runs about $40, and it can be a great way to get your feet wet for next to nothing.

However, the Lee kit is somewhat primitive in comparison to an adequately outfitted reloading bench. On a correctly set up workspace, your reloading press does the heavy lifting on your bench. It'll handle resizing the cases and knocking out the spent primers in conjunction with the die sets. A press can also install new primers, flare case mouths of the straight-walled cartridges, seat new bullets, and crimp the bullets. There are different types of presses, and each has its benefits and drawbacks. Before we delve into presses, though, let's start with the foundation of your system — the reloading bench.

THE RELOADING BENCH

You'll need a dedicated space to reload ammunition, though it doesn't necessarily have to be a massive operation. For most handloaders, the reloading bench is the foundation of their entire process. It's a place where your tools and components won't fall into the wrong hands. You should locate your bench in a quiet area, free from distraction, climate-controlled, and comfortable. Over the years, my reloading bench has evolved from a temporary spot at the kitchen table to a metal office desk to a fully dedicated commercial operation that occupies the better part of a large outbuilding. Each situation allowed me to get the job done, but it sure is nice to have a dedicated space that doesn't need to serve any other purpose but reloading. It's a controlled environment where all my tools have their spot, and I can organize all of my stuff in my own fashion. By the last count, I've got over 80 sets of dies (some duplicates) and a healthy collection of reloading gear, from the simple to the complex.

I have a custom-built wooden bench, attached to my garage's wall, about 12 feet long (much longer than I need) and 2 1/2 feet deep, with a storage shelf underneath

The author at his reloading bench.

and three cabinets above. A pair of fluorescent light banks keep it well-lit. I keep the reloading press bolted to the forward edge of the bench, just far enough over the edge to allow for free movement of the ram and associated linkage. Because I'm right-handed, I keep my powder dispenser and scale next to the press (on the left), so it's a short trip from the powder measure to the primed case and then to the seating die in the press. The trimmer can be off to one side or another, used during a separate operation.

I like my reloading bench of a height where I can stand to reload or sit on a stool, as my back tends to stiffen up if I remain seated in the same position for several hours. Depending on how much room you have, you should store other gear when not in use. You can use a wooden bench or a sturdy wooden table, and I've even employed a heavy metal desk in the past, bolting or clamping the press to the desktop. Sometimes, you must make do with what you have available. You primarily need a sturdy working surface, which doesn't wobble or move, so your scales and other tools give accurate readings and operate as they should. An inexpensive way to make any bench more rigid is to screw it to the studs in your wall using a couple of 90-degree brackets purchased from any hardware store. Add 2x4 and 2x6 crossbracing to the back of the bench and under the tabletop to further reinforce it.

STORAGE

Storage may be an issue, depending on how much space you have available. When storing powders and primers, keep them separated and stow them where

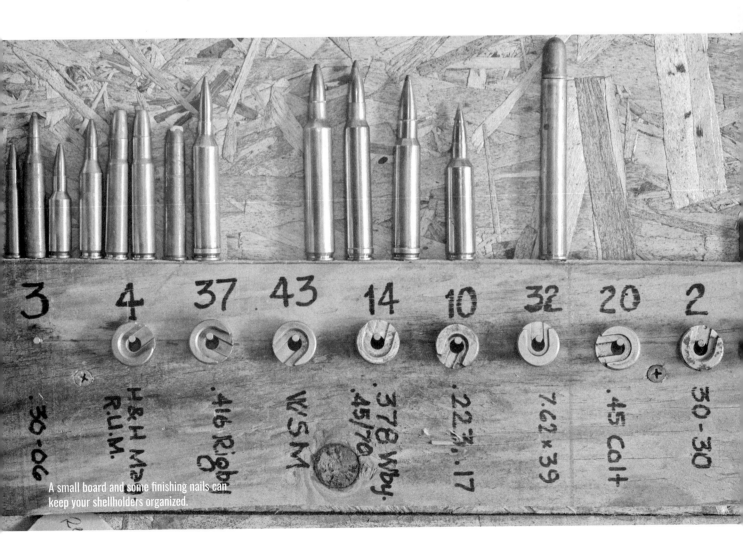

A small board and some finishing nails can keep your shellholders organized.

other folks can't access them. I have a wooden shelving drawer unit where I organize my primers, component bullets, and brass cases, and I keep the powder on the other side of the room in a lightweight metal cabinet. I always keep primers in their original package and use scotch tape to close the box when finished. The tape prevents the little silver buggers from falling out and getting into the drawer's mechanism or rolling under a chair. I always respect Murphy's Law. The accidental detonation of a primer in my reloading room would be disastrous. Keep your supplies of powder as far away from the primers as possible.

Storing powder is not difficult. Keep in mind that whatever box or cabinet you keep it in needs to be open to the air in case of ignition. What you want is the ability for the powder to burn openly and not under pressure. I knew of a local gun shop that sold reloading supplies, and it kept its powder supply in an oversize gun safe. Perhaps they didn't realize it, but what they'd created was a one-ton bomb, which would've flattened the joint. Keep your powder in a cool, dry place, away from the risk of sparks, and out of direct sunlight, and all should be well.

COMPONENTS AND PARTS ORGANIZATION

Since I reload many different cartridges, I often use the same shellholder for multiple ones. For example, the .22-250 Remington, .243 Winchester, .280 Ackley Improved, .30-06 Springfield, and .45 ACP all use the same RCBS No. 3 shellholder. If I were to keep that shellholder in the .30-06 die box, I'd be reaching in there all the time. Instead, I use a series of small finishing nails driven into a board, label each of the most common shellholders (I use the RCBS naming system) by number, and write the parent cartridge or family underneath it. This process has saved me a bunch of time. (A shellholder is one of those pieces of gear that is much like a 10mm socket — you set it down, and then you can't find it.)

I've also come to appreciate those plastic parts cabinets used to store small items in the workshop's garage. Mine has ten drawers that rotate out from the center and one lower drawer that pulls straight out. It's not expensive, and there are many variations, but I like it because it screws to the wall, conserving bench space, and it keeps all my smaller tools and parts nicely organized. Look for something similar at your local home improvement stores. My chamfer/deburring tools and primer pocket cleaners stay in one drawer, case lube in another, replacement decapping pins and other die parts in another, so on and so forth. While I'm not the most organized human on the planet, I know where my reloading tools and parts are when I need them. An adequate supply of spare parts — things such as decapping pins, the small nuts that lock the seating plug, and other breakable or easily lost items — is a good idea to keep in your tool kit. I keep my case brushes, resizing bushings, 9v batteries, a small tube of grease, paperclips for feeler gauges, spare shellholders, and other odds and ends in that wall-mounted container.

A set of tools, some basic and some specialized, will be needed for maintaining your reloading setup. Keep plenty of Allen keys — metric and standard — as you'll use them frequently for set screws on the die bodies. You'll also use screwdrivers (Phillips-head and slotted) in sizes from the tiny ones used for eyeglasses and other delicate work up to the larger models. Channel locks and needle-nose pliers will be handy, as will a small set of adjustable wrenches, as some dies have hexagonal nuts for lock rings.

RELOADING PRESSES

There are three main types of reloading presses: the single-stage, holding one die and performing one function at a time; the turret press, which contains multiple dies in a rotating head yet still performs one process at a time; and finally, the progressive press, an impressive machine that performs multiple operations with each stroke of the handle and can manufacture a considerable amount of ammunition in a short amount of time. The progressives are also the hardest to keep

A vintage RCBS RockChucker O-frame press. RockChuckers are common as dirt and built solid as a tank.

an eye on, and when something goes wrong, it can be a royal pain. I do most of my work on a single-stage press or a turret press, but the progressive has its place for an experienced reloader.

Looking at the single-stage presses first, you'll see several different designs. The O-frame presses look like the letter "O," and the frame's shape is rigid. There is little flexure in this type of press, which will help keep your end-product as consistent as possible. I find the O-frames to be among the best values in the reloading industry, as they produce excellent ammo without breaking the bank.

Some of my favorite O-presses are the famous RCBS RockChucker, the new RCBS Rebel (I like its heavy cast-iron frame), the Redding Boss and Big Boss II, and Lyman's Brass Smith Victory. These are solidly built for a lifetime of service and have tolerances tight enough to produce match-grade loads. Each of these — except the RCBS Rebel — offers the capability of installing primers from the press. I spent years behind a RockChucker; it is a simple, reliable, and effective press, and you won't be disappointed if you choose the modern iteration, the Rock Chucker Supreme.

The C-frame presses are, not surprisingly, shaped like a capital C and have a slimmer profile than the O-frames. Historically, the C-frames were not as strong nor rigid as the O-type, and in some of the more inexpensive models still available, that may remain true. Even so, I

A simple Lee C-frame press offers beginning reloaders a lot of practical value.

The innovative RCBS Summit Press, technically a C-frame, has a massive 2-inch ram for rigidity and consistency.

The Redding T7 turret press is the author's favorite. It has seven openings to accept multiple dies and the 27-lb. cast iron body provides the rigidity to crank out match-grade ammo.

like the affordable models such as the Lee Breech Lock for removing primers with a Universal Decapping die; it takes up little room, and I can leave that die set up in the press for that function alone. Lyman still offers a traditional C-press in its Brass Smith line known as the Ideal, and it's a beefy, cast-iron workhorse perfect for the beginner.

Another type of press provides a top-notch performance level, technically C-shaped, but is tough as nails. The unique RCBS Summit, which uses a huge 2-inch ram, and moves the reloading die up and down while the case stays stationary, works for all reloading

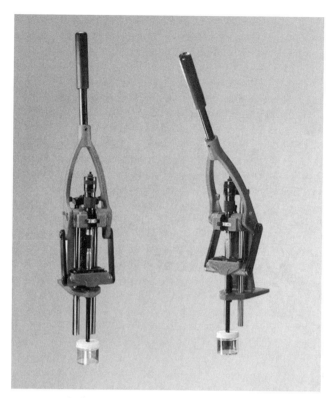

The Forster Co-Ax press uses twin parallel rams to keep the case body, and reloading dies, as concentric as possible. Instead of a shellholder, it uses steel jaws to hold the case.

duties; it's ambidextrous and features a 4-1/2-inch operating window for the long magnum cases. The Summit's design is very 'open': there's not much to get in the way, as it doesn't have a frame, so seating bullets and performing other operations is much easier for those with large hands. RCBS provides a zerk fitting for greasing the press, and despite the 'C' frame's reputation for flexing, the Summit isn't going to move. I've used it for pistol cartridges large and small, and for rifle rounds from the diminutive .17 Hornet and .17 Remington to the .375 H&H Magnum and .458 Lott, without a single issue.

I suppose the turret presses fall under the C-press category, and over the years, I've come to enjoy them. I learned how to reload on a Lee Turret press but have settled on the Redding T7 turret. The Redding is built like a tank, extremely rigid, and is a pleasure to use. The seven-station rotating head saves time screwing and unscrewing dies into the press, and you can keep up to three different calibers on the press simultaneously.

The T7 has a 1-inch hollow ram, which allows the spent primers to run through the center and into a collection tube. Equipped with a powerful compound linkage and a 4-3/4-inch opening, the T7 can handle nearly all cartridges, save for perhaps the longest. Its seven holes take the standard 7/8-14 die bodies, and its cast-iron body weighs more than 27 lbs.; Redding provides four mounting holes, and once you bolt the T7 to your bench, it isn't going anywhere. Redding sells additional turret heads, so you can swap them by removing a screw, leaving your dies set up permanently. I especially like the T7 for loading straight-walled cartridges —such as the .45 ACP or .40 S&W or the .45-70 Government and .458 Lott — as I can keep the resizing, flaring, bullet seating, and taper crimp dies on the turret. Should I need to load an extra cartridge or two, or if something goes wrong along the way, I can simply rotate the turret head to use the die I need. The Redding T7 sits right in the middle of my bench, and I use it more than any other.

Other choices probably don't fit well in any category but can be a fine choice for reloaders of all levels. The Forster Co-Ax press uses twin parallel rams to keep the case body and reloading dies concentric. Instead of a shellholder, the Co-Ax features steel jaws to hold the case. Instead of a threaded hole to screw in the 7/8-14 thread die body, it has a precision-milled slot in the frame to hold the die by the lock ring, again to maximize concentricity. The Co-Ax gives you a significant mechanical advantage, resulting in a smooth feel. Its handle is ambidextrous.

For the lengthy cartridges such as the .45-120 Sharps, or the bigger safari rounds, such as the .500 Jeffery and .505 Gibbs, I like Redding's Ultramag press. It has a 4-3/4-inch opening, and a ram stroke of 4-1/8 inches. The beefy press has a linkage that connects to the top of the frame, generating tons of pressure. This leverage is beneficial when I'm converting cases from one caliber to another. For example, to create cases for my .318 Westley Richards loads I need to trim down .30-06 Springfield brass to length and then run it through the RCBS resizing die. While it's possible to perform this action on several different presses, the Redding Ultramag makes short work of it. Its mechanical advantage and massive leverage give you a smooth pull without exerting excess pressure, which could bend a rim. While it doesn't see as frequent use as my T7, the Ultramag handles the biggest cartridges. The 7/8-inch threaded insert can be removed, leaving a 1-inch threaded hole for the larger die bodies. Like the T7, the Ultramag's ram is hollow, with the spent primer collection system.

The progressive presses can generate a bunch of ammo in a hurry and are the favorite of the high-volume shooters. A progressive press has multiple stations. Each station performs a different function; each lever pull rolls a completed cartridge off the line. The more stations available, the more options you have. Quite obviously, the normal processes of resizing, decapping, priming, charging, flaring, bullet seating, and crimping, must be completed. But there are powder checkers to prevent uncharged cases and other options

The MEC 600 Jr. shotgun press is a popular choice among shotshell reloaders.

to make life convenient. A progressive press, when running correctly, is a joy to use. When things go out of adjustment, they can test your patience. As this is the *ABC's of Reloading*, we'll touch on these presses and how to set them up briefly, but I suggest that if you're a new reloader, you begin on a single-stage press until you're familiar with all the processes involved. That way, you can keep an eye on all of them as they happen simultaneously. Think of a progressive like a series of single-stage presses that operate in unison with each handle pull. There are many quality models. I'd wager the Dillon machines are the most popular, but I've also made quality ammunition on RCBS and Hornady machines as well.

Shotgun reloading presses work in much the same manner, using a pair of vessels containing powder and shot and various bushings and charge bars to limit the amount of each loaded into the shotshell. The MEC presses are a popular choice (the MEC 600 is a favorite of mine) as they deliver a great value. Also, check out the Lee Load All II and the RCBS Grand Progressive. You can even purchase an automated MEC shotshell loader for the highest production rates. Let's look more closely at the presses available today.

CHOOSING A RELOADING PRESS

Among the many choices mentioned above, I've had great results with the RCBS RockChucker. The latest iteration, the Rock Chucker Supreme, can be had for a street price of about $160 and will provide you with a lifetime of service if cared for properly. You can set it up for left- and right-handed operation, so it's flexible. You can purchase the Redding Boss single-stage press for about the same money and equal value. If you're on a budget, the RCBS Partner is a smaller, more lightweight press, priced at under $100, and it can give good service. The Lyman Brass Smith Victory press is pricier and offers a solid cast-iron O-frame, plus a primer feeder.

Any of these designs will handle your regular

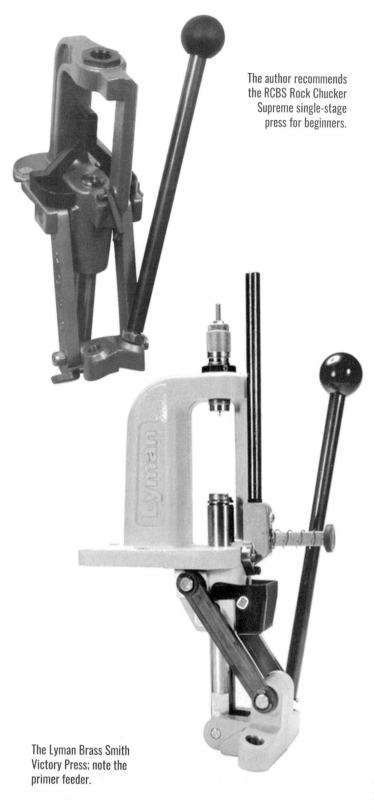

The author recommends the RCBS Rock Chucker Supreme single-stage press for beginners.

The Lyman Brass Smith Victory Press; note the primer feeder.

reloading duties well and have a large enough platform to be bolted down securely yet don't take up a ton of room. Today's press manufacturers build them tough enough to last for decades. But they can only hold one reloading die at a time, requiring you to change between resizing, flaring, and seating dies when each

is needed. More expensive presses like the Forster Co-Ax single-stage press still only hold a single die at a time yet produce a higher level of precision. The Co-Ax will set you back $500. I know reloaders who swear by this press, which doesn't use a threaded hole to support the die. Instead, it relies on the lock nut's flat surface for support.

Let's look closer at the Redding T-7 turret press. As mentioned, it holds seven dies on a rotating head and maintains tolerances much tighter than you would think achievable from a turret press. Though still a single-stage design, I like the ability to hold all three dies for a pistol cartridge. This configuration allows me to switch from resizing die to flaring die quickly, then load and seat as many bullets as I want, going right back to the resizing die should I choose to make more ammunition. It provides enough clearance for the longest magnum cartridges and has sufficient leverage to convert brass cases from one caliber to another. The one drawback with the T-7: it accepts only 7/8-14 die bodies, so you'll need another press with a 1-inch die body for the larger cartridges. If you have no intention of loading huge cartridges such as the .505 Gibbs and .500 Jeffery, that point is moot.

Suppose you intend to form brass cases from one cartridge into another, such as making .338-06 A-Square brass from .30-'06 Springfield or forming .416 Taylor cases from .458 Winchester Magnums. In that case, you'll need a press with additional leverage. For that task, I like the Redding UltraMag, a beefy single-stage capable of handling the most challenging brass-forming duties. With a street price of about $340, the UltraMag gives you all the leverage you'll ever need.

If you're going to take the plunge into the world of progressive presses, the Dillon machines make the most sense. Dillon seems dedicated to making nothing but progressives, and while the RCBS and Hornady models have some excellent qualities, the Dillon XL650 checks all the boxes for me. I'm not a

The mighty Redding T7 turret press features endless setup options for the reloader while maintaining the stability of a single-stage, single-hole press.

The Redding UltraMag press is a massive piece of gear, perfect for loading the biggest cartridges. It has more than enough leverage for forming brass.

high-volume shooter, so I don't do any rifle cartridges on my Dillon, but I appreciate how a well-tuned Dillon will produce handgun ammunition. I'll cover the progressive presses in greater detail later, as an awful lot is going on simultaneously, but they can be a fantastic tool for the experienced reloader.

SHELLHOLDERS

The shellholder — aptly named — holds the cases (or shells) during each process. The shellholder snaps into the recess at the top of the press ram. They are specific to each family of cartridges or a single cartridge, and you must consult the necessary chart to obtain the proper one. Find them segregated by number, but note that the numbers aren't universal between brands. In other words, a Hornady No. 1 isn't used for the same cartridge as an RCBS No. 1 or a Redding No. 1, so the brand/cartridge correlation is necessary.

Irrespective of numbers or brand, a shellholder designed to fit the .30-06 Springfield/7mm Mauser/.308 Winchester/.45 ACP family of cartridges, for example, from any manufacturer will work with any set of matching dies. The same holds for all the cartridges based on the Holland & Holland belted case, and so on. You can use a Redding shellholder with Lee dies, a Hornady one with RCBS dies, etc. While you can own many different shellholders, when you're concerned with precision, always use the same shellholder with the same set of dies, as there will be slight variations in dimension. You want to minimize the effect those variations can have.

Redding offers its specialty Competition Shellholder Sets. Redding manufactures these to varying depths, in increments of 0.002 — from 0.002 to 0.010 inch below standard, to control headspace. The idea is that you can adjust the location of the shoulder to best match your particular chamber. We'll cover this technique later but realize you'll use these shellholders for a specific technique.

Just as each reloading die set is cartridge specific (some sets can handle two cartridges, such as the .38

SHELLHOLDER INTERCHANGE CHART
(Popular Sizes-Not A Complete Listing)

REDDING	HORNADY	RCBS	LYMAN
1	1	3 & 11	2, 8 & 27
2	2	2	6
3	7	1	10
4	4	11 & 15	5
5	8,10 & 12	1, 19 & 27	12 & 15
6	5	4 & 26	13
7	N/A	3	N/A
8	11	7 & 24	7
9	9	26 & 28	N/A
10	16 & 36	10 & 23	9 & 26
12	6 & 17	6 & 27	1 & 21
13	8	16	12
14	3	12	4
15	23	13	17
16	N/A	22	N/A
17	31	8	N/A
18	14	14	17
19	27 & 30	18 & 28	7 & 14B
20	25	5	N/A
21	29 & 33	21 & 30	30
22	22	17	19 & 23
23	32	20	11
24	20 & 21	9	N/A
25			
26	N/A	31	N/A
27	37	29	32
31	55	46	N/A
33	N/A	N/A	N/A
404	53	41	N/A
34	37	45	N/A
35	43	48	17
36	52	44	N/A

Shellholder Interchange Chart, provided by Redding. As you progress as a reloader, you'll collect all sorts of useful reference material with which to decorate the walls of your reloading room.

Special/.357 Magnum and .44 Special/.44 Magnum), you'll need the appropriate shellholder for each cartridge you intend to reload. One shellholder may serve an entire family of cartridges. For example, the .30-06 Springfield, .308 Winchester, .270 Winchester, 7mm-08 Remington, .243 Winchester, and more all use the same shellholder because their rim diameter is 0.473 inch. So, check the shellholder charts to avoid duplication. The numbering system for each brand of shellholder isn't universal; in other words, a Redding No. 3 isn't the same as an RCBS No. 3 or a Hornady No. 3, so be careful when ordering the proper shellholder for your chosen cartridge.

The progressive presses use shell plates, matching the number of case recesses to stations in the press. You pull the handle, and the shell plates rotate. Like the shellholder, they're cartridge/cartridge family-specific, so you'll need as many shell plates as you have unique cases. Note they're typically specific to the model of progressive press you are using.

RELOADING DIES

Reloading dies are the cartridge-specific tools used for resizing, flaring, bullet seating, and crimping. They're screwed into the top of the reloading press and set at specific depths to give the exacting dimensions needed for proper functioning ammunition. Most basic bottleneck rifle die sets will come with two dies: a full-length resizer and a seater. The full-length resizing die forms the entire cartridge, from base to mouth, to the acceptable SAAMI- or CIP-approved dimensions. The bullet seating die serves two purposes: It seats the bullet in the case to a specific depth, and it can be adjusted to roll the case mouth into the bullet's crimping groove or cannelure, producing what is called a roll crimp. The roll crimp is desirable in the

Shellholders hold the case and snap into a recess on the press.

An RCBS three-die set for pistol cartridges. Note the flaring die on the left.

hard-kicking magnum rifle and pistol cartridges and is necessary on any straight-walled case that doesn't headspace off the case mouth.

Straight-walled cartridge die sets also typically come with a flaring die, which opens up the case mouth like a bell to allow the bullet to be seated in the case without crumpling the case walls.

The wide selection of reloading dies can be dizzying. I'm not sure there is one brand or type I'm married to as, during my reloading career, I've probably used ones from nearly every manufacturer at one point in time or another. That includes defunct brands such as Herter's, Pacific, and several custom-made ones. Among these, I've only had one defective set; the company is no longer in business, but the .300 H&H cases I was trying to resize wouldn't function in the gun no matter what I did.

REDDING DIES

I try to buy the best dies I can afford, and sitting at

the top of my list are those from Redding. Redding Reloading, from my home state of New York, has long been famous for producing products with exceptionally tight tolerances. Redding's high-end dies are no exception, though costly. Redding offers various levels of dies, and even the lower-priced standard sets are a worthy purchase. The components are very precisely made, and the surfaces are polished to a mirror finish. It's been my experience that Redding dies are polished so well that extra attention needs to be paid to the proper application of lubricant to avoid case sticking. The Redding Elite die set includes the Type S Bushing full-length resizing die, which extends brass life by reducing the necks only as much as is needed before drawing it over the expander ball. That set also includes bushing neck-sizing dies. Redding's micrometer-adjustable Competition seating die allows you to make quick,

accurate, and predictable adjustments to the seating depth. These die sets are expensive, but the results make the price well worth it.

Redding's Premium dies sets feature a standard full-length seating die, with a carbide expander ball and bullet seating micrometer. Redding builds its standard dies to the same tight specifications as its premium line, but it's the small things that you'll appreciate. The lock rings are blued, knurled steel and the set screw rests against a small lead shot instead of against the die body, so nothing gets scratched. I could spend the rest of my reloading days happily using Redding dies.

RCBS DIES

There were times, especially as a younger man, when a set of Redding dies were simply out of my financial reach. RCBS dies were the best I could do, and they

In the author's opinion, Redding's Premium die set (this one for the .308 Winchester) is one of the most precise tools you can buy.

were a smart purchase. The standard RCBS dies aren't full of bells and whistles but are simple affairs that get the job done. I've loaded a lot of ammo on RCBS dies and continue to use them to this day. RCBS basic sets have lock rings with wrench flats, and the seater plugs and decapping rods are held in place by small hex nuts. There are knurled rings at the top of the die bodies to grip when screwing the die into the press. Were I on a tight budget, I'd still look to the RCBS die sets to get the job done. They offer a full line of rifle and pistol dies and taper crimps, plus titanium carbide pistol dies that require no lubrication on the cases.

While the standard RCBS die set is probably the benchmark in the reloading world, RCBS has stepped up its game as of late. Its MatchMaster die sets are on

The classic RCBS two-die set is an affordable option for the beginning reloader.

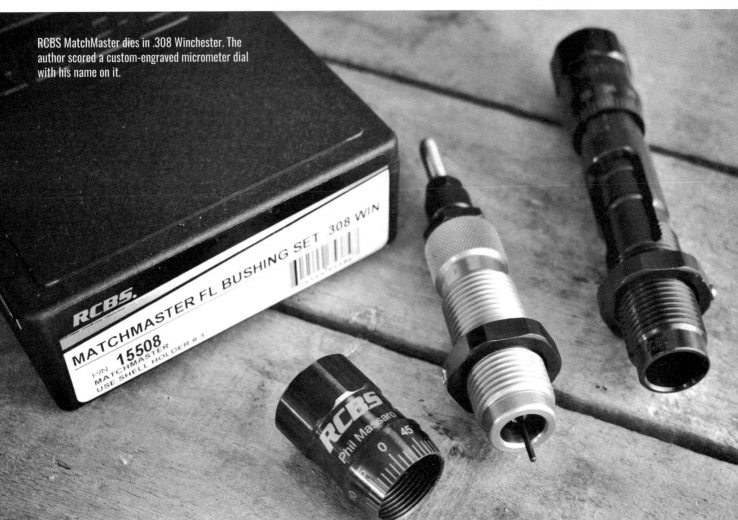

RCBS MatchMaster dies in .308 Winchester. The author scored a custom-engraved micrometer dial with his name on it.

par with the Redding stuff. Micrometer-adjustable seating dies with a window cutout in the body to drop the bullet onto the case mouth, full-length bushing resizing dies that will extend brass life — RCBS has met the demands of the modern reloader's needs.

HORNADY DIES

Hornady has a well-earned reputation for producing quality reloading products, and its reloading dies have some unique features that many prefer. I like Hornady's Custom Grade dies, which include the New Dimension sizing and seating dies. Both use a knurled, split lock ring with two flats, so you can use

an adjustable wrench if necessary. What's more, the lock ring tightens via an Allen-head screw, which tightens the ring around the die body (rather than against the die threads). The sizing die features wrench flats as well, and both have knurled bodies for a positive grip when screwing the dies into the press body. The sizing die has an elliptical expander ball, which aids in the smooth sizing of your cases. The Zip Spindle makes large and small adjustments simple. The finely threaded spindle makes precise adjustments, yet increased pressure on the rod will move the spindle up or down for rough adjustments.

The seating die included in the set is not cartridge

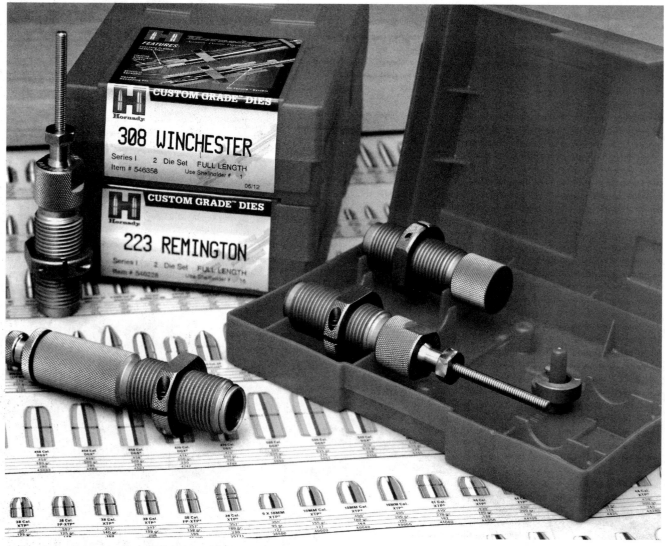

Hornady Custom Grade dies in .308 Winchester and .223 Remington.

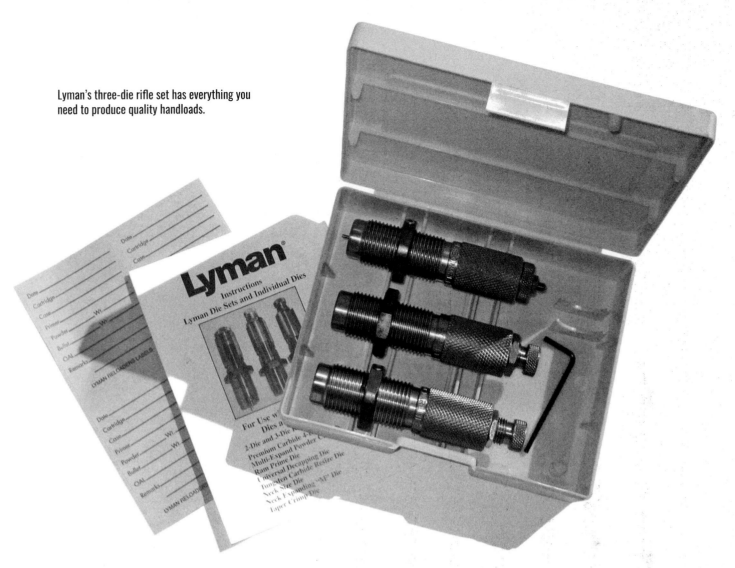

Lyman's three-die rifle set has everything you need to produce quality handloads.

specific; instead, Hornady produces them for the entire range of each caliber. Hornady uses an inline bullet seating system, including a floating bullet alignment sleeve, to enhance concentricity. You can set the seating die for a roll crimp or taper crimp (depending on which model you purchase), and some sets include various seater plugs. Hornady provides a pair of extra decapping pins in the die box, which come in very handy should you break one.

The American Series dies from Hornady are more affordable and are constructed of hardened steel, polished to a smooth finish. The dies come with a shellholder of appropriate size, and Hornady includes basic reloading data. The three-die sets for straight-walled cases feature a resizing die with a titanium nitride resizing ring to eliminate the need for case lubricant. The American series is available in five standard rifle cartridges and four different dual-purpose handgun cartridges.

The Match Grade Hornady die sets include a bushing resizing die. Bushings are not included and are sold separately. The Microjust seating die in this set has the same features as the Custom Grade New Dimension seating die, but with a micrometer adjustment on its top, in .001-inch increments.

Hornady can also make you a set of custom dies, based on the chamber reamer drawing used for your rifle or derived from spent cases fired in your gun. Custom dies are an excellent option for those wildcatters who enjoy shooting their creations. It's a costly process, but if you have an obscure or vintage firearm for which dies are nearly impossible to obtain, Hornady's customization service can mean the difference between a functioning gun and a wall-hanger.

Hornady also offers the option of using its Lock-n-Load bushings with its presses, which locks the dies into the press with a simple turn, saving you the time spent screwing and unscrewing dies.

LYMAN DIES

Lyman has long made excellent reloading dies and continues to do so. They are constructed of hardened, heat-treated steel, with the pistol cartridge dies featuring tungsten carbide sizing rings. Lyman's three-die rifle sets give you flexibility. Lyman includes a full-length resizing die and a neck sizing die, along with a seating die. These die sets also include the appropriate shellholder and an Allen key to set the lock ring. (Lyman lock rings look remarkably like the RCBS lock ring.) The resizing dies use a threaded rod to hold the decapping pin and expander ball, locked in place via a small hex nut at the top of the die body. The Lyman seating die features a knurled seating plug, locking down with a small hex nut.

The Lyman dies' replaceable decapping pins screw onto a one-piece rod and these slide into the expander ball. While the Lyman dies are relatively simple and lack the bells and whistles of some of the more complex models, they represent an excellent value to the beginning reloader. The simple design allows you to set up dies quickly and easily, ready to make top-performing ammo for a lifetime.

Lyman's Premium Carbide 4 Die sets offer the traditional trio of resizing, flaring, and seating dies in

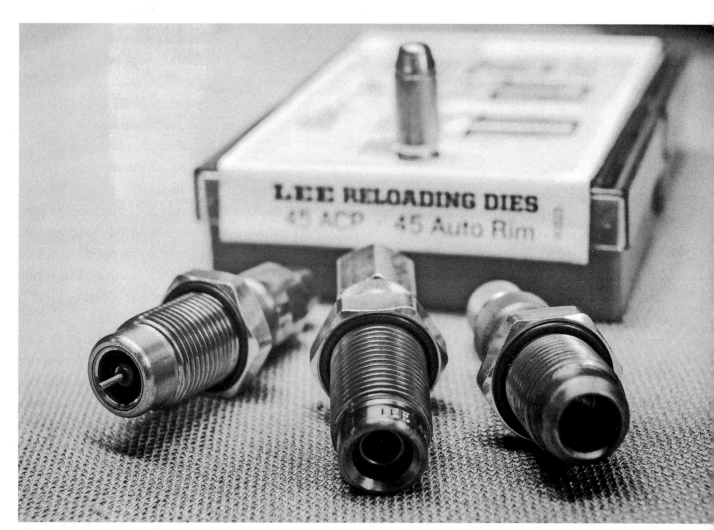

The Lee three-die taper-crimp set for the .45 ACP, note the aluminum lock rings with rubber O-ring.

a carbide setup that doesn't require case lube. A taper crimp die is the fourth in the set.

LEE DIES

My first reloading experiences were with Lee products, as my Dad had a three-hole Lee turret press and a set of Lee dies for his .308 Winchester. Lee uses steel bodies with aluminum lock rings held in place with a rubber O-ring. These dies are a great value even if they don't have other brands' more expensive features. Though I much prefer a die body with a lock ring that won't move, I've made a bunch of ammo using Lee equipment, resulting in some impressive accuracy from my guns.

Lee includes a shellholder with its die sets, and a plastic scoop of proper volume, as well as a chart depicting load data for the spectrum of bullets used in the chosen cartridge.

In Lee's straight-walled cartridge three-die sets, the flaring die is a 'Powder-Thru' design, so you can insert a powder funnel in the top of the die to charge cases. The company's Factory Crimp Die has a place of honor among many reloaders, as it operates differently than the standard roll or taper crimps. The die creates a segmented crimp of the end of the case mouth and is safe to use even with bullets lacking a cannelure. It's very popular among reloaders, even those who prefer the more expensive brands. The theory is that the crimp created by this die equalizes the pressure needed to

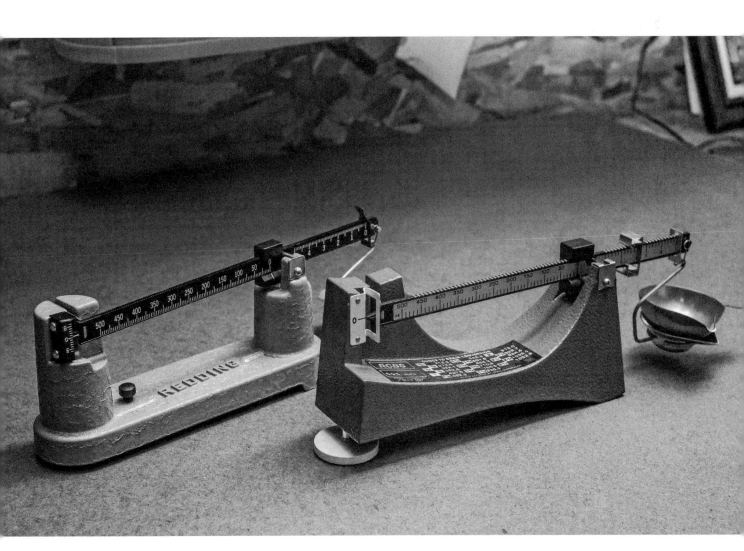

The Redding Model No. 2 is a premium scale, while the classic RCBS 505 balance beam is a proven performer for the value-minded.

get the bullet moving from the case to the barrel, and therefore helps to equalize velocities.

I've used a Lee Factory Crimp Die with good results in the past and will continue to do so. I feel this particular product is the best in the Lee lineup. Many reloaders appreciate the price advantage of the Lee dies. Still, I usually lean toward the RCBS stuff for a budget-friendly choice, though every reloader should try the Factory Crimp.

RELOADING SCALES

You'll need to weigh reloading components: predominately powder, sometimes cases, and even the projectiles themselves. Enter the reloading scale. Scales come in two types: balance beams and digital. Historically, the balance beam scale has been the preferred means of weighing loads, though there has been a definite shift toward digital models in the last decade. Digital measures utilize a piezo transducer to gauge pressure instead of weight. The balance beam scale, while simpler, is a must-have on your reloading bench. It's utterly reliable and will provide a lifetime of service if properly cared for and kept in good working order.

Let's look at the balance beam scales first. I learned how to reload using my Dad's RCBS 505 balance beam scale, and that has been a staple in the industry for years (Note: RCBS discontinued the 505.) I keep one on my bench to this day, probably more for tradition than anything else, and after many years of use, it's none the worse for wear. The 505 is a basic design, incorporating a die-cast body and a bold zero mark, with simple graduations on the beam. It features magnetic damping — a feature that settles the scale quickly for faster readings. Should you find a used 505, don't hesitate to purchase it if it's in good condition.

RCBS has introduced a new line of balance beam scales, and they are a good alternative. The M1000 is a unique design, with the main beam graduated in 20-grain blocks up to 1,000 grains and dual beams for finer adjustments; the larger being 1-grain increments up to 20 grains, and the lower beam graduated in 0.1-grain increments. I like the design, especially when dealing with the heavier cartridges. It's easy to use with a little practice and has a wide footprint and heavy die-cast frame. It comes with a heavy-duty clear plastic cover, keeping it free from dust and other debris. The scale levels out quickly via a wheel on the left side of the body, and the aluminum pan sits in a tip-proof cradle. The M1000 is a wise investment.

The RCBS M1000 scale is a unique beam-style measure graduated in 20-grain increments. It can weigh charges up to 1,000 grains.

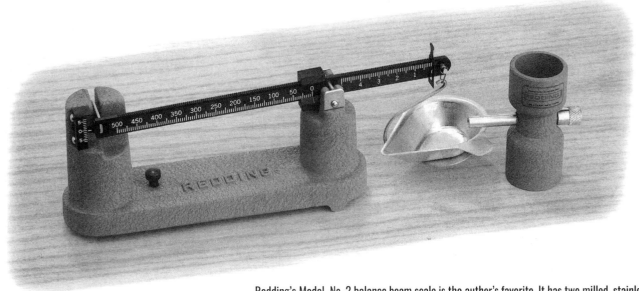

Redding's Model No. 2 balance beam scale is the author's favorite. It has two milled, stainless steel bearing seats to house the ground, knife-edge bearings on the beam.

Perhaps my favorite balance beam scale is the Redding Model No. 2; like most things Redding, this is a serious piece of gear and perhaps over-designed. The Model No. 2 uses two milled, stainless steel bearing seats to house the ground, knife-edge bearings on the beam. The left side of the beam is graduated in 5-grain increments (to 500 grains), the right side is in 0.1-grain increments. The total scale capacity is 505 grains. The pointer aligns with a plate, which is graduated in 0.1-grain increments (up to 1/2 grain above and below the zero marks). You can zero the scale using a set screw on the left side of the scale body, and the magnetic damping gives you fast, accurate readings. I think the Model No. 2 is one of the best balance beam scales on the market.

The digital scales aren't scales in the traditional sense of the term. Instead, they use pressure to correlate to weight. There was a lot of frustration associated with the early designs, but thankfully, that seems rectified. They have specific issues, like being susceptible to changes in readings caused by air currents (an oscillating fan can drive you nuts) and electromagnetic fields from cell phones that can cause interference. Keep your digital scales isolated and as free from interference as you can for the best results.

For years, my initial experiences with the digital scales made me skeptical, and I don't feel I was wrong. But by the time I came back to the electronics, I found things had changed radically, and for the better. The RCBS ChargeMaster 1500 digital scale — coupled with the ChargeMaster powder dispenser — changed my attitude toward digital scales altogether, though it was years before I trusted them completely. I still check once every 10 or 15 loads coming off the digital dispenser on a balance beam. I guess old habits die hard.

The Lyman Pro-Touch 1500 is an excellent design as well. With numbers on the digital display almost an inch tall (you younger reloaders will appreciate larger displays as you get into your 40s and 50s), it has a simple-to-use format. Lyman also provides a scale weight so that you can keep things calibrated.

Hornady's Lock-N-Load Bench Scale is another example of the type of digital measure that can improve your reloading operation. Use it when sorting bullets by weight or when using a powder thrower and trickler. Like the Lyman, the Lock-N-Load has a bold display, and the simple controls allow you to calibrate and zero the readout and switch measuring units quickly.

POWDER DISPENSERS

You'll need to dispense powder, and I've used the most primitive to the most complex tools for this part of the

Lyman's Pro-Touch 1500 digital scale. Its readout is large, a nice feature for aging eyes.

process. There have been times when I scooped powder from the top of a Yankee Candle jar with a spoon. I've used a well-calibrated powder thrower to dispense accurate loads that just needed some adjustment from the powder trickler. And I've also used state-of-the-art digital powder dispensers that throw a charge within 0.04 grain of the target weight.

Manufacturers ship powder in plastic containers, in increments between 1/2 lb. and 8 lbs., with 1-lb. cans being the most popular. But you need to measure smaller amounts accurately. As explained above, the scale is the final measuring tool. But getting powder from a 1-lb. container to the scale pan requires a tool. For years, Dad and I used a small cardboard box to hold our powder. It was the top of the RCBS Powder Trickler box. And we had a Lee volumetric scoop, one of the little plastic yellow affairs, with which we'd scoop out the powder into the scale pan. When we got close, we'd use the RCBS trickler to fine-tune the load. Crude as it may seem, I could show you some eye-popping groups we shot, and I have no idea how many tons of meat our handloaded ammunition procured for us from around the world.

There are a few methods of dispensing powder. That little yellow scoop still comes with the Lee reloading dies, along with some volumetric load data. While not the most accurate way (though there are benchrest shooters who load via volume rather than weight), the system works.

These days, I prefer to use either an adjustable volumetric powder measure or (more often) an automated powder dispenser. There are several models to choose from, and they can be wonderfully consistent. The concept is simple. A hopper holds the bulk powder. When you raise the handle, you fill an adjustable-sized chamber. The powder in the chamber is released through a drop tube and into your case on the downstroke. As a rule of thumb, these types of powder measures give the most accurate results in the middle third of their capacity, so depending on your chosen application, you may need one specific model or possibly several.

There are many choices at varying price points, but you get what you pay for — thus, I like the Redding and RCBS models. These companies build theirs to last, and I've found them to be the most repeatable.

Most of my reloading involves rifle cartridges. I spend a fair amount of time with the large-capacity safari cartridges, so I keep two Redding powder measures on my bench: the PR-50 'Precision Rifleman's Powder Measure' with a range of 35 to 75 grains of powder, which handles most of the standard rifle cartridges, and the Redding Competition LR-1000, which has a larger range of 25 to 140 grains, perfect for the big stuff. When dealing with cartridges like the .470 Nitro Express, .416 Rigby, and .505 Gibbs, powder charges can and will exceed 100 grains, so the LR-1000 is a perfect solution.

I keep a couple of powder tricklers on my bench as well to fine-tune the load. These handy little tools have a chamber for powder, and an interior-threaded tube, which acts as a worm screw. When you rotate the tube, the trickler drops small amounts of powder into the pan, allowing you to sneak up on the exact charge weight you want. The powder trickler is a simple affair, and you don't need to spend a fortune on one.

The graduated plate of the Redding Model No. 2 balance beam scale.

The Redding PR-50 Powder Measure has earned a place on the author's bench.

I favor the RCBS Powder Trickler. I've owned mine for decades, and it still works just fine.

The electronic powder dispensers are an entirely different animal. They'll make your reloading sessions much more productive. While expensive, they're worth the investment if you're a high-volume reloader. They use an automated programmable dispenser — think motor-driven trickler on a larger scale — in conjunction with a digital scale to dispense an exact amount of powder. Essentially, you fill the hopper with powder, punch in your chosen charge weight, and let the machine do the work. The dispenser rotates the tube, sending powder into the pan, and as it approaches the target weight, it slows down and trickles the last few grains.

Remember I said I had a mistrust of the electronic scales? That mistrust carried over to the automated dispensers, and for quite a while, I would check each dispensed load on a balance beam scale. Well, I found that there was only a minuscule difference between the two (if there was a difference at all) and that the loads dispensed were routinely consistent. I've since come to rely on the RCBS ChargeMaster 1500, as it is utterly reliable. As we'll discuss in greater detail later, my reloading technique involves charging a case with powder and immediately seating the bullet to avoid double-charged or uncharged cases. By the time I'm done seating a bullet, the next powder charge is out of the dispenser and ready to go with most cartridges. The ChargeMaster 1500 has some excellent features: you can store your favorite loads in the memory, and it has an auto-dispense mode — when you replace the pan, it dumps another charge. You can convert it from grams to grains and vice-versa, and it has a cartridge counter to make sure all the cases you think are charged do indeed have a charge counted for them.

Easily leveled on the bench by six adjustable feet under the unit, it'll warn you if a charge is overweight or underweight, and a button quickly zeroes the unit on the control panel. The drain removes the unused powder on the right side of the unit. (Close the drain, or you'll find a half-pound of powder on the bench instead of in the hopper.) Overall, the ChargeMaster 1500 is user-friendly and fast enough for me; a 50-grain load of extruded powder usually takes about 15 seconds to drop. With it, I load the .38 Special, requiring less than 5 grains of powder, all the way up to the safari cases taking well over 100 grains.

The ChargeMaster Lite is a similar unit, just boiled down to the essentials. It uses an LCD touch screen instead of the individual buttons of the 1500 and takes up less room on your bench. So, if real estate is at a premium, this might be the one for you. I've used it in the same manner as the 1500, with no disappointment at all.

The newest of the RCBS line of automated dispensers is one serious unit: The MatchMaster. It uses dual-dispensing tubes and runs in either Standard or Match mode. Where most dispensers and scales discern to the nearest 1/10th grain, the MatchMaster will give an accuracy of 0.04 grain in Match mode. It's twice as fast as the ChargeMaster 1500, capable of being run via Bluetooth with its downloadable app on your smartphone, and depending on the powder you're using, it can be customized to run as efficiently as possible. The MatchMaster is a sweet machine, especially when loading match-grade ammo. Still, it's costly, and the ChargeMaster 1500 or Lite may be a smarter choice for the beginner or recreational reloader.

There are other brands and models available, such

The author's RCBS Powder Trickler has served him well for decades. This simple device trickles grains of powder into your pan to fine-tune your charge weights.

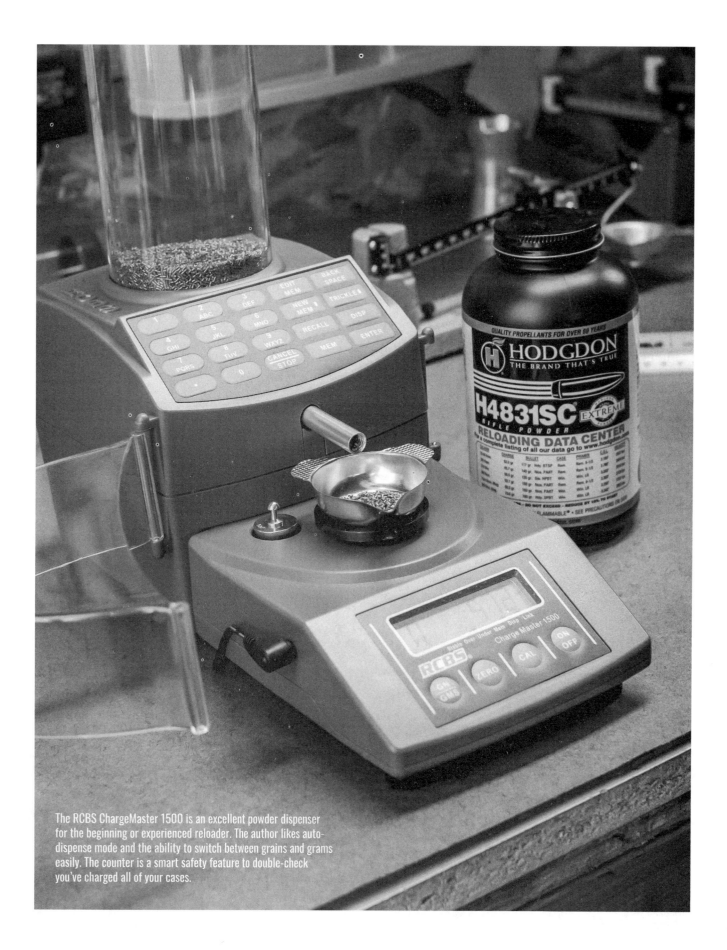

The RCBS ChargeMaster 1500 is an excellent powder dispenser for the beginning or experienced reloader. The author likes auto-dispense mode and the ability to switch between grains and grams easily. The counter is a smart safety feature to double-check you've charged all of your cases.

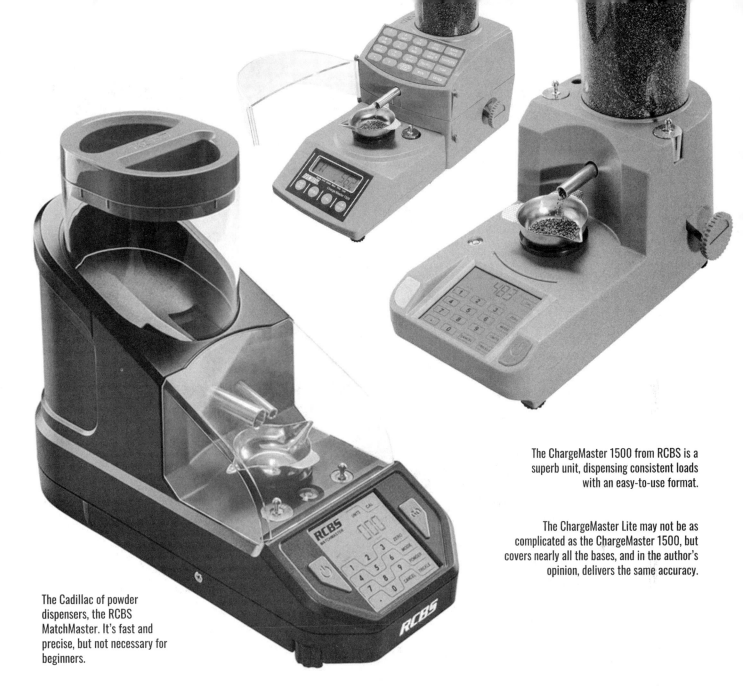

The ChargeMaster 1500 from RCBS is a superb unit, dispensing consistent loads with an easy-to-use format.

The ChargeMaster Lite may not be as complicated as the ChargeMaster 1500, but covers nearly all the bases, and in the author's opinion, delivers the same accuracy.

The Cadillac of powder dispensers, the RCBS MatchMaster. It's fast and precise, but not necessary for beginners.

as the Lyman Gen6, the Frankford Arsenal Platinum Series, and the Hornady Lock-N-Load Auto Charge. All have similar functions, but there may be a small feature or two that may sway your choice. I've used the RCBS models more than others, but I can report satisfactory results with all of them. I still keep that balance beam scale next to them, though.

CASE PREPARATION TOOLS

You'll need a case tumbler or ultrasonic cleaner to clean your brass cases. I use a Lyman or RCBS ultrasonic cleaner followed by an RCBS or Midway vibratory tumbler. My pal Chris Sells swears by his Thumler's Tumbler (Thumler makes rock-polishing tumblers and vibratory cleaners). If your budget is tight and you must choose between the two, opt for the vibratory tumbler, as it'll clean sufficiently and polish the cases simultaneously.

CASE CLEANERS

Brass cartridge cases tend to tarnish. I happen to have somewhat acidic sweat, so a week or ten days on safari under the African sun will tarnish my cartridges. This staining is one good reason for nickel-plated cases,

The new RCBS MatchMaster is a
fast yet costly powder dispenser.

which resists the effects of sweaty hands. But, as brass is most common, you'll need a means of cleaning and polishing it. The vibratory tumbler has been relied upon for decades, as it works efficiently and effectively. The machine itself simply creates a vibration in the tub, which holds the cases. You add some abrasive media — ground corn cob, walnut shells, or even stainless steel pins — to scour the brass cases and polish them to a sheen. There are some brass polishing pastes that you can add to the media to speed up the polishing process. I've long used Lyman's Turbo Brite to spruce up my crushed walnut shell media. An hour or so in the tumbler will leave your cases looking shiny and new. I use two models: the RCBS Vibratory Case Cleaner and an older Midway Model 1292; I've had them for years, and both get the job done well. Most reloading companies make a suitable tumbler, and I don't think brand matters all that much.

The vibratory tumbler/abrasive media is not the only means of getting those cases clean, though I feel every reloader should own one. There are chemical solutions such

as Birchwood Casey's Brass Cartridge Case Cleaner, in which you soak your cases. The chemical comes in concentrate, and you mix it with a prescribed amount of water. Once properly mixed, you can reuse the solution several times.

An ultrasonic cleaner is another excellent tool for cleaning brass. It uses high-frequency sound waves to

The RCBS Vibratory Case Cleaner uses a coarse media to polish your cases to a shine.

A Lyman ultrasonic cleaner and the company's specially formulated Turbo Sonic additive will keep dies and components clean.

create tiny bubbles that agitate the liquid contained in the tub. Liquid agitation removes burnt residue from the inside of the case. While I can't exactly prove it, I think that the ultrasonic cleaners are the best choice for match-grade ammunition, as the cleaning process keeps the internal case volume as uniform as possible, removing any internal debris from fired shells. Ultrasonic cleaners work well for cleaning reloading dies, too, and you may be amazed at what comes out of your dies. Bits of brass from trimmed cases, shavings

of bullet jackets, and burnt primer residue all mix with case lube to create a greasy, abrasive paste that can harden over time. A nice bath in the ultrasonic cleaner can vibrate all that gunk free and preserve your dies for a lifetime of use.

You can add liquid additives to distilled water or tap water to enhance the ultrasonic cleaner's cleaning performance. I like the Lyman Turbo Sonic solutions specially formulated for brass cases and steel gun parts, reloading dies, etc. I also use my RCBS Ultrasonic Cleaner II, as it has a large tub (it holds 6 liters), and I can fit a large number of brass cases in the basket, or even a full-size 1911 (its internal dimensions are 8x12x5 inches deep). Its digital display allows the quick and easy setting of run time, temperature, and switching between modes. A drain port quickly empties the tub, and the provided hose enables the unit to be emptied without spilling its contents all over the floor (ask me how I know about that). The ultrasonic cleaners get into areas where the vibratory tumbler has difficulty reaching: predominately inside the case. My preferred cleaning method is to use a universal decapping die to knock the spent primer out of a dirty, fired case. Next, clean the brass in the ultrasonic cleaner to remove all the burnt powder and primer residue. Then give the cases a ride in the tumbler to polish, all before they go to the resizing die. This cleaning process keeps my resizing dies as gunk-free as possible, for a lifetime of service.

Handheld case prep tools are the most straightforward and most economical means of dressing up your cases, as just a couple of tools can handle the primer pockets and case mouths, though that will come at the expense of aching wrists and forearms. At the bottom of the spectrum, Lee makes a chamfer/deburring tool, which will set you back a whopping $4. It works, though not as nice as the L.E. Wilson model, which runs about $18, fits much better in my hands, and cuts brass cleaner. Wilson also manufactures several of these tools for RCBS, and they will handle cartridges between .17 and .45 caliber. To clean up brass larger than .45 caliber, Wilson offers a larger model, which will take .17- to .60-caliber cases. I have several that I've picked up over the years, and they're great for when a buddy or two come over for a reloading session.

If you're picky like I am, Redding offers a case mouth chamfer tool that uses the case's flash hole as a pilot

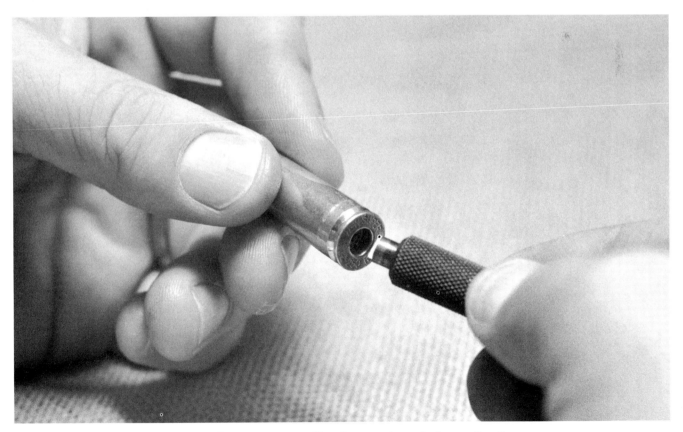

The Lee primer pocket cleaner has a scraper for large primers on one side and a scraper for small primers on the other.

to put a perfectly concentric chamfer on the mouth. The cutter's depth is adjustable for a wide variety of cartridges.

Also, Lee makes a dual-side primer pocket cleaner to scrape out the residue from large and small primer pockets for about $7. It's small and will last a lifetime.

RCBS makes a threaded handle that accepts inserts for all its case prep tools, including stainless steel brushes designed to clean both large and small primer pockets. The brushes work perfectly.

Lyman includes a set of rubber-handled tools in its Universal Case Prep Kit if you prefer a small toolbox-

Lyman's Ultimate Case Prep Kit has all the tools you need for preparing your cases.

type set for handling several tools. The kit provides standard and VLD (very low drag) chamfer tools, a deburring tool, large and small primer pocket reamers, uniformers, and cleaners. Should you like the kit idea, the Lyman Ultimate Case Prep Kit contains additional tools, including a bullet puller and a case length gauge. The former runs about $80, the latter $150, and each keeps all of your tools organized.

Like most other things, there are electronic versions of case prep tools that use an electric motor to spin the brushes, reamers, scrapers, and other implements. Lyman's Case Prep Xpress Case Prep Center is an example, with all of the primer pocket and case mouth tools located on the motor-driven unit's top. This model even has a sloping top, small brush, and dump pan to clean all the brass shavings off the machine. At a street price of $160, the Lyman unit saves you time, as well as wrist fatigue.

The RCBS Brass Boss uses a variable speed electric motor to drive six rotating heads, which you can load with various case prep tools. You can control the speed via a knob on the back of the device, and you

The RCBS Brass Boss drives its case prep tools with a variable speed motor, saving your hands and wrists and making the entire reloading process more efficient.

can customize it to include the tools you use most frequently. RCBS has two fixed stations — perfect for case neck brushes — in addition to the half-dozen rotating stations. Rather than spending time looking

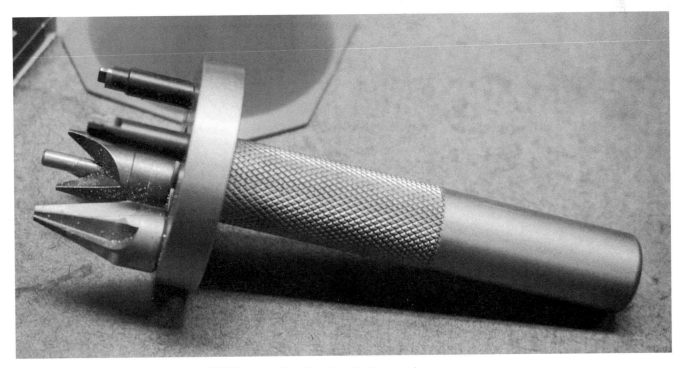

The Little Crow Gunworks Precision Prep Tool (P.P.T.) is one of the author's favorites for preparing cases.

The combination of Imperial Sizing Wax and Dry Neck Lube will prevent your cases from sticking in the die body.

for different tools for each phase of the operation, you hold the case in your hand and let the machine do the work.

I recommend you get a couple of handheld tools such as the L.E. Wilson chamfer/deburring tool, a Lee primer pocket cleaner, and the RCBS Brass Boss or Universal Case Prep Station with the motor-driven trimmer.

I used a simple Lee tool when I started reloading and have switched to a Wilson model. Little Crow Gunworks makes my current hand tool — the Precision Prep Tool (P.P.T.). It's a four-station rotating head that uses a fishing reel-type motion to chamfer, deburr, ream the primer pocket to the proper diameter and clean the primer pocket. It keeps all four of these tools in one place, and the motion is ergonomic and straightforward. The cutting surfaces are sharp and have stayed that way for years. Different tools can vary the angle of chamfer you put on the case mouth. For example, Redding sells its Model 15P Competition Inside Chamfering Tool, which uses a shaft that pilots from the flash hole to cut a steep, uniform chamfer to seat the VLD bullets. The chamfering cutter is adjustable for length and depth, so by adjusting the set screw for the proper size for your chosen cartridge, you can achieve the most uniform chamfer on your cases. This method keeps every step as uniform as possible for precision shooting.

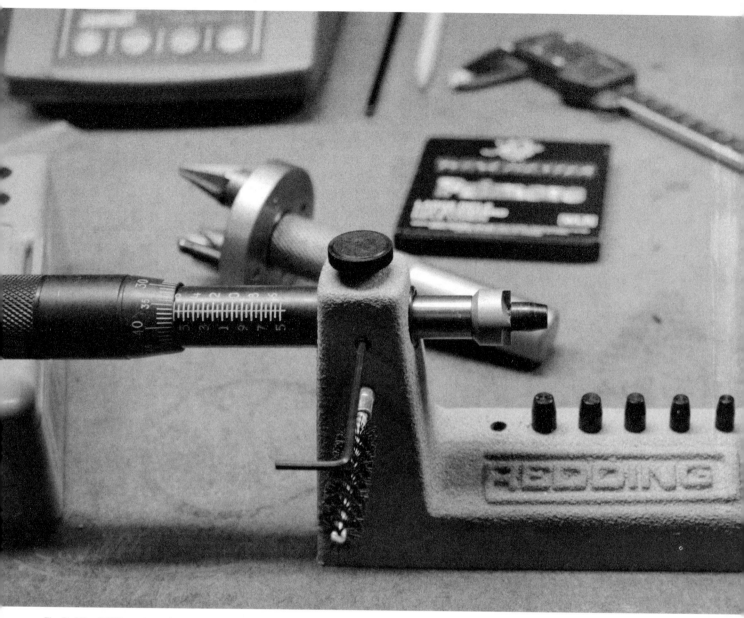

The Redding 2400 requires a bit of elbow grease but produces excellent results.

In some instances, you lubricate brass before being resized, so some form of case lubricant will need to be employed. There are aerosols such as Hornady One Shot, gels such as RCBS Case Lube 2, waxes such as Imperial Sizing Wax, and dry lubricants such as Imperial Dry Neck Lube. Of the lot, I used RCBS Case Lube 2 for quite a few years but have recently switched to Imperial's Sizing Wax. I rub some between my fingers and apply it to the cases. If I'm forming one cartridge case from another — say, turning .338 Winchester Magnum brass into .308 Norma or the .30/.338 wildcat — I like the way the Imperial Dry Neck Lube works. No matter which type or brand you choose, lubricant application can take some time to get right. Not enough lubricant can result in a stuck case in your resizing die, while too much will put hydraulic dents in your shells. Don't worry if it takes a while to get it right. It's something all reloaders learn.

Redding's 2400 Match Precision trimmer is quick and effective, delivering a uniform case length every time.

CASE TRIMMERS

You must trim your brass cases at some point. That's true for once-fired brass and new shells. There are several trimmers from which to choose. Some are simple dies that hold the case and expose the extra material so you can file it to the specified length. While this method works, I prefer the rotary trimmers, whether powered by an electric motor or hand-cranked.

Yes, steel-cased ammo will shoot, but steel cases are not suitable for reloading. Use only brass and nickel-plated brass cases. The length of your shells will play an essential role if you're using a roll crimp or if the cartridge design requires headspace off of the case mouth. Trimming cases to the proper length is especially critical.

Like most other reloading tools, there are options, and you can make it as elaborate or as simple as possible. On the simple side, Lee makes a tool that has a case length gauge of proper dimension and a shellholder for the cartridge to be trimmed, mated with a cutter and lock stud. You can manually cut your brass or use a cordless screwdriver or drill, and Lee makes a Quick Trim die that allows you to use your reloading press as a basis for trimming. I've used this system for years, cutting my brass manually, and was concerned about the possibility of a repetitive stress injury in my wrists. Hence, the addition of a cordless drill was most welcome. As the number of cartridges I was loading for and shooting began to increase, I adopted one of the rotary bench trimmers. But, for the beginner, the Lee system works just fine.

The rotary bench trimmers come in many brands, shapes, and sizes, as nearly all the major players offer one. Some are motorized, others are hand-cranked, but they all work similarly: chock the case and set a piloted

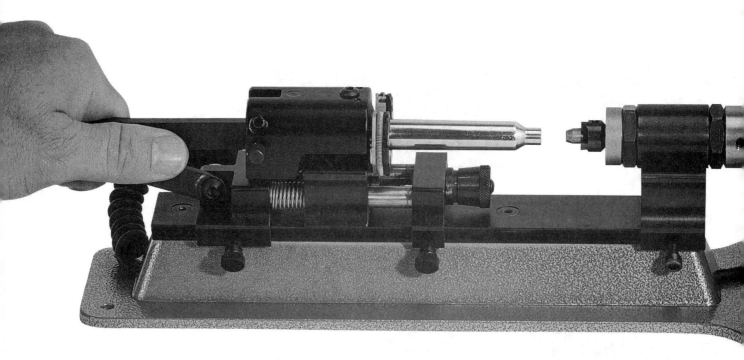

cutter to trim to a particular length. Again, the more inexpensive models will suffice for the beginner. Still, as you become more experienced and your reloading volume increases, you may want to invest in one of the more precise (and more expensive) units. The RCBS Trim Pro -2 is a compact unit, built with a spring-loaded universal shellholder handling cases up to 0.625 inch in diameter. It ships with nine pilots for the standard cartridge diameters. You set the length by locking down a ring on the cutting shaft, and with a crank of the handle, you can quickly trim your brass to size.

I also like the Redding 2400 Match Precision case trimming lathe. Its cast-iron construction and micrometer-adjustable cutter — coupled with a universal collet that holds almost any cartridge — makes for precise and quick trimming. Like most things coming from Redding, the 2400 is quick and easy to use and is repeatable. A shaft lock button on the trimmer's crank side locks the shaft to allow the universal collet to be tightened or loosened. The micrometer adjusts the trim length by the amount labeled on the cutter (some micrometer adjustments don't work as advertised). The titanium nitride cutter leaves a nice, square case mouth. Redding has conveniently placed some case preparation tools on the unit's side, including a case brush and large and

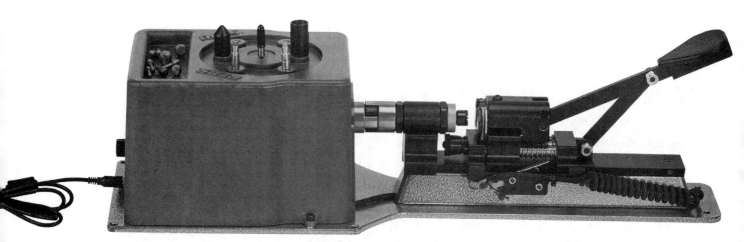

The RCBS Universal Case Prep Center has a micrometer-adjustable trimmer driven by a variable speed electric motor, as well as rotating heads for other case preparation chores.

The Lee Case Length Gauge and Cutter, and Lock Stud, allows you to trim your cases on a budget. You can mate the tool with a drill to speed up the process and save your wrists.

small primer pocket cleaners. You can use the 2400 in an assembly line style.

I've developed a penchant for micrometer-adjustable reloading tools, and when it comes to trimming, it's hard to beat RCBS Universal Case Prep Center. This thing has a variable-speed motor to drive not only a bunch of case prep tools but also has a micrometer-adjustable trimmer. RCBS ships nine pilots with the unit. This trimmer is my go-to, as it's quick and easy, even if the motor's sound gets a bit monotonous at times.

Lyman's Case Trim Xpress also uses a variable-speed motor and a carbide cutter to trim the brass. However, it relies on a set of 10 different bushings that contact the cartridge's shoulder (the unit doesn't work with straight-walled cartridges) to cut your brass to length.

An adjustment wheel allows for custom lengths in 0.001-inch increments.

Consider the amount of reloading you intend to do. If you're loading just a few boxes of ammo for hunting each year, a manual case trimmer makes sense. If you want to delve deeply into reloading, shooting year-round, or loading for your buddies, consider the motor-driven units.

On the complete opposite end of the spectrum, the Lee trimming system is very affordable and reliable. It uses four parts: a universal lock stud, shellholder (which screws into the stud), case length pilot, and a cutter that screws into the pilot. For less than $15, you can accurately trim brass cases. The pilot uses the flash hole for concentricity, butting up against the lock stud to establish the proper case length.

The RCBS Universal Hand Priming Tool uses spring-loaded jaws to hold the case and a primer tray to keep a fair amount of primers for long sessions.

use the little priming arm and cup on your reloading press to prime your cases, though there are a handful of presses that don't offer this feature, such as the RCBS Summit. The only drawback with using the press to prime your cases is that it generates massive leverage without giving the 'feel' of a hand primer tool. Some presses, such as the Lyman Brass Smith Victory, come with a primer feeder and a steel shield to protect you should a primer go off accidentally (yes, it can happen). Other presses have a priming cup on an arm that will swing into a slot in the ram of the press, and you'll have to load the primers one at a time. The down press of the ram will shove the primer into the pocket of your case. If I must prime from the press, I prefer this style so that should something go awry and I ignite a primer, it'll be just one, not an entire tube.

The second priming method uses a hand-primer, and this is the technique I prefer. I have two models: The RCBS Universal Hand Priming Tool and the Lyman E-ZEE Prime Hand Priming Tool. Both use a tray to hold primers and have a hand lever to seat them. They also use a shut-off gate to avoid chain detonation. The RCBS tool uses the RCBS spring-loaded universal shellholder, while the Lyman uses the appropriate shellholder for the cartridge you're priming. I like them both and happily use either, as I appreciate the feel they give me while seating large and small primers.

Should the idea of repeatedly twisting the cutter make your wrists and forearms hurt just thinking about it, you can chock the lock stud in a drill. It's a fantastic solution for the beginner, and I still have my collection of Lee trimmers. If finances or space present an issue, this one can be an excellent choice for the low-volume reloader.

PRIMING TOOLS

You've got to be able to install a new primer in the formed cartridge case to make things work, and there are essentially two methods of doing so. The first is to

CALIPERS AND MICROMETERS

Precise measurements are a vital part of the reloading process. Just as you use a scale to weigh reloading components, you need to measure case length, bullet diameter, length, datum line (the distance from the base of the cartridge to the shoulder), and cartridge overall length. You'll need a quality dial caliper or digital caliper to measure precisely. You'll generally use a micrometer to make precise measurements on round surfaces, such as lead balls, bullets, or perhaps case mouths you have turned to a specific diameter. Still, for general reloading, a caliper will suffice.

I use two digital calipers from RCBS and Mitutoyo. With these, you can easily switch between inches

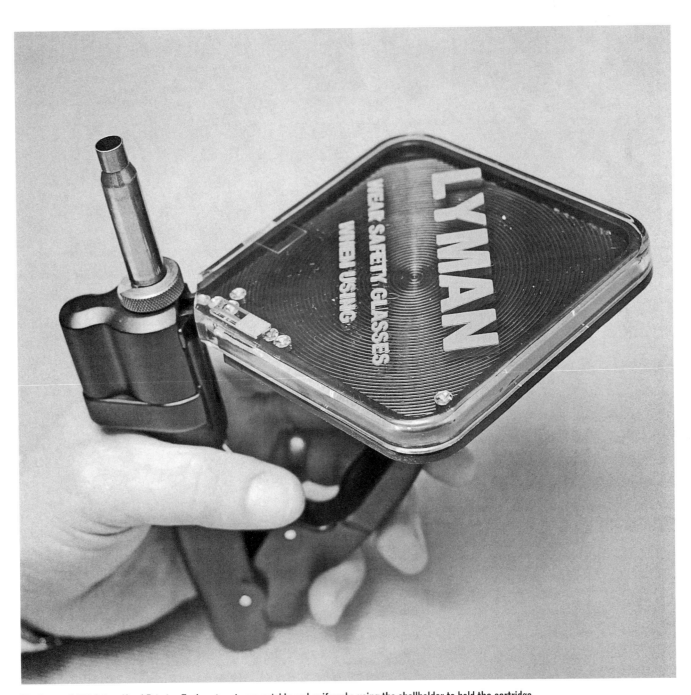

The Lyman E-ZEE Prime Hand Priming Tool seats primers quickly and uniformly, using the shellholder to hold the cartridge.

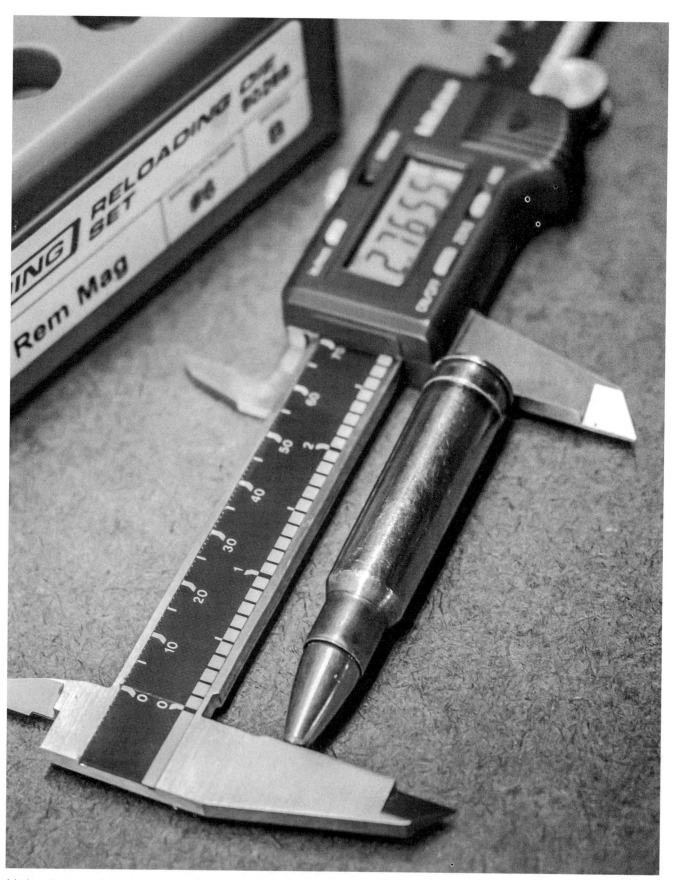

A high-quality dial or digital caliper is a must-have for the reloading bench.

and millimeters, and each has a bold LCD that even I can see without my reading glasses. Also handy is the fact that the digital models display quick, easy measurements. If you prefer to use the more traditional dial caliper and are comfortable reading the dial, you're free from batteries and have a tool that you'll keep for life, providing you take good care of it. Whichever style you choose, become familiar and confident with it so that you can monitor all the dimensions of your ammunition.

POWDER FUNNELS

For pouring powder into cases, you'll need a powder funnel. Many universal models will suffice for cases between .22 and .45 caliber. Some of the new case designs beg for a modified funnel (the Remington Ultra Magnums come to mind) with a shorter spout length, so the powder all goes into the case and doesn't pour around the mouth and along the neck and shoulder. Some companies make diameter-specific funnels; Satern has some static-free models. If you intend

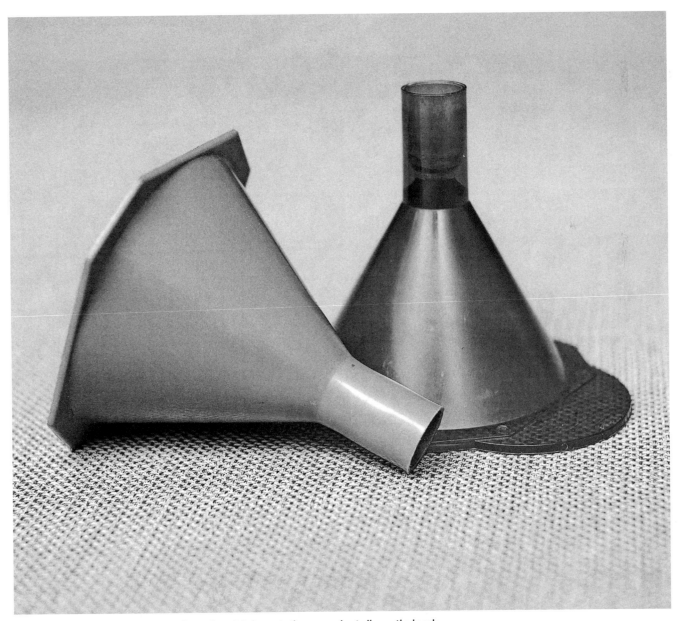

A simple powder funnel keeps the propellant where it belongs: in the case and not all over the bench.

to reload for just a few different bore diameters, a diameter-specific funnel is a useful tool to add to your bench. I've modified universal funnels for other projects and keep an assortment of ones I've collected over the years on my bench. If you intend to reload for the tiny .17-caliber centerfires, you'll need a specialty model to funnel the powder into those little cases.

LOADING BLOCKS

When dealing with many cases, even if you stand them up neatly like toy soldiers on your reloading bench, you'll invariably knock them over. If you're like me, they will roll all over the place, into crevices that you'll throw your back out trying to reach. A set of loading blocks keeps your cartridges arranged and organized neatly. They can range from simple wooden blocks with holes to molded plastic affairs designed to hold multiple rim diameters to anodized aluminum parts. Manufactured blocks typically use one of three standard rim diameters — .378 inch for the .223 Remington family, .473 inch for the .30-06 Springfield and its relatives, and 0.532 inch in the belted H&H case family. I've had a couple of RCBS case blocks designed for .30-06 rims on one side and

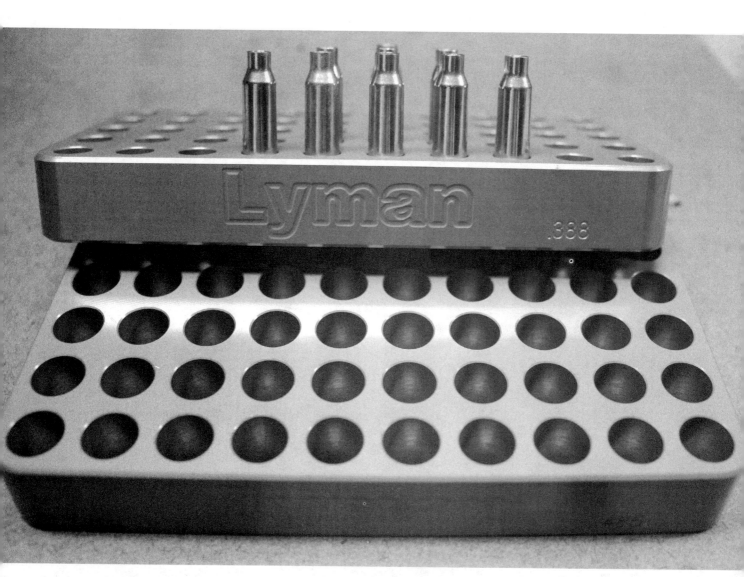

The Lyman Deluxe Anodized Loading Blocks are built to last a lifetime; they clean up easily, never warp or crack, and are heavy enough to keep cartridges from being knocked over.

.375 H&H rims on the other for decades, and they work just as well today as they did when I got them. I also use Lyman molded plastic Bleacher Blocks and the Deluxe Anodized Aluminum Loading Blocks. While on the more expensive side, the aluminum models are a useful tool, as there is a hole drilled through the center of each receptacle to allow debris to fall through, and they're heavy enough to stay where you put them.

ADDITIONAL TOOLS

Get a small toolbox for your reloading equipment. A set of Allen keys (to adjust the lock rings on reloading dies, trimmers, and other tools) is a must, as well as various Phillips head and slotted screwdrivers. Pliers of multiple types, from needle-nosed, to channel locks, will come in handy should things get stuck. Some dies use hex nuts, and a small assortment of wrenches isn't a bad idea to keep in your toolbox.

RELOADING MANUALS

I include reloading manuals in the tool section because information is arguably the most valuable tool for any reloader. There is an absolute wealth of data

The Wilson chamfer/deburring tool is simple and effective.

available online, and many of the bullet and powder companies have published their information digitally. However, I am still a book guy, and never more so than when it comes to reloading manuals. You can think of the reloading manual as a combination of a recipe book and a laboratory report; it gives you useful data based upon the rifle used while testing the various bullet/primer/powder combinations. Invariably, you'll end up with several manuals. Makers introduce new powders, innovative bullets, and wild cartridges, and

sometimes data changes. It can be confusing to see two manuals list data for a cartridge with a particular bullet weight and have a discrepancy of 5 percent or more. Remember, the manuals and their long lists of powder charges are just a report, a snapshot in time, and variances in test barrels or conditions can and will create minor discrepancies.

At any rate, you'll refer to the load data contained in the manuals frequently when developing your recipes. Some bullets are unique enough to require their own

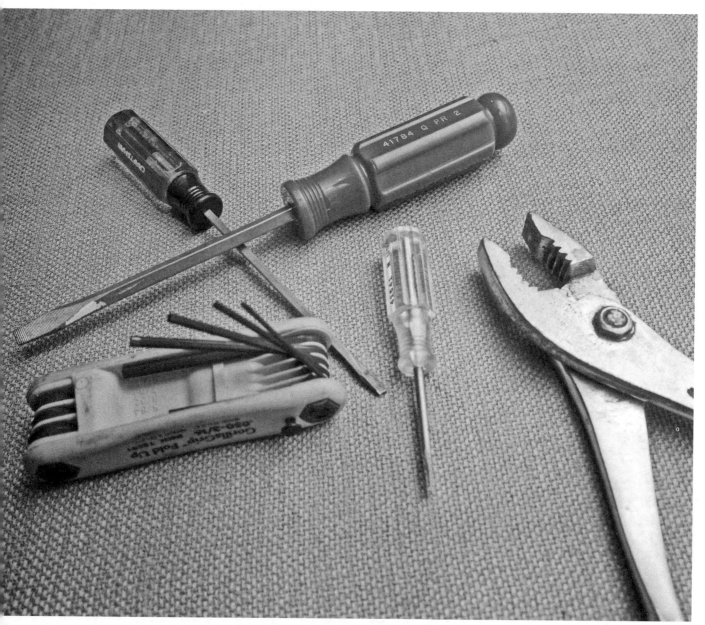

Some simple tools such as pliers, screwdrivers, and Allen keys will make life easier at the reloading bench.

prefer the hand-written notes that accompany the load; I also take a notebook to the range with me to keep notes on the accuracy, velocity, and other aspects of the load I've developed. Over the years, your notebook and accumulated data will become priceless to you, so start from the beginning to preserve your work for posterity. ⫼

set of data, so you may want to purchase a proprietary reloading manual from the bullet manufacturers. What's more, individual bullet companies don't test with the full spectrum of powders available, so the powder manufacturers' manuals are also valuable. As we delve further into the reloading process, you'll see how we rely on these books.

NOTEBOOKS

Record keeping is also imperative when it comes to reloading. Throughout your reloading career, you'll develop your reloading diary, a history of the trials and tribulations you experience. Everyone has their means of keeping records (some more organized than others), but you must keep your personal loading information written down to refer to it later. Never start loading cartridges with a powder charge/primer/bullet combination recalled from memory; sooner or later, it'll backfire on you. Sometimes variations in powder charge as little as 1/2 grain can push your loads into the dangerous pressure zone. Each time you sit down to load ammo, refer to your previous data, and write down, in detail, the parameters of the ammo you're loading. It's a good idea to build a computer database of your load data as a secondary system. Even so, I

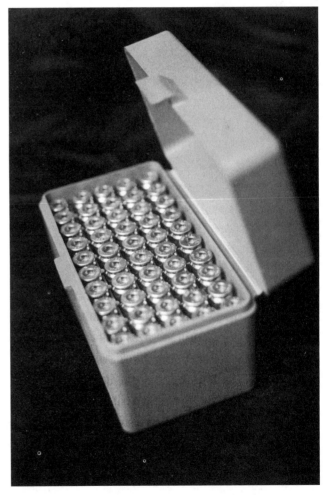

You can keep your cases and loaded ammunition protected and organized in a box made specifically for that purpose. This molded plastic model is from MTM.

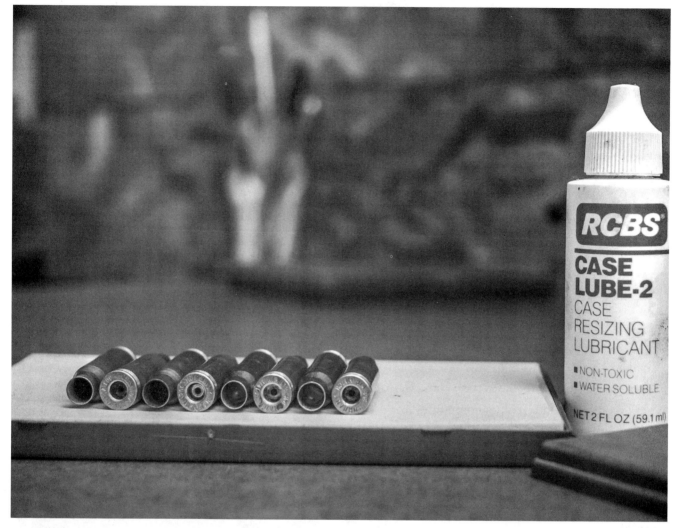

The RCBS Case-Lube 2 is a water-soluble gel that you can spread across a lube pad, and then you can roll your cases across the pad for proper lubrication.

Reloading Bench Features

The most important feature of any reloading bench, whether newly constructed or repurposed and adapted to suit your needs, is that it be steady. A wobbling table, a board set on sawhorses, you name it, and I've seen it over the years, with varying degrees of success. When I first learned the fundamentals of reloading, we had neither room nor money, so we improvised to the best of our ability and used what we had. Dad would mount the Lee press to a suitable piece of wood and then use a pair of C-clamps to attach it to the kitchen table — much to my mother's chagrin. I remember having to sit statue-still while Dad measured out powder; if the table shook, it would throw an incorrect charge.

The next improvement was to clamp the press to a metal desk, which made a big difference. We removed the wobble, and the balance beam scale was performing much better. Though we attached it almost permanently to our office desks, we could move it if necessary. We had gone to an auction to outfit our land surveying office. Since we need to lay large maps out for our work, we picked up a trio of heavy, solid metal desks for nearly a song. These made an excellent reloading bench on a budget (providing you have the space for the desk and the means to move it). You can drill mounting holes in the desktop or mount a

The Frankford Arsenal Reloading Stand has foldable legs so you can collapse it for storage when not in use.

3/4-inch sheet of plywood to the top for easy mounting of various tools.

I've created some impromptu reloading benches over the years for various reasons, such as lack of room or the need for a portable rig to teach reloading classes at gun clubs. I've used a rolling tool cart to mount a reloading press, and while it wasn't the ideal platform for using a balance beam scale or automated dispenser, it did work. Again, it wasn't my dream setup, but in a pinch, it worked.

Commercial Bench Options

There are several manufactured reloading bench options if you prefer to buy a pre-made bench, but most seem to be slightly on the shaky side for what I like to use for a permanent bench. Frankford Arsenal's Platinum Series Reloading Stand has folding legs, much like an ironing board, making the unit collapsible for storage. The wooden tabletop measures 12x13 inches. You mount the top to a frame of 1 1/2-inch tube steel. It has wings that extend the overall tabletop dimensions to 12x39 inches. The steel tube legs open to give a footprint measuring 34x21 inches. The unit is height-adjustable from 28-1/2 to 45 inches,

The Lee tripod stand uses a concrete block for stabilization (not included)! Should you want to build a custom wooden reloading bench, there are plenty of plans available. While I'm not a carpenter, I enjoy making things, admittedly with varying degrees of success.

so you can use the stand when you're seated or standing. Reviews are typical for a bench of this nature. Some reloaders noted that it wobbled with a heavy progressive press on board or that they needed to add weights to the feet to keep the bench steady. However, for someone whose space is severely limited, this may be a solution. The street price is $145.

Lee produces a three-legged reloading stand, in powder-coated steel, topped with Lee's Bench Plate System, which will work with all of the company's reloading presses. The unit has rubber feet and will work on carpeting and hard surfaces alike. To stabilize the stand, Lee has provided supports that will hold a concrete patio block (block not included). A steel shelf located about halfway down the tripod allows for storage of additional reloading tools. The legs have eight mounting holes each, allowing you to customize the location of various shelves or accessory racks (sold separately).

Presses all use mounting holes. Many of them have considerable room in the placement of the mounting screws. RCBS' Accessory Base Plate has many threaded holes in patterns that coincide with their tools' mounting holes. You mount the Base Plate to the bench and then mount the press, trimmer, or whatever tool to the plate — reducing the number of holes drilled in

The RCBS Accessory Base Plate will save the number of holes drilled into the top of your bench.

the top of your bench. Lee's Bench Plate (mentioned earlier) provides a convenient means of switching between Lee presses. Many different adapters are made for other presses, both by the manufacturers themselves and by aftermarket companies, which will raise the press off the bench slightly, moving it closer to your eyes. Inline Fabrication makes some excellent tools for the Redding line of presses, and Hornady offers a Quick Detach Universal Mounting Plate for those with limited space. Two cam locks secure a variety of tools to the base so that you can switch between a trimmer, then a press, and so on.

04

CASE PREPARATION

"**R**eloading." The term implies the reuse of some part of the cartridge loading system. Otherwise, we would simply refer to it as 'loading.' The brass cartridge case's beauty is its ability to withstand multiple firings and resizings. The magic of reloading is the ability to rework and reuse those cases confidently and safely. However, you can reuse a brass cartridge case only so many times before it becomes unsafe. You need to know where to draw that line. Picking up spent shells at the range and assuming they're safe to use can be a grave mistake, and there needs to be a rigorous inspection and preparation regimen. Once the cases have passed muster, they will

begin a process that will bring them back to the original specified dimensions or the dimensions you specify. Follow this multi-step process, and your cases will be ready to be reloaded.

INSPECTION

Shotshell preparation will consist of a simple inspection, as the resizing will happen just before the loading of the shell unless you intend to load your hulls one stage at a time. Pistol cartridges — mainly due to their relatively low pressures — will present fewer issues than rifle cases. Unless you need to trash them because they are so damaged or warped, they will be simple

Happiness is a pile of spent brass.

to prepare for loading. Rifle cases can be an entirely different story. As rifle cartridge design continues to evolve and cartridge pressures increase, the strain on brass increases. So, a thorough inspection of all your brass will undoubtedly save you the trouble of loading a cartridge that may be on its last legs, preventing a potentially dangerous situation upon the next firing.

When preparing cases for reloading, give your brass a thorough visual inspection. This rule applies to new brass, as I've seen some defects in stuff from the factory that has rendered them unusable. Remove all aluminum or steel cases from the mix of fired cases. If you're unsure whether you're looking at brass or steel, a small magnet will help identify them; you want to remove steel cases from the mix, as steel is not malleable like brass, therefore, is not suitable for reloading. Also, look for any cases with a military headstamp and crimped

primer pockets. You'll need to remove that crimp before reloading the case.

In brass and nickel-plated brass cases, look for cracks in the case mouth or neck and watch for excess stretching above the rim, which can appear as a shiny area. As the cases are resized and fired, the brass will flow from the rim to the mouth, and eventually, the area just above the rim will become progressively thinner until the case head separates from the body. This condition is known as "case separation," and it's a dangerous situation, one you will want to avoid at all costs.

Should you find a case exhibiting excess stretching, a shell with a crack in the mouth or neck, or one with a badly bent rim, separate it from the herd, and use a pair of pliers to crush the case mouth, so it doesn't find its way back into the mix. If your eyes aren't what

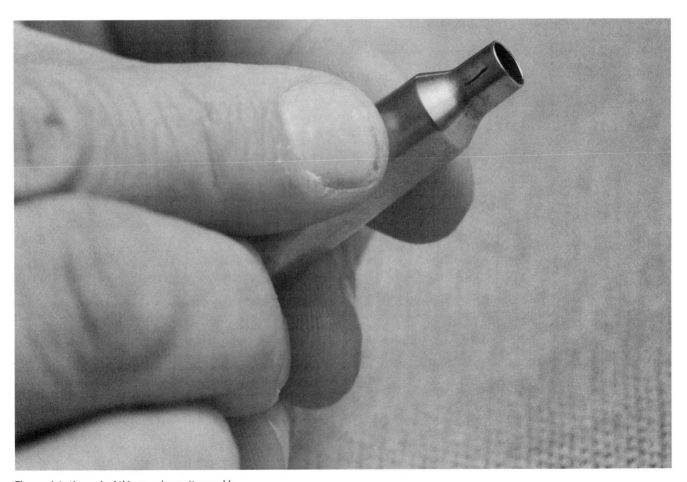

The crack in the neck of this case deems it unusable.

they used to be, a simple pair of reading glasses or magnifying glass can be a great aid. The cases with that tell-tale shiny ring are not always beyond hope; use a homemade feeler gauge to see how bad things have gotten. With the last ¼ inch bent at right angles, a straightened paper clip will serve to inspect the inside of the case wall. If you feel a severe dip around that shiny ring, indicating that the case wall has stretched excessively, that case faces the pliers as well.

Cases that have made it to this point are then segregated by brand, as there can be discrepancies in case volume between makes. Depending on the cartridge you're inspecting, ensure that all the primer sizes are equal; the .45-70 Government, .45 ACP, 6.8 SPC, .308 Winchester, and even the .22-250 Remington came at one time or another with both small and large primers. Ensure that none of the oddballs make their way into the mix. Separate the nickel cases from the brass ones, as there can be enough variation between the two (especially in rifle cartridges) to make a difference in accuracy and pressure. I'll use the nickel cases for one bullet and the brass cases for another. Look at all the headstamp markings, as it isn't hard to confuse a 7mm-08 Remington case with a .308 Remington, .280 Remington, or .30-06 Springfield — or 6.5mm Creedmoor with a 6mm Creedmoor. I use freezer bags to keep cartridges separated by type and brand, so I know when grabbing a bag of once-fired Federal .308 Winchester cases, my inspection process will pretty much assure that's all that's in the bag.

Now that things are sorted and inspected, the next step is to clean the cases.

CASE HYGIENE

Fired cases will have some residue built up on the inside of the case and in the primer pocket, and you

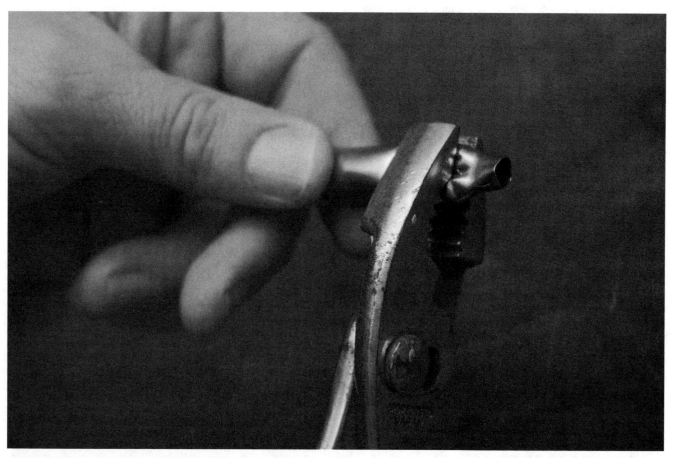

Crushing bad cases with pliers ensures they don't find their way back into rotation.

should remove that stuff. You can use a Universal Decapping Die to remove the spent primer from the case before resizing it. Then clean the primer pocket, flash hole, and inside of the case to keep residue out of your resizing die.

I use a combination of an ultrasonic cleaner and a vibratory tumbler, as I feel the former removes the most residue, while the latter polishes the brass cases the best. The nickel cases don't need the polishing phase, but I like to let them swim in the ultrasonic cleaner. I then use the RCBS Rotary Case Media Separator to get all the media out of the cases. Once cleaned and polished, use a primer pocket scraper to remove all the primer residue. Also, visually inspect all the flash holes, firstly to make sure small bits of tumbling media didn't get stuck in there (which could potentially prevent ignition of the powder charge) and make sure the flash hole is uniform. If it isn't concentric, use the small flash hole reamer to set things right.

The RCBS Rotary Case Media Separator will clean the bits of media out of your cases, preserving the media for reuse.

My hands can tarnish a brass case quickly — especially on the warmer hunts or when handling the same cases throughout the season — so once my brass is clean, I handle it as little as possible. Some shooters will use latex gloves while reloading. Others make certain to wipe the cases down after being touched to avoid tarnishing.

RESIZING CASES

Once the cases are clean, it's time to resize them. Use the resizing die provided with each die set. Set it up per the instructions to resize the entire case body. Snap the appropriate shellholder into the slot of the press's ram, and extend the ram all the way upward by pulling down on the handle. Keeping the lock ring loose, screw the resizing die into the press until you feel the bottom of the die body touch the top of the shellholder. Lower the ram, screw the die body down an additional 1/4 to 1/3 turn, and lower the lock ring until it hits the top of the press. Tighten the lock ring to keep the resizing die at that depth. When you fully extend the ram, you should feel the shellholder hit the bottom of the die body, and with a bit more effort, you'll feel the press cam over to the full extension of the stroke. This configuration will resize the case body to the SAAMI-specified dimension. Adjust the expander ball/decapping rod, so you expose about 1/4 inch of the decapping pin below the case mouth; that will be enough to remove a spent primer, yet not so much that the bottom of the expander ball will hit the case web during resizing.

Before you insert a case into the shellholder, you'll

The author uses the RCBS Universal Case Prep Center's rotating brush to clean residue from a dirty primer pocket.

need to lubricate the case; without lube, you'll rip the rim clean off when you try to remove the case from the resizing die. (An exception to this rule is the titanium carbide dies for pistol cartridges, which require no lubrication. I recommend you lube all rifle cases.) These days, I'm using Imperial Sizing Die Wax from Redding more than any other lubricant, though, for years, I put the RCBS Case Lube and Lube Pad to fair use. The Imperial wax feels like Chapstick. I rub a minimal amount between my index finger and thumb and apply a thin layer over the case, concentrating it toward the base. One application to my fingers will usually lube four or five cases, and the two tins of wax I purchased six years ago are still going strong. You'll need lubricant on the inside of the neck, too, to give a smooth transition over the expander ball. I like Imperial Dry Neck Lube. It's a fine powder that handles the task

correctly. My pal Marty Groppi prefers the aerosol lube from Hornady, and his cases come out just fine, so the choice comes down to personal preference. You need enough lubricant to prevent the case from sticking in the die (we'll deal with how to remove a stuck case later on), but if you put too much lubricant on a case, you can cause hydraulic dents, especially in the shoulder of a bottleneck cartridge. It may take a while to get the procedure down, but practice makes perfect.

Insert an adequately lubricated case into the shellholder. Pull the handle to run that case up into the resizing die, which will squeeze the case body down to the proper dimension. That motion will simultaneously bring the case mouth down to its appropriate size to ultimately grip the bullet. If you haven't popped out the spent primer yet, the decapping pin in the expander ball will handle that process on the upstroke of the ram.

Cases can get quite grimy, as shown in the comparison between a clean case on the left and a dirty one on the right.

The case mouth is drawn over the expander ball on the ram's downstroke, returning the inside dimension of the neck/case mouth of the bottleneck cartridge to the diameter that will offer the proper bullet tension. In a straight-walled cartridge — which you will need to flare — the expander ball serves less of a function. Once run through the resizing die, the brass is ready for the next phase of preparation.

Use the neck sizing die for bottleneck cartridges; it only resizes the neck. Reserve this process for bolt-action rifles, which have the most camming power to close the bolt. The reason? When neck sizing, you must use the cases fired in the gun you're loading for, as neck-sized ammo won't be useable in other rifle chambers. That's because when you fire a cartridge, it expands to become a mirror of the chamber; in theory, it is perfectly concentric, or at least as concentric to the bore as is the chamber. The neck sizing operation doesn't touch the body or shoulder of a fired cartridge. It only resizes the neck, reducing it below the target diameter and bringing it down over the expander ball to give the proper inside diameter for bullet tension. Yes, when using neck sized ammo, you'll feel a considerable amount of resistance when closing the bolt. This pressure is due to the cartridge remaining so close in dimension to that of the chamber, but you should see an accuracy improvement because it is so tight. Neck-sized ammo is ideal for target shooting or precision work when hunting woodchucks, prairie dogs, and other small targets. I've used it for deer hunting with no issue, but the follow-up shots were a bit slower, or perhaps not as smooth loading as regular ammunition. I would not use neck-sized loads for dangerous game hunting. Whether or not you want to try neck sized reloads in your bolt gun is your choice; the process isn't any different than full-length resizing, but make sure you

A disassembled resizing die, showing the expander ball and decapping pin.

Redding's three die Premium Sets include a full-length resizing die and neck sizing die, in addition to the micrometer-adjustable seating die.

clearly label the ammunition for its intended rifle to avoid any mix-ups.

After resizing, inspect the cases again. The stress of working the brass through the resizing die and over the expander ball can cause weak spots in the brass to crack. Any cracked cases should be crushed by the pliers and sent to the recyclable brass bin.

TO THE TRIMMER

The next step is to measure your cases' length with your calipers, trimming off any excess so that they are of a proper, uniform length. Consult your reloading manual to get the correct data on your cartridge and adhere to the case length dimension, checking it with

your calipers. The more you use your trimmer, the more familiar it'll become, and the faster the process will go.

Once you trim the cases, use the chamfer and deburring tools to dress the case mouth. The chamfer tool works inside the case mouth, smoothing the brass so the bullet can be seated with a minimal scraping of the copper or lead bullets. The deburring tool works the outside of the case mouth, removing burrs that cause ammo feeding issues. This process shouldn't remove a lot of metal; you should only smooth things out. The chamfer angle on the inside of the case mouth can differ, depending on the tool. While many tools deliver the 'standard' chamfer, Redding offers a VLD chamfer tool that pilots off the flash hole — optimizing concentricity — and puts a steeper angle on the inside of the mouth to facilitate the loading of bullets with steeper boattail angles. These are known as "very low drag" or VLD bullets.

FLARING THE CASE MOUTH

For the straight-walled cases, both pistol and rifle, the flaring die is the next stop on the tour. The straight-walled die sets come with a flaring die, for these cartridges need the mouth flared out to accept a bullet. The flaring die uses a plug to open the case's mouth like a bell; I like to use the minimal amount of flaring to avoid overworking the brass, which can shorten case life. Also, excessive flaring can stress the brass at the mouth to the point where you'll see premature cracking in that area. On the other hand, insufficient flaring will cause the bullet to crumple the case wall when it's seated. It's all about balance. I prefer about 1/8 inch of flared case mouth on my cases, so

I keep about ¼ inch of space between the top of the shellholder and the bottom of the flaring die, lowering the flaring plug to get the desired amount of flare. Like any reloading process, it'll take some experimentation, and you'll probably ruin a few cases along the way. Still, reloading is a process that requires hands-on learning, so chalk those ruined cases up to experience.

The dual-sided RCBS chamfer/deburring tool.

L-R An unflared pistol case, a correctly flared pistol case, and an over-flared pistol case.
Flaring is required to prevent the case wall from crumpling during bullet seating.

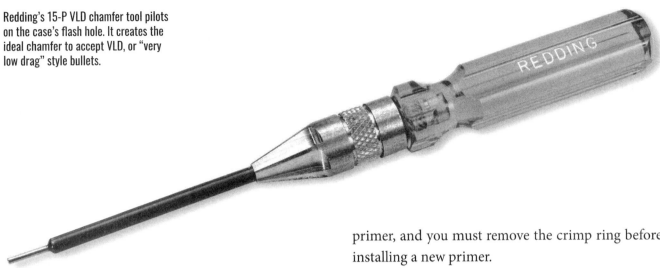

Redding's 15-P VLD chamfer tool pilots on the case's flash hole. It creates the ideal chamfer to accept VLD, or "very low drag" style bullets.

REMOVING A MILITARY PRIMER CRIMP

If you're using military brass, you'll find crimped primers. A small band of brass at the primer pocket's rim holds the primer in place during the most rigorous battle conditions and rough handling of military ammunition. Crimping poses a pair of problems to the reloader: it is more difficult to remove the spent primer, and you must remove the crimp ring before installing a new primer.

I recommend installing a hardened decapping pin to remove those wedged-in military primers. You'll feel the difference in the first few rounds of military brass you try to resize; there is a considerable amount of extra resistance when you attempt to pop primers out. The hardened pin will not bend or break easily and allows you to use more force.

Once you remove the primer, you have to get rid of that little crimp ring built into the primer pocket.

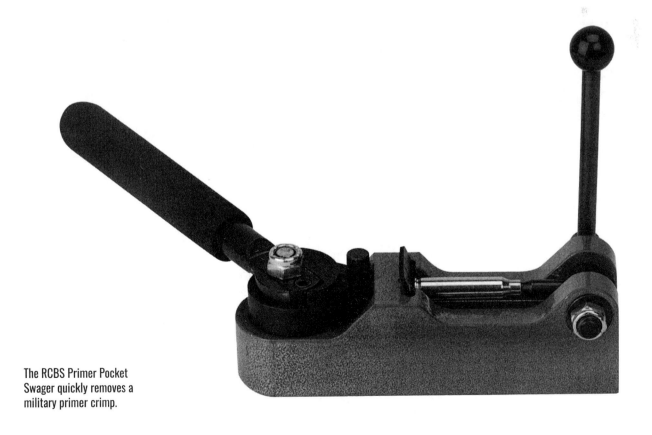

The RCBS Primer Pocket Swager quickly removes a military primer crimp.

There are two methods: either cut it out or swage it out. Many hand tools will cut or ream it out. Some are amazingly simple, like the Hornady or Lyman pocket reamers. Like L.E. Wilson's reamer, others operate on a hand crank principle in conjunction with their case trimming device. Electric case prep machines drive some cutting tools used for military primer removal. The RCBS Case Prep Station has an attachment specially designed for removing the military crimp from large and small primer pockets. It uses the rotating heads on the top of the machine and easily cuts out the crimp at the higher RPM settings. Hornady offers a similar tool for its case trimming machine. The second method, swaging, squeezes the brass ring back into the case head. Some swaging tools mount to the press and use leverage to squeeze out the crimp.

My favorite tool for swaging military brass primer pockets is a separate bench-mounted device. The Dillon

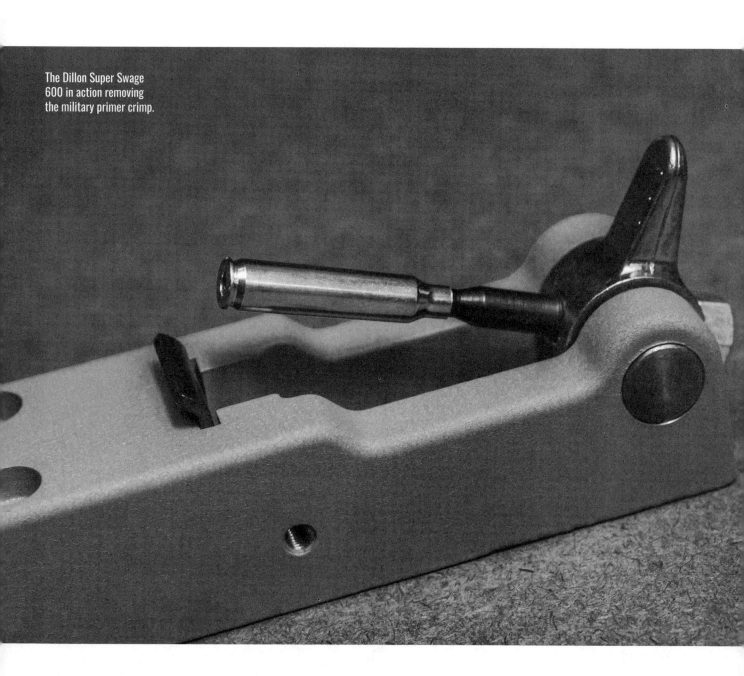

The Dillon Super Swage 600 in action removing the military primer crimp.

Super Swage 600 is a simple little unit that uses leverage to swage the crimp. The RCBS Bench Mount Primer Pocker Swager is another fine tool. Both are available in small primer pocket size (for .223/5.56mm) and large primer pocket size (for .308/7.62mm NATO and the .30-'06 Springfield).

Once the brass is clean and well inspected and the primer crimp removed, look further at the primer pocket for excess primer sealant. Scrape out this stuff as well. Examine the flash hole for burrs, metal protruding into the primer pocket. You see, most military brass has a punched flash hole (unlike sporting brass cases that feature a reamed flash hole). The flash hole punch enters through the case web from the mouth, and it sometimes leaves jagged brass in the primer pocket. The primer pocket scraper is essential here to remove the excess sealant and bits of brass left over from the punching process. Use a flash hole tool to true-up the hole and ensure you have a concentric flash hole for perfect ignition in your reloaded ammunition. |||

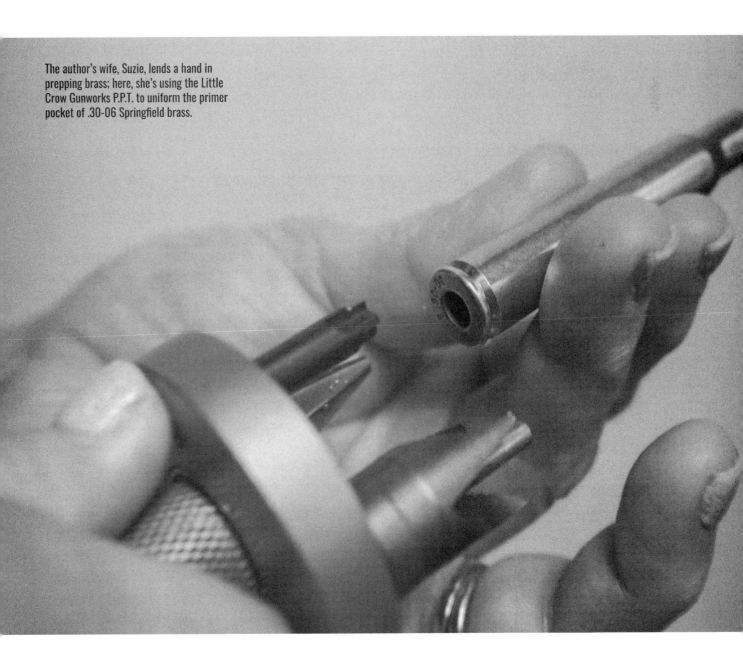

The author's wife, Suzie, lends a hand in prepping brass; here, she's using the Little Crow Gunworks P.P.T. to uniform the primer pocket of .30-06 Springfield brass.

CARTRIDGE ASSEMBLY

PRIMING

You've inspected, cleaned, prepped, and resized the cases. Now you'll install the new primers. For this part of the process, you can use the priming arm on your press or opt for a hand-priming tool. I've used both methods and have settled on hand-priming, as I like the 'feel' it affords. What's more, the pressures generated by the press can be excessive, and you can seat primers too deeply or overstress the metal cup.

When installing primers, be aware that they can go off if crushed. It is just the nature of the beast. And if you have a bunch of primers in the hand primer's tray and one goes off, a chain ignition can occur. When priming cases, I keep the powder off the bench in the event of a primer ignition, and I always ensure no primers spill on the floor. I've seen a primer go off under the leg of a chair when someone sat down, so you want to keep them in their original package and a safe place until

Lyman E-ZEE Prime tool is a safe and efficient device for installing primers; it uses the appropriate shellholder for your cartridge.

they're ready to be installed.

With the hand priming tool, you can feel the primer sliding into the primer pocket, and you'll want to use a smooth, even squeeze each time. With the press' priming arm, the feel is a bit less sensitive, but the same even stroke is necessary. The result should be a primer seated flush with the case head or slightly recessed. You never want a primer to protrude beyond the surface of the case head, as you'd run the risk of detonation when the firearm goes into battery. Primers seated more than 0.004-inch deep can be damaged internally and might not go off. Once installed, check each primer by running a fingernail over them to ensure none are sticking above the case head. You can also set the primed cartridge on its base, on a hard, flat surface — if it stands without rocking, the primer is seated flush or recessed. If the case rocks or wobbles, the primer

isn't seated deeply enough.

Once you've developed a feel for installing primers, you'll know when you feel one seated too easily or one that goes in with difficulty. Various brands of cases will create different "feels" when seating primers. For example, Norma cases typically offer more resistance than other brands. At first, I thought the primer pockets were cut too small, but it's just how they make their cases. I'm not concerned when I feel extra resistance when using Norma brass, as the extra resistance makes no difference, so long as the primers are correctly seated. If the tighter pocket dimension bothers you, a quick twist of the primer pocket reamer will loosen things up.

Should a primer slide in too easily, you may have a case with a stretched primer pocket, and this can be dangerous, as, upon ignition, the gases can escape

Norma brass has a 'tighter' feeling primer pocket. As you gain experience, you'll accumulate expertise in recognizing nuances such as this.

rearward, toward the shooter's face. I had an eye-opening experience when I purchased my first dangerous game rifle. It was a Winchester Model 70 chambered in .375 Holland & Holland. Among the big-bore rifles, ammunition for the .375 H&H is one of the most affordable, but factory loads were still too much for my budget, so I bought a set of RCBS dies and some Sierra bullets. A friend had some spent cases that he generously donated to my cause. I set up my dies, resized and prepped the cases, primed them (from the press), charged and loaded them. When I sat down at the bench on our backyard range, I noticed loose powder on the bench. Examining the cartridges, I found one without a primer, and the powder was spilling out of the flash hole. I was immediately embarrassed, convinced I'd forgotten to prime the case, but I soon found the primer on the bench. I could slide the primer in and out of the pocket with ease. Perhaps the factory loaded the ammunition hot, or there was a pressure issue generated by the rifle. Still, something stretched the pockets of those cases so severely that the ammo was unsafe to use.

Evenly seated primers can enhance the accuracy of your reloaded ammo, though you would think that as long as the shower of sparks makes it through the flash hole, it shouldn't matter. However, it does. Having toured several commercial ammunition factories, I've seen the high-end companies, which create some of the most accurate and dependable ammunition, routinely check their primer seating depth. If the primer is out of spec, that cartridge gets weeded out. Judging by the result, I brought the idea into my procedures, which is one of the reasons I've adopted the hand primers from RCBS and Lyman. I've found the most consistent results when I use them to prime my cases. The process doesn't take up any more time than priming from the press. You don't have to touch the primers at all — you can transfer them from the packaging to the priming tray and install them without touching the anvil or risk getting oils from your hands onto the priming compound.

Let the cartridge and the test data in the reloading manual dictate your primer choice. For example, a .30-06 Springfield case will always take a large rifle

These .300 Winchester Magnum cases have new primers appropriately installed. There is no sign of deformation or excessive primer depth.

primer, and a .223 Remington will take a small rifle primer. Some magnum cartridges use a standard large rifle primer. A standard cartridge might use a magnum rifle primer instead of a standard rifle primer with some powders. Check the test data, paying attention to the brand and type of primer used to develop the load data. Changing primers can have a drastic effect on the pressures generated by a specific powder charge. And I'll state this here, though I'll reiterate the point later in the book: if you have to deviate from the primer specified in the test data, you need to start with the lowest powder charge weight and work up slowly, watching for pressure signs.

Take load recipes with a grain of salt. It isn't easy to replicate the factories' exact component combinations. (Think of them as specific formulae that manufacturers tested within a particular rifle.) So, as we'll see when discussing the other parameters in load development,

There are many different types and brands of primers, and you'll need to pay attention to the specific ones used in the test data.

primer choice is an integral part of the equation.

Once you've primed the resized cases, put them into the loading block, and begin the loading process.

SETTING UP THE SEATING DIE

Now we turn to the seating die. This die, quite obviously, is responsible for seating the bullet into the case but can also apply a roll crimp onto the case mouth. It accomplishes this by using a small shelf built into the die body. Unlike the resizing die, setting up the seating die keeps a gap between the bottom of the die body and the top of the shellholder. Snap the shellholder in the ram, extend it all the way upward, then screw the seating die body down to the shellholder, and back it off a full turn. Set the lock ring and back out the seater plug almost all the way to make sure the plug won't contact the bullet.

Some seating dies are equipped with a micrometer adjustable stem so you can make exact adjustments to your bullets' seating depth. Redding and RCBS make quality micrometer dies, and I have come to appreciate the adjustments' accuracy. If I'm working with specific bullets and want to make precise changes in the seating depth, it sure is a nice feature and convenient to know exactly how much you are altering the seating depth. As you'll find out later, these slight adjustments can significantly affect accuracy and velocity. You can also check to ensure seating depth hasn't come out of adjustment by merely glancing at the dial.

If you need a roll crimp on the case mouth, the process changes. The die body, not just the seater plug, needs to be set to the proper depth to roll the case mouth over slightly so it will crimp the mouth into the groove in the bullet shank (that groove is known as the cannelure). With the lock nut loose on the die body, take a trimmed case of proper length (just the case,

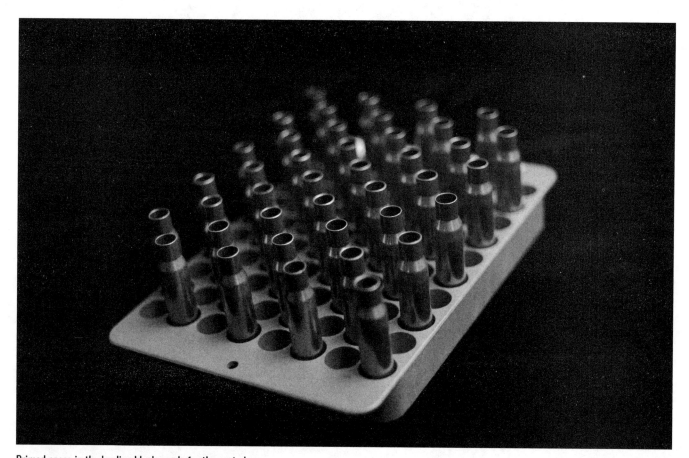

Primed cases in the loading block, ready for the next phase.

no bullet) and slip it into the shellholder, extending the ram all the way upward. Screw the die body down until you feel that small shelf barely engage the case mouth. Lower the ram, screw the die body down an additional 1/8th turn, and lower the lock ring to make contact with the press's top. Run that case up into the die body, and when you lower it, you should see the case mouth rolled inward (see photo for the proper amount of roll crimp). If there's too much crimp, back off the die body slightly, and if there isn't enough crimp, lower the body. Usually, a small amount of adjustment will have the proper effect on the case mouth. You'll

A pair of .458 Winchester Magnum cartridges, which require a roll crimp. The left one has too much crimp (the die body is set too low) and has crumpled the case. The other cartridge (right) has a proper crimp.

then need to set the bullet seater plug in the manner I described initially, and it may cost you a few cases and projectiles to get the proper combination of seating depth and roll crimp.

Because the roll crimp is a product of the depth of the seating die in relationship to the shellholder, you can now see why it is crucial to maintain a consistent case length when a roll crimp is required. Time spent at the trimmer is an essential investment to load correctly crimped cartridges.

Never try to apply a roll crimp to a bullet that doesn't have a cannelure. When the die squeezes the case mouth into the bullet's shank, you can distort the bullet and damage it, drastically affecting its accuracy. If you're loading a bullet without a cannelure and still need to crimp the bullet in place, or if you're reloading for a cartridge that uses the case mouth for headspacing, you'll need to use a taper crimp, which squeezes the case wall around the bullet. There are seating dies that offer the taper crimp instead of the roll crimp. The process

These .38 Special cartridges — loaded with the excellent Barnes XPB bullets — have a proper, uniform roll crimp to keep them seated.

is the same as I described above for the roll crimp, and you'll still want to adhere to the recommended cartridge overall length in the reloading manual.

There are times when a crimp is required, and there are instances where it is optional. All the straight-walled cases require a roll crimp or taper crimp to prevent the bullet from slipping into the case or pulling out of it. Cartridges designed for the tubular-magazine lever guns, in which you insert the cartridges nose-to-tail into a spring-loaded tube, need a roll crimp to prevent the bullets from being driven into the case each time you load them in the rifle. This rule applies to straight-walled cartridges such as the .38-55 Winchester and .45-70 Government — and bottleneck cartridges, including the .30-30 Winchester and .348 Winchester.

Cartridges destined for a revolver also require a roll crimp, as the recoil of the handgun can cause the bullets to pull from the case mouth. If they dislodge too far, you run the risk of the bullet extending past the edge of the cylinder and preventing the cylinder from rotating, locking up the entire operation. No matter the cartridge, from the easy-going .38 Smith & Wesson to the hard-kicking .44 Magnum and .454

Casull, use a roll crimp to keep your pistol bullets where you want them.

The .45 ACP, 10mm Auto, .40 S&W, and 9mm Luger cartridges are popular choices for the semi-auto handguns, and all use the case mouth for headspacing. As such, the roll crimp is out of the question. These cartridges are the classic application for the taper crimp; it's the only means available to keep your bullets where you seat them. The violent action of popping a cartridge up from the magazine and slamming it into the chamber can cause the bullets to pull if they're not properly crimped. You can go with the taper crimp seating die, or you can purchase a separate taper crimping die to get the job done.

For most bottleneck rifle cartridges, avoid a crimp unless it's needed. Most have enough neck tension to hold the bullet in place unless you are loading competition ammunition for the autoloading rifles such as the M1 Garand or M1A1. Even with the bottleneck designs (such as the .30-06 Springfield and .308 Winchester), the stresses caused by the cycling action can still cause the bullets to pull out of the case enough to affect accuracy. However, there is no concern in a bolt-action

These .40 S&W cartridges feature a taper crimp to keep their bullets in place.

rifle whether the rifle is a target shooter or hunting gun.

Even the heavy-recoiling dangerous game cartridges, including the .338 Winchester Magnum, .375 H&H Magnum, .416 Rigby, and .404 Jeffery, have sufficient neck tension to keep their bullets seated in place.

Despite sitting in the bottom of the magazine for several shots during my safaris, I've yet to see one of these cartridges have a bullet change location and require a crimp. Some of the Weatherby cartridges — famed for their large case capacity and high velocities — have

This easy-to-understand overview shows the step-by-step reloading process. Be sure to review the author's explanation within this chapter for the finer details. Photos courtesy RCBS.

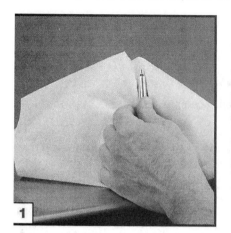
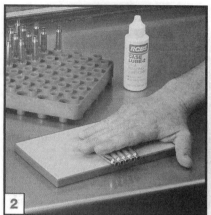
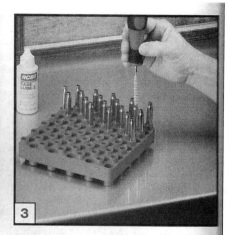

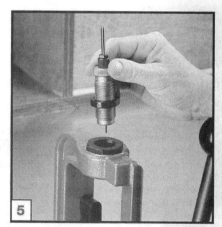

Follow this step-by-step guide using the tools from the Rock Chucker Supreme Master Reloading Kit and you'll soon be reloading like a pro.

1. Clean and Check
Using a soft cloth, wipe each case clean to prevent dirt from scratching the case and the sizing die. Inspect the case for anything that would keep it from being safely reloaded, such as split case mouths, case head separations, excessive bulges and other case defects. Any case found to be defective should be thrown away.

2. Lubricate the Cases (Part 1)
Because of the force involved, you'll need to lubricate the cases before they go into a sizer die. Spread some lube on the pad and lubricate the body of the case. Make sure not to lube the neck of your cases as this can cause dents. If you're using a carbide sizer die for reloading straight-wall pistol cases, you can eliminate this step. The carbide ring in the sizer die is so smooth that cases simply can't get stuck in the die.

3. Lubricate the Cases (Part 2)
Clean dirt and powder residue from inside case necks and simultaneously add a light coating of case lube with a case neck brush. This will reduce the sizing effort and prevent excess working of the brass. Roll the brush across the lube pad after every three or four cases for just the right amount.

4. Install the Shell Holder
Snap a shell holder into the press ram with a slight twisting motion. The shell holder will securely grip the head of the cartridge case. Check out our latest catalog or see your local dealer for help in selecting the correct shell holder. A Quick Reference Table on page 11 lists shell holder numbers for our top 30 calibers.

5. Install the Sizer Die
Thread the sizer die into the press until the die touches the shell holder when the ram is at the top of the press stroke. Raise the press handle and turn the die down another one-eighth to one-quarter of a turn and set the large lock ring. If you're using a carbide sizer die, leave a 1/16" gap between the bottom of the die and the shell holder.

shown more consistent results with a roll crimp. The crimp seems to help even out the velocity figures and enhance accuracy.

Take a look at the data and recommendations for your cartridge in the various reloading manuals. A bit of experimentation with crimping can change the results you see on your targets.

POURING POWDER

Your cases are now nestled in their blocks, primed and ready for the powder. You'll need to weigh out a specific powder charge and drop it into the case before a bullet can be seated. Powder type and the charge weight will depend on the cartridge and the data available in your reloading manual. While I discuss this in greater detail under load development, let's assume that you

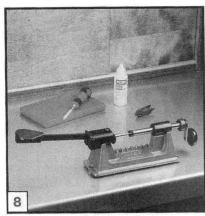
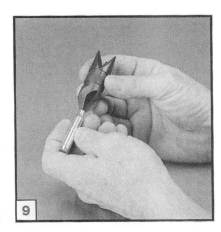

6. Insert the Case
With the press handle in the up position, slide a case into the shell holder.

7. Size the Case
Gently but firmly lower the press handle all the way to the bottom and run the case all the way into the sizer die. This will size the case to the proper dimension and push the fired primer out of the case. Next, raise the press handle. This will lower the case and expand the case mouth (on bottle-neck cartridges), correctly setting the case neck diameter to hold the bullet tightly.

8. Check the Case Length and Trim if Necessary
After several firings, cases sometimes stretch and become longer than the specified maximum length. These cases must be trimmed to allow for proper chambering and for safety reasons. The trimmer works like a small lathe and can be used to trim most cases up through 45-caliber. Check the Speer Reloading Manual for maximum case length and trim length.

9. Chamfer and Deburr
Cases that have been trimmed need to also be chamfered and deburred. This will remove any burrs left on the case mouth after trimming

and will allow a new bullet to be easily seated into the case. Insert the pointed end of the Deburring Tool into the case to remove burrs and chamfer the case mouth interior. Fit the other end over the case mouth to remove exterior burrs.

10. Expand the Case Mouth (applies only to straight wall cases)
Because of their design, straight-wall cases need to be expanded in a separate expander die. Install the expander die in the press, place a sized case in the shell holder and run it into the die. The expander should be adjusted so the case mouth is belled outward just enough to accept the new bullet.

11. Prime the Case (Part 1)
Use the Primer Tray—2 for fast, easy primer handling. To use, first scatter primers onto the grooved surface of the tray. Then, shake the tray horizontally until all the primers are positioned anvil side up.

12. Prime the Case (Part 2)
Place a fresh primer, anvil side up, into the cup of the primer arm and insert a case into the shell holder.

STEPS 13-23 CONTINUED ON NEXT TWO PAGES.

have appropriately matched the powder charge to the application at hand.

How you dispense your powder is your choice, but you'll need a means of accurately weighing the charge. You can scoop powder into the pan of your scale, use a powder measure and trickler, or try one of the automatic powder throwers. I've used them all, and so long as you're careful and diligent, the outcome will be the same, though some methods will be faster than others. I've come to appreciate the automated powder dispensers' accuracy and speed (check out the RCBS ChargeMaster and its ilk). They've proven themselves to be reliable and efficient.

When it comes to your powder charges, consistency

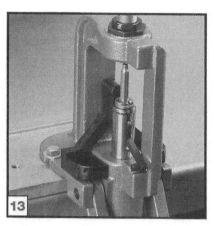
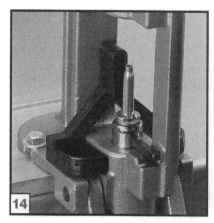
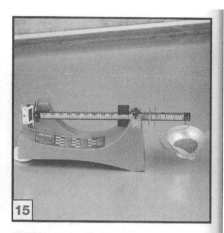

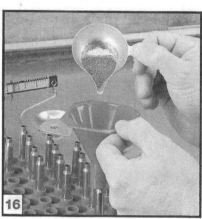
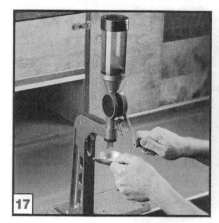

13. Prime the Case (Part 3)
Lower the handle and flip the primer arm into the slot in the shell holder ram.

14. Prime the Case (Part 4)
Now, gently and slowly raise the press handle. As the case is drawn out of the die it will be lowered onto the fresh primer which will be seated into the primer pocket. Push the handle all the way up. Inspect the primer to make sure it is properly seated. In order to gain optimum primer sensitivity, the primer must be seated firmly to the bottom of the primer pocket.

Tip for Priming the Case
For a faster way to prime cases, use the Hand Priming Tool that is included with your Rock Chucker Supreme Reloading Kit or purchase separately the Rock Chucker Supreme Auto Prime. Primers drop one at a time into the primer arm on the press.

15. Powder Charging (Part 1)
Consult the Speer Reloading Manual to learn what kind of powder, and exactly how much is recommended to reload your cartridge. Then weigh the recommended charge on your scale.

16. Powder Charging (Part 2)
After accurately weighing the powder charge, pour it into the case using a powder funnel.

17. Powder Charging (Part 3)
You can dispense a precise charge, without weighing every charge on a scale. Fill the measure with powder and dispense several charges to establish flow and settle the powder in the hopper. Return this powder to the hopper. Use your reloading scale to adjust the powder measure. Weigh every charge until several consecutive charges show the desired weight. Re-check the weight about every 10 cases.

will be a critical factor in reloading accurate ammo. I'm going to stress the safety factor here once again, as an overcharge — or undercharge — of powder can be catastrophic. So, get in the habit of double-checking the data and your scale each time you sit at the bench. Keep a notebook to record every loading session, including the cartridge, brand of case, new or fired, primer brand and type, brand and weight of powder, and the bullet used. After you consult your reloading manual, write down the powder charge in that book, and keep it open to that page while you're reloading. While I use dozens of different powders, I only keep the container of powder I'm using for that session on the bench, so there can be no confusion. I recommend you do this, too. Using the wrong powder can result in catastrophe at best and death at worst.

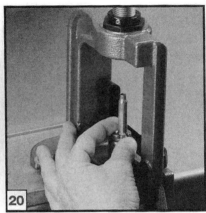

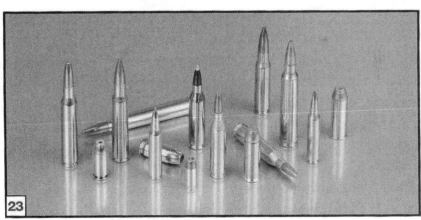

18. Bullet Seating (Part 1)
Thread the seater die a few turns into the press. Put a case in the shell holder and lower the press handle, running the ram with the case to the top of the press stroke. Turn the die body down until it stops. The crimp shoulder in the die is now pressing against the top of the case mouth. Back the die out one turn, raising the crimp shoulder above the case mouth. Secure the die in position with the die lock ring.

19. Bullet Seating (Part 2)
Next, unscrew the seater plug enough to keep the bullet from being seated too deeply.

20. Bullet Seating (Part 3)
With the handle in the up position, insert a properly primed and charged case into the shell holder.

21. Bullet Seating (Part 4)
Take a bullet and hold it over the case mouth with one hand while you lower the press handle with the other, easing the case and bullet up into the die. After raising the handle, note the seating depth of the loaded round. If the bullet needs to be seated deeper into the case, turn the seater plug down.

22. Bullet Seating (Part 5)
Run the loaded round back up into the die, raise the press handle and check the seating depth again. A few more adjustments may be needed for the proper bullet seating depth; then, you simply tighten the small seater plug lock ring.

See our reloading die instructions for more detailed information about bullet seating and crimping.

23. That's It!
Your first reloaded cartridge is ready to be fired. Of course, we've described only one case going through all the reloading steps. When actually reloading, you'd take a batch of cases through each operation before moving on to the next step.

The author used a Lee powder scoop and a glass candle jar top to hold and dispense powder as a youth but has since come to appreciate more complex tools.

Do you have to weigh each powder charge? That's a debatable question. The thought processes differ, with one camp trusting powder charges dispensed by volume and the other relying on weighed charges only. Some folks feel the higher-pressure rifle cartridges require weighed powder charges. Alternately, you can charge the pistol cartridges by volume. Some folks think that any rifle cartridge they don't use in competitive matches or long-range shooting can safely be loaded by volume. Many benchrest competitive shooters indeed load their ammunition by volume. I cannot argue with the results, as they measure groups with calipers in fractions of an inch. However, their reloading field experience is usually considerable, and the loads are well within the safe pressure limits. Many people load their pistol ammunition by volume — typically on progressive presses — perhaps checking the first few charges thrown on a scale, some in the middle, and then again a few at the end.

I'm a believer in weighing all powder charges. The powder dispensers are more consistent than they have ever been, but certain propellants' grain structure can create variations in the weight of a particular charge volume. My goals as a reloader are safety first, followed by consistency second. Accurate and safe reloads are the byproduct of consistency. Most load data give powder charges based on weight. Lee still offers data based on the volumetric powder scoops, so you'll want to weigh these charges. That's especially true for near-maximum load handgun ammo, where 0.3 grains of powder can make a drastic difference. The capability to easily weigh every powder charge is another reason to consider an automated powder dispenser such as the RCBS ChargeMaster 1500 or MatchMaster. They are nearly as fast as using a manual powder dispenser, but you get the benefit of having each charge weighed. You can even check the automated dispenser's digital reading on a balance beam scale. That way, there are no surprises when you squeeze the trigger.

If you use a progressive press, you'll have to rely on a volumetric powder dispenser, but you should periodically double-check the powder weight even in that situation. Should you prefer to use a volumetric powder dispenser (and there's no reason not to), I recommend dispensing the charge into the pan of a balance beam scale and then using a powder trickler to dial in the exact weight required. Then you can pour the powder charge into the case with the powder funnel.

There are two mindsets on case charging methods. The first is to charge all the cases, then seat all the bullets. The second (my preference) is to charge a single case with the appropriate amount of powder, then seat the bullet. I do this to avoid the possibility of double-charging a case or seating a bullet into a case with no powder. Once you weigh your powder charge, pick up an empty case, set the funnel on top, pour in the load, and seat the bullet. Then weigh another charge, seat another bullet, rinse, and repeat. This process has worked for me for decades, and I feel very confident in my loads' safety, especially when I'm reloading defensive handgun ammunition.

I remember sitting down at the Sheriff's office,

Pouring the weighed charge into the case with a powder funnel.

The powder dispenser on an RCBS Pro2000 progressive press. While very consistent, you should check the charge periodically.

putting a new handgun on my permit, and chatting with the deputy about reloading ammo. "Let me show you something," he said. "Here's why I'm not a fan of handloads." He produced a plastic handgun case, the contents of which were rattling as he set it on his desk. Inside the case was a pile of mangled parts, a handgun at one point in time. "This was a double-charged handload. The shooter lost three fingers." Because the .45 ACP case uses a low volume powder charge, there is space inside for a double load, with room to spare. According to the Deputy, a double charge blew the handgun apart, and he considered the shooter lucky to come away with his life.

Pay strict attention while charging cases. Make sure you check and recheck the powder charge throughout the reloading session. If you feel you may have made a mistake — by double charging or neglecting to charge a case — you can weigh your loaded ammo. While case weights may vary slightly, the assembled cartridges should weigh within a grain or two, and you can detect any deviations from the norm.

SEATING AND CRIMPING

With the seating die all set up, you can take a charged, primed case, loosely seat a bullet on the case mouth, slide it into the shellholder and guide it up into the seating die by working the press handle. Extend the ram all the way, and you should feel the bullet sliding into the case mouth. If you set the die up correctly, the bullet should now be seated to the proper depth, and your cartridge overall length (C.O.L.) should be correct as well. If not, now is the time to adjust. If you opted for a crimp, check that also, as you may have to make minor adjustments as you go along.

Depending on the cartridge, there may have been more than one seating plug provided in the die set or additional seater plugs available for purchase. For example, the .375 H&H, .416 Rigby, and .416 Remington are all commonly used with round nose and spitzer bullets alike. Some die sets provide two bullet seaters — one for each bullet shape — so you can effectively load each style. The recent popularity of long-range shooting has resulted in a wide range of long, sleek, high ballistic coefficient bullets. Sometimes if you use a standard seating plug for seating these bullets, you'll find a ring cut into the bullet jacket. Or even worse, you can deform the bullet's jacket in the process. In that case, you'll need a seater explicitly made for these VLD (very low drag) bullet shapes, and your extreme long-range ammunition will come out much better.

Specific seating dies (such as the Hornady Standard Seating) have floating seater stems that help establish concentricity before you press the bullet into the case. Bullet concentricity is an essential part of precision reloads. Why? A concentrically seated bullet will touch the lands and grooves equally. Perfect alignment keeps the bullet uniform, producing repeatable results, and repeatability equals accuracy. The RCBS' MatchMaster Die has a window where you insert the bullet from the side rather than underneath. RCBS designed the die to produce the most accurate ammunition possible, and the price reflects that. While it may not be necessary for the beginning reloader, if you intend to extend the distances you shoot, you'll more than likely end up with a set like these.

Now that you've made your first cartridge, I'd like to welcome you to the world of reloading officially. You've done it, but beware: it's the first step of a long journey down the rabbit hole, and there may be no looking back. ⫶

The Hornady seating die shown cutaway. Note the floating bullet seater.

The RCBS bullet window is a very convenient feature.

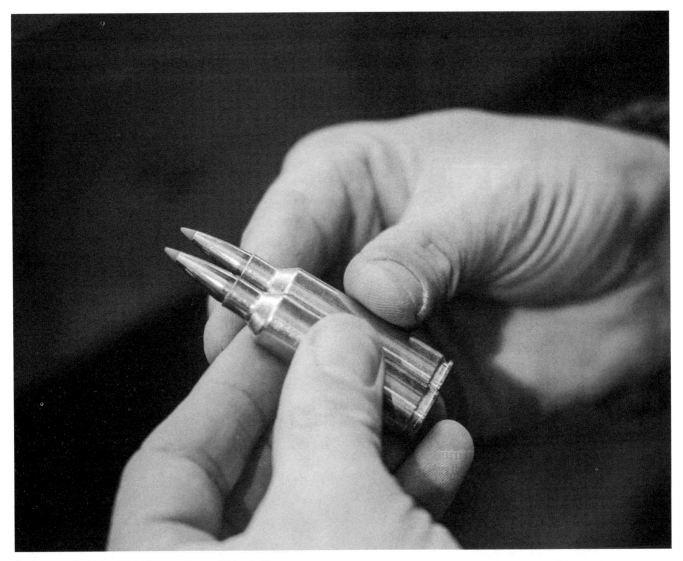

Seeing your efforts come to fruition can be a gratifying feeling.

Pro-Tip: Make a Dummy Round

I like to make a dummy cartridge for each type of bullet I load, using a resized case without a primer installed to identify it as inert quickly. A dummy round makes press set up simple each time you change cartridges. Here's how to create one.

Loosely place a bullet in the case mouth of an unprimed, uncharged case, and lower the press handle to raise the case into the die body. Screw the bullet seating plug down until you feel it contact the top of the projectile. Grabbing the calipers to measure the cartridge's overall length, consult the reloading manual to find the proper seating depth for your bullet/cartridge combination. Next, screw down the seating plug a half-turn or so, measuring the overall length from the case bottom to the bullet tip until you get close to the target length. Fine-tune the seating depth until you get the measurement needed, setting the lock nut on the seating plug. Using a permanent marker, you can label the cartridge as a dummy, with the overall length, bullet make and type, on the case. Keep this dummy round in the die box for that cartridge. If you need to adjust the die for a different press, or perhaps for another bullet, you can use the dummy to quickly reset your seating die very close to the proper depth, with only minimal fine-tuning needed. At the cost of one case and one bullet, this can save a considerable amount of time down the road.

06

HEADSPACING

Those shooting factory ammunition give little consideration to how their cartridge headspaces. However, once you begin reloading, you start to develop a thorough knowledge of how things work and how to make them perform better.

Wikipedia defines headspace as follows: "In firearms, headspace is the distance measured from the part of the chamber that stops forward motion of the cartridge (the datum reference) to the face of the bolt." There are four primary means of headspacing, represented in four cartridge types, though we can manipulate specific ideas to work best for us as reloaders.

Rimmed cartridges. The simple yet effective rimmed cartridge was among the first designs available and remains a popular choice today. Almost all of our revolver cartridges use a rimmed base, as it is strong and has lots of area for the extractor to work reliably.

The rimmed cartridge is one of the earliest designs and remains an excellent choice for the lever, single-shot, and double rifles, as well as revolvers.

The rimmed cases work perfectly in the break-action single shot and double rifles, as the cartridges are fed into the gun by hand, and the lever-action repeaters have long been the domain of the rimmed cases. For the reloader, the rim is probably the most straightforward means of headspacing a cartridge. The rim does all the work. If you resize the cartridge to SAAMI specs, even the bottlenecked rounds such as the .30-30 Winchester, .32 Winchester Special, and .470 Nitro Express will operate. I'll also lump the semi-rimmed cartridges such as the .45 Colt into this group.

Rimless bottleneck cartridges. Because the rimmed cartridges don't feed well from a box magazine — the rim often hangs up when feeding — rimless cartridges feature a groove machined into the base of the case for extraction, a bottleneck shoulder for headspacing. The original inception of the 8x57mm Mauser, the Patrone 88, was among the first rimless cartridge designs. Hands down, the rimless cartridge is the most popular cartridge type we have, and almost all of the cartridges the military employs are of the rimless design. The .223 Remington, .308 Winchester .30-06 Springfield, .35 Whelen, .404 Jeffery, .416 Rigby, and even the .50 BMG are all rimless. These use the shoulder and neck joint as the headspacing point, and the vast majority

have a shoulder of at least 15 to 20 degrees, with some exceptions. The .404 Jeffery has a shoulder of just over 8 degrees, while the .416 Rigby and .350 Rigby Magnum have shoulders of 45 degrees. This group also includes the rebated rim cartridges, such as the .300 Remington Ultra Magnum and 6.5-284 Norma, as the rim's size plays no part in the headspace equation.

Belted magnums. To develop a round with a rimmed cartridge's positive headspace, yet the easy-to-feed characteristics of the rimless type, Holland & Holland developed the belted magnum. Its case uses a brass belt above the extractor groove that acts as a miniature rim yet doesn't protrude outward so far as to hang up during feeding. Though some historians credit the .375 Holland & Holland Magnum as the first belted case, that isn't correct. H&H had a shorter .375-inch-diameter case called the Velopex that predated the .375 H&H Magnum by seven years, though it proved to be relatively weak in the field. Regardless, with the popularity of the .375 H&H Magnum and its little brother, the .300 H&H Magnum, the design would ensure the belted case would live on for over a century. That belt allowed designers to use a shoulder of nearly any configuration, as the belt handles the headspacing, though you'll shortly see how you can modify that. The

The rimless bottleneck cartridges remain popular choices for both target shooters and hunters alike. They include such revered designs as the .30-06 Springfield, 7x57 Mauser, and .308 Winchester.

The rebated rim cartridges include the Winchester Short Magnum (WSM) and Remington Ultra Magnum (RUM) families, the .284 Winchester and 6.5-284 Norma, and the .500 Jeffery.

belted case is synonymous with the word magnum, and many shooters believed designers intended the belt for strength to handle the magnum loads. The belted case would be the basis for many different family branches, including the line of Weatherby Magnums, the Winchester Magnums of the 1950s and 60s, the Remington Magnums of the 1960s, the Norma Magnums, and more. Recently, many shooters, reloaders, and wildcatters have negatively cast the belted magnum because of the case stretching associated with it and the modern trend of lower velocities with higher B.C. bullets. Nonetheless, the .300 Winchester Magnum and 7mm Remington Magnum continue to be top sellers among today's hunting cartridges.

Rimless straight-walled cartridges. The revolvers that were so popular during the late 19th century had begun to give way to the autoloading pistols in the early 20th century, and those new designs used a rimless, straight-walled case with the case mouth as its means of headspacing. The 9mm Luger and .45 ACP were two early designs that headspace from the mouth. Modern designs include the .40 S&W and 10mm Automatic.

The ammo industry has gone through various design phases over the years, and it has left us with several families of cartridges. Your approach to reloading specific cartridges can take differing paths, yet you can handle some only one way. I have, up until this point, stressed the fact that reloaders of metallic cartridges use the resizing die to return the cartridge to the SAAMI-specified dimensions of factory ammunition. Here I want to discuss how and when you can deviate from that rule and use the ideas to make your handloads perform better.

Let's jump in with a look at the belted magnum cartridges. Again, these cartridges use the small brass belt just above the extractor groove to headspace the cartridge. Straight-walled belted cases — .458 Winchester Magnum or .458 Lott — or those with a slight shoulder —.375 H&H, .416 Remington Magnum, and .300 H&H — headspace from that belt. But looking at most bottlenecked belted cases, from the Weatherby Magnums to the Winchester, Norma, and Remington Magnums of the 1950s and 60s, they have a shoulder more than sufficient for headspacing in the same manner as a rimless cartridge. Suppose you measured the distance from the cartridge base to the shoulder

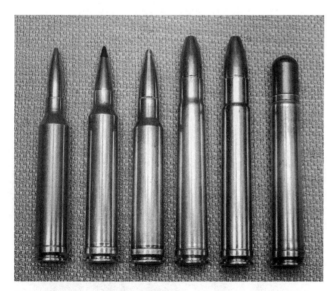

Holland & Holland's famous belted magnum case went on to begat an impressive family of cartridges. Though the straight-walled variations need the belt for headspacing, you can resize most of the 'children' to headspace off the shoulder.

The 9mm Luger, .40 S&W, and .45 ACP all use the case mouth for headspacing.

of a .300 Winchester Magnum or 7mm Remington Magnum factory load before and after firing. You could see as much as a .020 inch difference as the case stretches during the firing process. If you were to use the resizing die to bring the case back within the SAAMI tolerances, you could see how all that stretching and resizing would cut short the life of the brass. The more you work brass, the more brittle it becomes, and it will crack prematurely.

If the belted cartridge used the shoulder to headspace, not only would it extend case life, but it would significantly improve concentricity, and in theory, improve the precision/accuracy of the ammunition. There are a couple of ways to handle this, and I do this quite often for my guns and reap the benefits. A neck sizing die resizes only the cartridge's neck to the proper diameter required to hold a bullet with the correct tension. The case's shoulder will not be changed, making the case a perfect match for the chamber. The cartridge will rest on the shoulder, reducing the amount the case will stretch with each firing and extending the number of times you can reload the brass. The downsides of neck sizing? You won't reduce the case's body diameter, so you'll feel additional resistance when chambering a round in your gun. And the expanded body dimension restricts the use of neck-sized ammunition to bolt-action rifles, as they have the camming power to handle the larger diameter cases. Where the target community

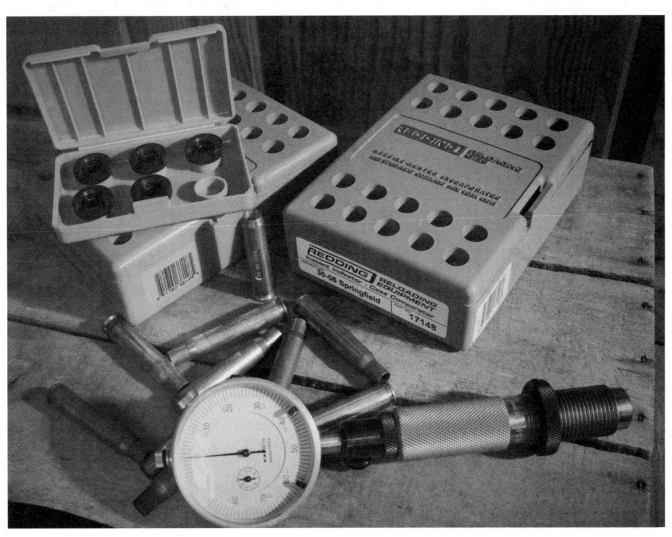

The Redding Instant Indicator Headspace and Bullet Comparator and Competition Shellholders allow you to match the shoulder position to the chamber of your rifle.

might not be as concerned about the additional effort required to close the bolt on neck-sized cartridges, hunters looking for rapid follow-up shots might not like this characteristic. The neck sizing principle is also applicable to rimless cartridges, which already use the shoulder for headspacing. While it doesn't change the means of headspacing, it improves concentricity, and you'll usually see an improvement in group size and extended case life.

There is another means, similar in principle, but I much prefer the result. Redding has a couple of products that can help you make customized loads, giving the neck-sized ammunition's enhanced concentricity while still reducing the case body diameter for easy feeding. You can combine Redding's Instant Indicator Headspace and Bullet Comparator (that's a mouthful) and Competition Shellholders to load ammunition that uses the datum line of your particular chamber. The idea works like this: the Comparator uses a dial indicator to compare the difference in headspace (case base to shoulder) dimension between a SAAMI-spec dummy and your fired cases. Because all chambers have slight variations in that dimension, the Comparator will tell you how much your fired cases differ from the SAAMI dimension. Therefore, the difference between factory ammo (held to the SAAMI spec) and your chamber.

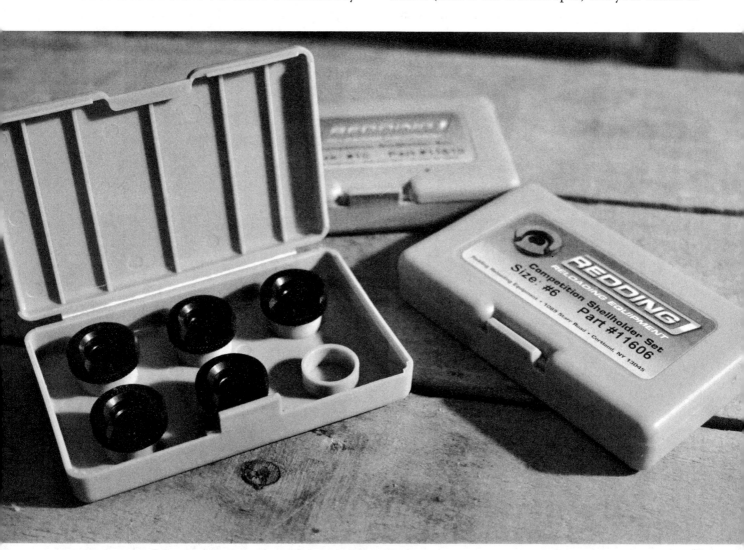

Redding's Competition Shellholder Set is an excellent tool for controlling shoulder bump while still full-length resizing. You can achieve match accuracy with ammo that feeds easily in hunting guns.

A hypothetical example: examining fired cases from your .30-06 Springfield, the Instant Indicator is set up and zeroed to the SAAMI datum line of the headspace gauge. Observing a dozen fired cases, you see an average difference of 0.004 inch from the unfired cases; therefore, the chamber is 0.004 inch longer than SAAMI spec. While this small difference is entirely acceptable from a gunsmith's perspective, you want to create ammunition that will match that chamber as closely as possible. If you set up the resizing die in the usual manner, you'll bump the shoulder back 0.004 inch, and there will be wiggle room.

The Redding Competition Shellholder Set has five shellholders of increasing depth, from 0.002 to 0.010 inch, in increments of 0.002 inch. You set your resizing die up in the typical fashion and grab the shellholder labeled .004 inch — to increase the datum line by that amount. When you resize your fired cases, the body and neck will be reduced by the proper amount, giving the same easy feeding of factory ammunition, yet the shoulder will be of the dimension to best match your rifle's chamber.

The above example was with a rimless bottlenecked case, which uses the shoulder for headspacing. You can apply the same principle to any of the steep-shouldered belted magnums. That's because the fired case's shoulder position will supersede the belt for headspacing. I've had great results using this method in the .300 Winchester Magnum and .338 Winchester Magnum, and several rimless cartridges. Manufacturers would cut every chamber to the ideal SAAMI dimension in a perfect world, but this is an imperfect world. One of the benefits of handloading is the ability to modify the ammunition for the best performance.

Neck sizing your loads isn't a bad idea. But the concept Redding put forth with its Competition Shellholder Sets works much better for hunting rifles, keeping cartridges feeding smoothly.

When it comes to the rimmed, semi-rimmed, and rimless straight-walled cases, what you see is what you get regarding headspacing. However, it can be exciting and fun to experiment with the ideas I've outlined in the belted and rimless rifle cartridges to see how much of a performance improvement you can get.

SIGNS OF HEADSPACE PROBLEMS

If your firearm has headspace problems, you'll want to know it and have the problem rectified before you start loading for it. One of the first signs of excessive headspace is a backed-out primer in the fired case. Excessive space in the chamber can cause the primer to back out of the pocket upon ignition. This very thing happened to my Dad's 1905-vintage Marlin Model 1893 in .30-30 Winchester, and I had to discontinue its use. In a rimless case, which relies upon the shoulder's specific location for proper headspacing, the resizing process can affect the cartridge's headspace. Should the resizing die be set up incorrectly and the cartridge's shoulder moved too far rearward, the case can move in the chamber. While the rifle's extractor should hold the cartridge in place for firing, the case's violent stretching can result in head separation in just a few firings. Check the dimensions of your resized case, especially the datum line on any case using the shoulder, and make sure your resizing die is doing its job correctly.

Should the resized cases measure correctly and symptoms of excessive headspacing continue, have a competent gunsmith look at the rifle to see what's going on, but by all means, stop shooting that gun until it's fixed. |||

07

CARTRIDGE PRESSURE

Perusing the reloading manuals, you'll see "maximum load" listed for each powder. What determines the maximum amount of each type of powder in a particular cartridge case? It isn't the case capacity, as many of these loads are well below 100% capacity. The simple answer is pressure.

Modern cartridges generate a healthy amount of pressure to launch a projectile out of a barrel at today's standard velocities. Whether that pressure is created by compressed air as in the high-speed airguns on today's market, or by the expanding gases produced from the latest highly flammable smokeless powder, or even yesteryear's coarse blackpowder, the concept is the same. More pressure usually equates to a higher muzzle velocity. However, there can be too much of a good thing. When you exceed the acceptable pressure for a given cartridge or rifle, all sorts of things can happen, from difficult extraction to burst barrels and cracked receivers. Without the laboratory-grade tools needed to measure cartridge and chamber pressures accurately, you need to heed other telltale warning signs letting you know you're approaching dangerous pressures.

I've stated before that reloading manuals are a lab

The author's .404 Jeffery handloads.

report based on a particular set of parameters. While the data reported are assuredly legitimate for an individual test firearm, those figures may not translate well to your gun. For example, while I began developing my .404 Jeffery load, I consulted several reloading manuals, as I'd been testing different bullets, and found a considerable discrepancy. I was planning to use Alliant's Reloder 15 powder, as it mates well with the .404 Jeffery, and I had quite a bit on hand. Comparing the Hornady manual's data with the Woodleigh's (both are reputable and well-researched), there was a maximum load difference of almost 9 grains of powder. That is no small amount.

In each manual, test shooters fired similar 400-grain bullets in rifles with conventional barrel lengths (not in a universal receiver with an abnormal barrel length). I was shocked to see such a wide variation in powder charges. The Hornady manual lists a range of 66.9 grains to a maximum of 74.1 grains, while the Woodleigh manual starts at 75.0 grains and goes all the way up to 83.0 grains. What's more, the velocities aren't exactly out of whack, with the maximum Hornady load generating 2,200 fps and the lowest Woodleigh load doing 2,150 fps. Why, then, would Hornady stop at just over 74 grains of Reloder 15 when Woodleigh doesn't start for almost a grain heavier? The answer is that Hornady hit high pressure at a much lower charge weight than did Woodleigh.

I started my charge weight at 72 grains and worked up carefully, looking for signs of pressure. My Heym rifle gave me the best blend of velocity and accuracy at 80.0 grains of Reloder 15, driving 400-grain bullets (including the Hornady DGX Bonded and DGS Solids, and the Woodleigh Hydros) to a muzzle velocity of 2,280 fps, with no pressure signs, even in Africa's blistering heat. That load and rifle have been around the world with me. The load remains an excellent choice *in my rifle*. Like the CZ550 that Hornady tested their bullets with, a different rifle might give a whole different set

The author found accuracy in the .404 Jeffery at 80.0 grains of Reloder 15.

of data, and that is why you always work up from the bottom of the suggested load range.

PRESSURE SIGNS

What are the pressure signs you need to recognize? How do you know when your load is too hot and you need to back it down? Several signs can be seen or felt on the fired cartridge. The first indicator is a difficult case extraction. Whether it's a revolver that requires additional effort to get the cases from the cylinder or a bolt-action rifle with a bolt that is difficult to lift, an overly expanded case is a telltale sign. A semi-automatic firearm may fail to cycle the action or extract the cartridge at all, or a lever-action may lock up completely. No matter the gun, if a cartridge is stuck in the chamber or is challenging to extract, that should be the first sign of trouble.

The spent primer can tell you much about what's going on inside the cartridge. Become familiar with how a primer looks when newly installed, properly seated, and fired at normal pressures. It should have a clean mark from the firing pin. The edges of the spent primer, where it contacts the edge of the case's primer pocket, should have the same curved appearance when you installed it. If the primer seems to have a sharp, square edge along the primer pocket, or it seems distorted in any way, that is an immediate sign of high pressure. (Many reloaders refer to this as a 'flattened primer.') Also, look at the firing pin mark: if the dimple made by the pin has a raised crater on its edges, this is an example of the pressure blowing the metal in the primer backward and around the firing pin. It's highly indicative of excessive pressure.

If you see a bright, shiny spot on the case head where the extractor sits, this is another sign that the pressure is too high for the cartridge/rifle combination. I've also

The case on the left shows normal, safe pressures, while the one on the right has a flattened primer and a cratered firing pin mark.

seen excessive pressure blow the primer entirely out of the case and have found the cup and anvil of the primer down in the rifle's magazine.

However, lest you should fear the handloaded cartridge, I have seen all of these symptoms in factory ammunition and on more than one occasion. Some shooters like to stuff +P ammunition in older revolvers, and the result can be a cracked cylinder, rendering an otherwise perfectly good handgun useless. I've also seen people push a classic, century-old lever-action rifle to the brink with the faster, modern ammunition such as Hornady's LEVERevolution. Both the +P handgun ammo and Hornady's great lever gun cartridges have their place, so long as you understand the pressures they generate and use them in the appropriate firearms.

STAYING WITHIN THE LIMITS

You'll need to recognize the pressure and velocity limits of the cartridge you're loading. My first bolt-action big game rifle was a Ruger Model 77 MKII chambered in .308 Winchester and was a Christmas gift from my Dad, Ol' Grumpy Pants. He shoots .308 Winchester, so we started handloading for the pair of rifles and had success. It was quite a good feeling to take deer with the ammunition we'd created together, and that rifle and cartridge were responsible for my journey into reloading. I began experimenting with all sorts of loads for that rifle. Some were middle-of-the-road recipes that the .308 likes and others pushed the limits, as I was essentially trying to beat .30-06 velocities from the much smaller case. With my cartridges demonstrating all of the symptoms I described above, Grumpy Pants gave me that look of parental disappointment, and I knew I'd be hearing about it. "Why don't you use that rifle for what it was designed for and just go deer hunting? If you want a .300 Magnum, go buy one, but

These 6.5 Creedmoor cases show shiny extractor marks, flattened primers, and cratered firing pin marks — all are indicative of excess pressure.

stop torturing that rifle." He was right.

There was no point in generating those high pressures in that rifle, and once I came back to the realm of sanity, the groups went back to the sub-MOA size they had been, primers and cases appeared as they should, and I still enjoy that rifle to this day. The point is that even though you can control the parameters of your ammo, wringing every last bit of velocity out of the cartridge at the cost of high pressures is a poor tradeoff.

WHEN PRESSURE CHANGES

What causes the pressures to change? What are the parameters involved in generating pressures? Examining the example of the .404 Jeffery, we can interpret, and perhaps assume, some reasons for the lower Hornady charge weight versus the higher Woodleigh. The top-end Hornady charge of 74.1 grains gave a velocity of 2,200 fps, while the 75.0-grain charge in the Woodleigh data generated only 2,150 fps. Could this suggest that the CZ550 test rifle's barrel listed in Hornady's data had

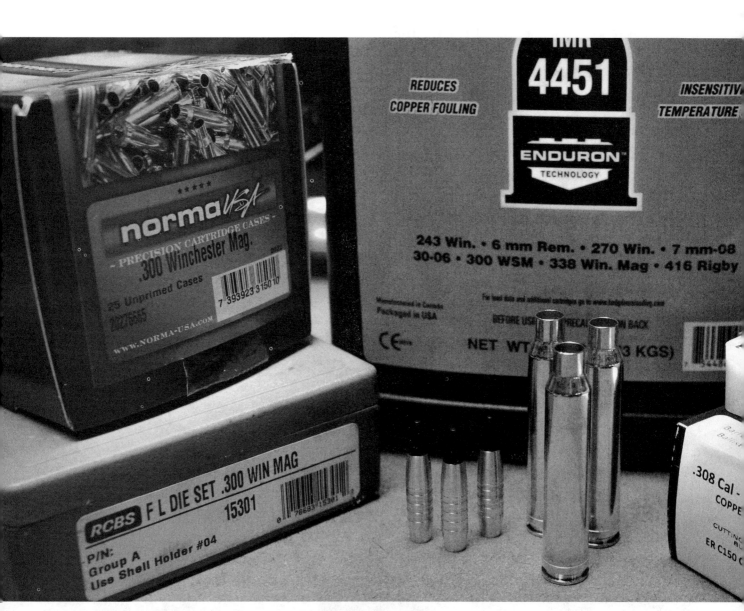

The author loaded his .300 Winchester Magnum ammo for a plains game safari with IMR 4451 because of its temperature insensitivity. It performed when temps rose to over 110 degrees!

a tight bore, generating velocities higher than usual? It's a possibility. Something caused Hornady to stop at that charge weight, and as I found in my own .404 rifles (I have two, and each likes the 80.0-grain load of Reloder 15), you can shatter that ceiling safely. So, the barrel's dimensions can play a role in generating higher pressures sooner than expected. I've had 'fast' barrels and 'slow' barrels, which is why load data are a guide, but not the last word on a safe load for a particular rifle or handgun. It is also the reason you need to start at the lowest charge weight and work up.

Temperature is another factor that can push pressures to a dangerous level. While today's propellant makers designed the new powders to be as insensitive to temperature swings as possible, some of the older designs were notorious for reacting to temp swings. The old rule of thumb, which applies to many of the older powders still in use today, is that the muzzle velocity in a rifle would increase or decrease roughly 2 fps for every degree in Fahrenheit the temperature changed. Loads developed on a warm early fall day where the daytime high was 70 degrees will have a lower muzzle velocity on Thanksgiving Day when the high struggles to break 20 degrees here in the Northeast. Likewise, on a hot July day waiting for that woodchuck to poke its head over the horizon in an alfalfa field, with the summer sun beating on the rifle and ammo, you can expect an increase in both muzzle velocity and pressure.

I've made ten safaris to Africa, and for all of them, I've used handloaded ammo. Some of those trips saw temperatures in the mid-80s, but others soared to 110 and even 115 degrees. I can only imagine how hot my rifle was on those hunts. To combat those brutal temps, I'd develop my handloads and let them sit in the direct summer sunlight, so I could verify that the African temperatures wouldn't cause any pressure issues. I didn't want a stuck case when pursuing dangerous game such as elephant or Cape buffalo! When developing your handloads, consider the season and conditions you expect to encounter. These days, I've been slowly switching to the new temperature insensitive powders such as the IMR Enduron, Hodgdon Extreme, and Alliant powder lines.

Primers can also influence pressure generated within your cartridge. I've gotten myself into trouble when switching primers in an established load. Cratered, flattened primers and sticky extraction were the results, not to mention excessive bolt thrust. I reduced the load, and only then did things function correctly. This example shows why the powder charges need to be

started from the manual's lightest load and worked up in small increments. Also, pay attention to the primer brand and type listed in the reloading manual, as there may be some surprises — for example, a magnum primer used in a standard cartridge, or vice versa.

Case capacity is another factor in the pressure equation. As thicker brass has a smaller combustion chamber, it can reach maximum pressure sooner than thinner brass. The military brass, and especially cases for the 7.62x51mm NATO (known commercially as the .308 Winchester) or the .30-06 Springfield, are long known to have thicker case walls. Adjust your data accordingly. It'll take less powder to achieve the same pressure in a smaller combustion chamber. Thus, you may see a different set of data for military cases than in sporting components. The Speer Reloading Manual traditionally offered data for military cases. In some instances, such as the Hornady Reloading Manual, you may see different data for a military rifle than for the sporting rifles, as the actions differ, and the pressure limits do as well.

While most of the handgun cartridges run at much lower pressures than the high-powered rifle cartridges, there will be variances in case capacity (though it will play a much lesser role). Measure the case capacity of the various brands of rifle cases by weighing the resized case empty, then fill it with water (you'll need to leave the primer in the pocket to hold the water in the case), and you should see a difference in the capacity. This procedure will give you a good idea of how the volumes of different brands vary and how the correlating pressures change. This variance is why I segregate my cartridges by brand, to keep the case volumes as uniform as possible.

A dirty chamber, especially a dirty barrel, can affect the ammunition, as an overly fouled bore will constrict the bullet's path and significantly increase pressures. ⫼

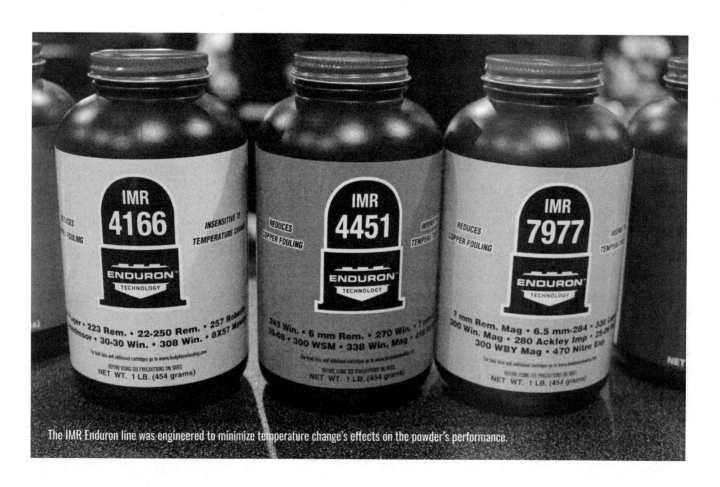

The IMR Enduron line was engineered to minimize temperature change's effects on the powder's performance.

Massaro used IMR 4451 Enduron in his .300 Winchester Magnum to take this 55-inch bull kudu in the 112-degree South African heat, with no signs of excessive pressure.

08

LOAD DEVELOPMENT

W e've discussed the tools, the processes, and the various options available to the new reloader. I'd like to discuss practical considerations and several different ideas for you to ponder while developing your ammunition.

LOAD DEVELOPMENT

"Load development" is the process of, well, developing a load for *your* firearm. It's the process of trial and error, of systematic testing and adjusting components and component values, and fine-tuning the variables to

These new Hornady cases are destined for safari; the author put together a load for the classic .450-400 3-inch Nitro Express.

These defensive loads resulted from extensive load development to determine which formula performed best in the author's gun.

arrive at the desired goal. Producing new ammo requires you to be diligent in creating the most repeatable results. You must be much more particular in your choice of components, sometimes insisting on using the same lot of powder, bullets, or primers, even going so far as to buy the brass cases from the same lot to keep things as uniform as possible. If you're serious about handloading, leave no stone unturned, and expect things to get downright geeky.

Our reloading manuals — both in print and digital form — have become much more complex over the years. Just a couple of decades ago, things were much more straightforward, though the results were not usually what we are achieving today. Modern manuals are updated more frequently as powder manufacturers introduce new propellants and as bullet technology

evolves. Reloading data is becoming more refined — primarily because the bullet shape is playing a much more significant role. That's a good thing for us.

I've said this before, but it warrants repeating: a reloading manual is not gospel. Consider it a laboratory report based on a particular set of test parameters, which will be different than your own in some manner. So, to develop your specific load data, you'll use the reloading manual as a starting point and a reference to stay within the realms of sanity, but your data will be specific to your firearm. Sometimes your findings will agree with the test data provided in the reloading manual. Other times, your results will differ greatly. Let me give an example of how I would start load development for a rifle cartridge.

The .30-06 Springfield is one of our most popular

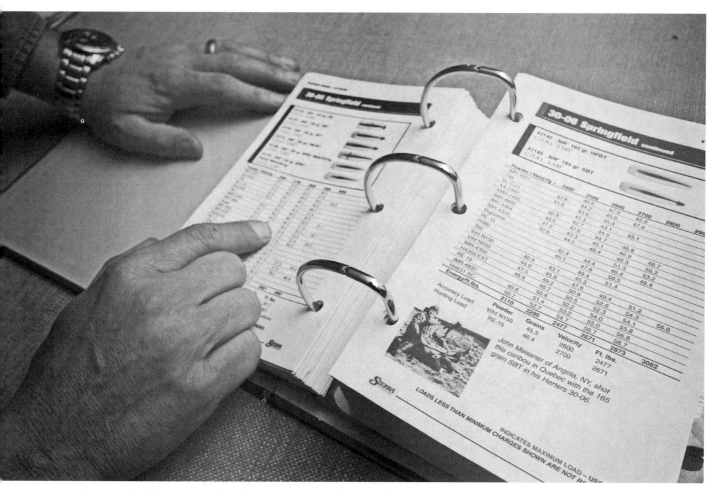

A reloading manual is a lab report, sometimes based on a particular rifle or barrel in a universal receiver, and may not apply perfectly to your gun.

hunting cartridges, being fully capable of handling almost all big game, save the big beasts. The 180-grain bullet is an appropriate choice for general hunting, as it will take deer, antelope, elk, moose, bear, and many other common species. The Nosler Partition, the godfather of premium bullets, is equally universal in its application. Soft enough in the front for good expansion (which destroys more vital tissue) yet built with a partition of copper to protect the rear core for deep penetration (two holes are better than one), the Partition has been getting it done for decades.

To begin my handload development, I'd consult the Nosler Reloading Manual (a great reference book to have on hand, but which Nosler has made available on its website) and take a close look at the data provided. First, I look at the test materials used and compare them to my own. I have a bolt-action .30-06 with a 24-inch barrel, and I can quickly see that my barrel length matches what Nosler used to develop its data. They used Nosler cases (Nosler makes fantastic brass cases), but I've got a whole bunch of Remington-Peters once-fired brass, so that may have a potential effect. Nosler used standard Winchester WLR (large rifle) primers. Still, I've got a supply of Federal Gold Medal Match GM210M primers on hand, so that may also be a source of potential trouble, in that the performance of various primers can affect the pressures generated.

Nosler also 'bundles' its bullets into one group of data — in this case, lumping 175- and 180-grain bullets together — with differing bullet shapes. Quite obviously, the Nosler AccuBond and Ballistic Tip have a much different profile than the Partition, so this data set will probably be an average for the bullet lineup, erring on the side of caution.

When looking at the list of potential powders for a rifle cartridge, I prefer a powder that nearly fills the case when using a particular bullet. In my years of experimentation, doing so has led to excellent accuracy and consistent velocities. I tend to pay attention to load densities, which Nosler provides for us in its load data. Load densities are a product of powder weight and powder grain structure (ball powder has fewer air voids than does an extruded stick powder). I want a density somewhere in the mid-90 percent range, filling the case, but not so much that I run the risk of over-compression, which could break the grain structure. Smokeless powder is treated with a retardant to keep the burn rate consistent. So, if you break the grain structure when you seat a bullet, you'll expose untreated surface areas to the sparks and run the risk of changing the burn rate. At the very least, inconsistent velocities could result.

Several propellants fit the bill — H4350, IMR 4350, and Alliant 4000-MR. Let's say I have a healthy supply of IMR 4350 on hand. Nosler's IMR 4350 data starts with 52.5 grains and stops at 56.5 grains. Again, that's Nosler's observation, based on its test equipment. Because I'm going to use a different primer in the other brass case, I'll want to start at the lowest charge weight and work up slowly until I find the blend of velocity and accuracy I find acceptable.

DEFINING YOUR GOALS

It is only human nature that every reloader tries to wring every bit of velocity out of a cartridge at some point in time. There will also be the desire to deliver one-hole accuracy from every cartridge/bullet/powder combination, or the unstoppable need to have single-digit velocity spreads, always. These goals may not be attainable or realistic.

Before you even sit at the bench, take a minute to think about the goals you're trying to achieve and what is and isn't acceptable. Indeed, our rifles are more

accurate than they've ever been, and handloading for them is much more rewarding than it was in the days when manufacturing wasn't what it is today. I remember when a hunting rifle that repeatedly gave MOA (minute of angle) groups was a big deal; nowadays, it has become the norm, and with some shooters, anything less is a disappointment. However, not all rifles are capable of MOA accuracy. Even so, that doesn't mean that such a rifle is unusable. I have a few rifles that will routinely shoot 1.5 MOA, making an effective hunting rifle to 400 yards. Does that mean that I'll stop pursuing accuracy at the first inch-and-a-half group I see? No, but when I see that a rifle shoots that level of accuracy with several projectile/powder combinations, sometimes you just have to accept that fact.

For handguns, you'll need to work within the limits of what the gun can provide. While handloading can be a problem solver, as we'll see shortly, you'll need to be realistic about what the handgun is capable of and if it can fulfill your goals.

I generally strive for accuracy over velocity in my hunting rifles. My theory is that I'll give up a hundred feet per second in a high-powered cartridge to have the ability to put the bullet where I want it. I know many people who feel differently and chase energy values over tiny groups. But I find that placing the bullet in the vitals is paramount and is critical as a hunter concerned about ethically and humanely taking a game animal's life. As a target shooter, the answer is accuracy, which is the point of their exercise.

There are instances where velocity matters, though, and the ability to measure your velocities accurately will be an essential part of knowing what will happen downrange. If you shoot in the handgun competitions, there are minimum energy values needed to adhere to the rules. In that instance, velocity is an issue. You must follow those rules. Double rifles use regulated barrels (Heym solders the barrels together), so each barrel strikes the same impact point at a specified distance with a particular muzzle velocity. Suppose the handloaded ammunition — or even the factory ammo — deviates too much from the regulation velocity. In that case, you'll see your right/left group start to separate and begin to print all over the map. Knowing the velocity of your double rifle loads is very important, which will also need to be measured using a chronograph so you can adjust the velocities to the proper levels.

The chronograph will become your friend when it comes to velocities, so plan on having at least one reputable unit on hand to observe the speed of your handloaded ammo (see sidebar for more on chronographs).

But let's get back to the example .30-06 Springfield/180-grain Nosler Partition loads. Once I decide on a starting point, I'll load three rounds of each powder weight, starting at the bottom of the scale at 52.5 grains of IMR 4350 and increasing in 1/2-grain increments. I'll stop at the top end of the listed charges in the manual and take these cartridges to the range.

For most of my hunting rifles, I'll test for accuracy at 100 yards. Hunting rifles generally tend to have thinner barrels than target rifles, so I limit my groups to three shots. I'm testing the gun's precision — I don't care where on the target my groups are hitting, so long as I can see the group — and looking at the fired cartridges to ensure that the pressures generated are safe. At the first sign of difficult or sticky extraction, or when I see cratered or flattened primers, I know it's time to stop — I've reached the limit of acceptable pressures or even exceeded them.

This exercise isn't about your shooting skills; it measures how the firearm is performing. You should shoot groups from a solid bench rest, off sandbags, or some form of dead rest where the gun can be held as steady as possible. Limit your influence on the shooting equation. Keep diligent records of how the groups performed in your gun, noting the weather conditions such as temperature, wind, and atmospheric pressure, and you'll start to notice a pattern. What you're looking for is the proper harmonics for your barrel. For example,

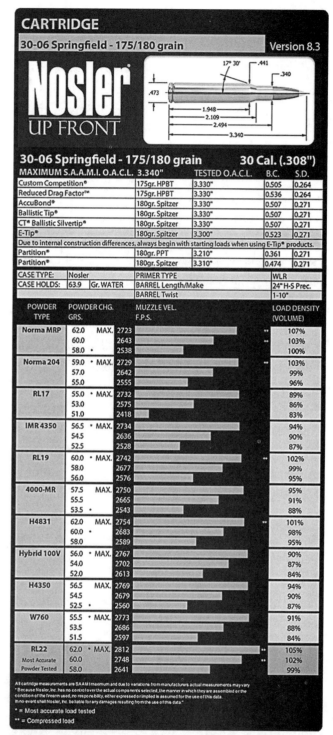

CARTRIDGE				
30-06 Springfield - 175/180 grain				**Version 8.3**

30-06 Springfield - 175/180 grain — **30 Cal. (.308")**
MAXIMUM S.A.A.M.I. O.A.C.L. 3.340"

		TESTED O.A.C.L.	B.C.	S.D.
Custom Competition®	175gr. HPBT	3.330"	0.505	0.264
Reduced Drag Factor™	175gr. HPBT	3.330"	0.536	0.264
AccuBond®	180gr. Spitzer	3.330"	0.507	0.271
Ballistic Tip®	180gr. Spitzer	3.330"	0.507	0.271
CT® Ballistic Silvertip®	180gr. Spitzer	3.330"	0.507	0.271
E-Tip®	180gr. Spitzer	3.300"	0.523	0.271

Due to internal construction differences, always begin with starting loads when using E-Tip® products.

Partition®	180gr. PPT	3.210"	0.361	0.271
Partition®	180gr. Spitzer	3.310"	0.474	0.271

CASE TYPE:	Nosler	PRIMER TYPE	WLR
CASE HOLDS:	63.9 Gr. WATER	BARREL Length/Make	24" H-S Prec.
		BARREL Twist	1-10"

POWDER TYPE	POWDER CHG. GRS.		MUZZLE VEL. F.P.S.	LOAD DENSITY (VOLUME)
Norma MRP	62.0	MAX.	2723	107%
	60.0		2643	103%
	58.0	•	2538	100%
Norma 204	59.0	• MAX.	2729	103%
	57.0		2642	99%
	55.0		2555	96%
RL17	55.0	• MAX.	2732	89%
	53.0		2575	86%
	51.0		2418	83%
IMR 4350	56.5	• MAX.	2734	94%
	54.5		2636	90%
	52.5		2528	87%
RL19	60.0	• MAX.	2742	102%
	58.0		2677	99%
	56.0		2576	95%
4000-MR	57.5	MAX.	2750	95%
	55.5		2665	91%
	53.5	•	2543	88%
H4831	62.0	MAX.	2754	101%
	60.0	•	2683	98%
	58.0		2589	95%
Hybrid 100V	56.0	• MAX.	2767	90%
	54.0		2702	87%
	52.0		2613	84%
H4350	56.5	MAX.	2769	94%
	54.5		2679	90%
	52.5	•	2560	87%
W760	55.5	• MAX.	2773	91%
	53.5		2686	88%
	51.5		2597	84%
RL22	62.0	• MAX.	2812	105%
Most Accurate Powder Tested	60.0		2748	102%
	58.0		2641	99%

All cartridge measurements are SAAM I maximum and due to variations from manufacturers actual measurements may vary. * Because Nosler, Inc. has no control over the actual components selected, the manner in which they are assembled or the condition of the firearm used, no responsibility, either expressed or implied is assumed for the use of this data. In no event shall Nosler, Inc. be liable for any damages resulting from the use of this data."
• = Most accurate load tested
•• = Compressed load

The Nosler load data for the .30-06 Springfield in the Reloading Manual No. 8.

the lightest load at 52.5 grains may give a broad group of over two inches, but you may see it shrink to an inch when you shoot the 54.5-grain load. It could start to open up again until you find the first pressure signs at 56.0 grains.

That 54.5-grain load may meet all the requirements you have, but you could start to experiment with smaller graduations of, say, 0.2 grain, loading 54.3 and 54.7 grains of IMR 4350, to see if there's an improvement in the group size. Once I find the group size that satisfies me and have verified it with several more groups of the same charge, I'll measure the muzzle velocity with the chronograph. If it's comparable with the advertised velocities for the cartridge, my work is done. If the velocities are glaringly low, which can happen, I might look at another powder and start the process all over again. It may sound like a lot of work, but the time spent with your rifle or handgun will make you a better shooter and much more confident in your rig. It's also an excuse to be on the range with a purpose, not just burning powder.

My buddy Frank Campana recently asked me to help him develop a load for his new 7mm Remington Magnum. He wanted a single load to hunt a wide variety of game. He chose the 175-grain Nosler AccuBond bullet, as it would handle the lighter game but would make longer shots at larger animals, too. The higher B.C. of that bullet resists wind deflection, and that's always a good thing for distant game in open country. We went through several different powders, and while accuracy was acceptable with all of them, we found that his rifle liked Reloder 23. At a near-maximum load of 63 1/2 grains, we obtained sub-MOA accuracy and a muzzle velocity of more than 2,800 fps. Some of the faster-burning powders gave excellent accuracy on par with the Reloder 23 load. The velocities were almost 200 fps slower. Reloder 23 is temperature insensitive. That makes it a perfect choice for a hunter like Frank, who may find himself in the Rockies for elk in knee-deep snow or sitting in a leopard blind in the African heat.

While we all want a specific bullet and load that will handle our dream hunts, reality may dictate a different choice of bullet, at a different speed. For example, Frank Campana and I worked on the load that will handle elk, moose, bears, eland, kudu, leopards, and more. But it might not be the optimal choice for a deer load

in my native New York. Here, typical shots are inside 100 yards, and the only other possible game you might encounter is a coyote or, if you're lucky, a black bear. The 175-grain AccuBond will work, but there are better tools for the job. If you wanted to use the 7mm Remington Magnum, it wouldn't be hard to whip up a handload, using a lighter bullet at a lower muzzle velocity. Such a load would still do the job nicely at 'woods' distances, without putting all the strain on the bullet and destroying too much meat. Perhaps a 150-grain Sierra GameKing or similar cup-and-core bullet, reduced to velocities somewhere in the 7mm-08 Remington and .280 Remington neighborhood would do just fine. It could be zeroed at 100 yards to precisely place your shots, threading the needle among the many branches in the hardwoods of the Northeast, yet could be easily used at longer distances if needed. For this particular purpose, a load that prints 1.5 MOA or more isn't a handicap. So without too much work, Frank's 7mm Remington Magnum could join him on all sorts of hunts during several seasons and would probably suffice for most of his hunting needs. That is the versatility of handloading your hunting ammunition.

Handgunners can enjoy the same kind of versatility, especially in the ammunition drought we are once again experiencing at the time of this writing. Trying to find a box of 9mm Luger or .45 ACP ammunition in the fall of 2020 is like finding a needle in a haystack, but if you squirrel away enough components, you'll have a steady supply on hand. Look at the varying powders that'll work with your chosen handgun cartridge. Some of them will yield more than 1,000 shots per pound. Hodgdon's Titegroup powder will give you reliable performance with a 4.5-grain load in the .45 ACP with a standard 230-grain bullet for more than 1,500 shots per pound of powder. Hodgdon's Titewad — at 3.2 grains under a 124-grain bullet — will produce better than 2,000 shots to the pound in the 9mm Luger. While this is a classic example of handloading's value (where the ammo volume outweighs any other feature), it makes perfect sense to have a surplus of ammunition for self-

John Rigby & Company designed the classic, behemoth .416 Rigby cartridge to withstand the variations in pressure and temperature between England and the Tropics.

defense, training, teaching new shooters, and more.

If you're a handgun hunter, you can follow the processes used by rifle cartridge handloaders. Your hunting ammunition will need special attention, as you'll want it to be the best you can get. Still, the opportunity to develop practice ammunition that is equally effective and affordable is another of the positive points of reloading ammo. And that brings me to another point regarding handloaded ammunition: can it be trusted when facing game that hunts you back?

HANDLOADS AND DANGEROUS GAME: CAN HANDLOADS BE TRUSTED?

Safari is one of my passions, and pursuing the dangerous game of Africa is possibly the most exhilarating hunting on earth. It is also aptly named, in that the animals you're hunting have the means — quite often the desire — to kill you. Therefore, it's an instance where your ammunition is also your life insurance policy. The cartridges suitable for dangerous game will start with the 9.3mms and the .375s and go as large as one can effectively carry and shoot, including the behemoth .577 and .600 Nitro Express.

The hunt is generally in Africa's remotest areas, in the dangerous game blocks, where the animals still roam free. The hunting is as close as you can get to those experiences relayed in the classic hunting literature. You'll need to depend on your gear, from boots to optics to clothing, especially your rifle and ammunition. Some are adamant about using factory ammo only on a dangerous game hunt, whether that hunt is in Africa for elephant, Cape buffalo, or lion, or in Alaska for the coastal brown or polar bear. I feel nothing could be further from the truth. There is nothing wrong with using factory ammo, of course, but to claim that you can't trust handloaded ammo is frankly preposterous. With ten safaris under my belt, not to mention the dozens I've loaded ammo for, I find that handloading gives me an advantage over factory ammo: I can closely examine the projectiles, powder charge, and primer. I can also control the load parameters for my dangerous game rifles and use several different bullets that are only available in component form and not offered in any factory load. For example, I've settled on a pair of Heym rifles for dangerous game work: one is a bolt-action Heym Express by Martini in .404 Jeffery, the other a Heym Model 89B double rifle in .470 Nitro Express. While there is quality factory ammunition available for both, I've come to rely on handloading's flexibility. The .404 Jeffery gives three-shot groups measuring 1 MOA with several 400-grain bullets over a load of 80.0 grains of Reloder 15 for a muzzle velocity of 2,280 fps. That load leans more toward the modern factory loads that scoot along at 2,350 fps.

Because Heym regulated that double with a load at specified velocity, I'm 'married' to the 500-grain bullets at roughly 2,150 fps for the best results. That's fine, but how I get to that velocity value is up to me. For example, I could use H4831, IMR 4350, or many different powders, but I found that Reloder 15 attains that velocity with considerably less powder, and therefore less recoil. A charge of 88.0 grains of RL-15 gives me the velocity I need for good accuracy, with about 75-80 percent of the felt recoil of the slower-burning powders. Because the load density is lower, a Kynoch No. 2 foam wad is employed to compress the load rearward against the primer for even ignition and consistent velocities.

If you're careful, diligent, and confident in your abilities, there's absolutely no reason not to use handloads on a dangerous game hunt. Other than rimfire ammo, I've yet to fire a factory cartridge in Africa and have never had an issue, no matter the weather conditions. And if you were ever concerned about the effects of temperature on your ammo, Africa is the place to test it.

TEMPERATURE'S EFFECT ON POWDERS

Most folks know the story of why the .416 Rigby case is so large: the differences in temperature between England and the Tropics had such an effect on cordite that the cases were sticking in the receivers, and the oversized Rigby case lowered pressures. While even the smokeless powders at the end of the 20th Century were much less sensitive to temperature fluctuations, the general rule of thumb was to expect a two fps increase or decrease in velocity for every degree (Fahrenheit) above or below the test temperature. (This is why I keep notes, including the weather conditions, when I test my data.) If you develop your loads on an 80-degree day, and you then set off to track Cape buffalo in 110-degree heat, which is not out of the question, you'd be looking at a 60 fps increase; that can cause a 'safe' load to become dangerous. Thankfully, several powders are available that minimize the effects of temperature, and I've come to rely on them.

Instead of my usual choice of IMR 4350, I took IMR 4451 — part of the temperature-insensitive Enduron line — to South Africa in my .300 Winchester Magnum

The author handloaded these 500-grain Peregrine BushMaster monometal soft points for his Heym .470 double rifle, they are not available in factory-loaded ammunition.

loads. The two have a similar burn rate and work ideally in the .300 case, but as the hunt was late in the season, I was interested in seeing how the weather would affect my loads. I was happy to have loaded that powder for that safari, as on day two, temps soared from the low 80s to over 110; it felt much like a blast furnace. Of course, that's when the kudu bull of my dreams presented a shot, but happily, IMR 4451 stayed consistent, and not only were there no pressure problems, but the shot flew true. If you're concerned about pressure issues

when traveling from home, test your ammunition in the heat of summer and the cold of winter. If time is pressing, you can put the ammo in a cooler, on an ice pack to simulate cold weather conditions, or leave it on the car's dashboard with the windows closed to heat it. Record the point of impact changes, as well as velocity changes. You may be surprised at the results.

So, whether you want to tailor the velocity of your hunting ammunition — my .404 Jeffery load isn't "hot," though I enjoy the recoil level and accuracy —

or you want to use a projectile that isn't available in loaded ammunition, handloading for a hunting trip is a perfectly viable means of checking that box. Add in the hefty cost of factory ammunition for a big-bore rifle, and you'll quickly see the value of handloading.

TARGET LOADS FOR THE PRECISION SHOOTER

Handloading goes hand-in-hand with target shooting, whether it's a 100-yard benchrest competition or extreme long-range work. Never before have we been able to pull a relatively cheap rifle off the rack, say a Savage Axis II in 6.5 Creedmoor, screw a decent scope on it, and stuff the magazine full of Hornady Match factory ammo and shoot 1,000-yard steel. This reliability is truly a testament to the quality and uniformity of

The 220-grain .30-caliber bullet will settle down much faster than will the 180-grain spitzer boattail .30-caliber bullet.

modern rifles and ammunition. However, once you get serious about target shooting, handloaded ammo will likely become a part of your gear.

Barrels are finicky things. If you thought that consistency was important at 100 and 200 yards, out past 1,000 yards, any flaws in the ammunition would show themselves quickly. Since accuracy (more appropriately, precision) is repeatable results from the entire chain of gear, including the shooter, one would think that no matter the charge weight or type of powder, ultra-consistent ammo should suffice. That consistency should be immediately visible on the target. Not so. The reality is that you're dealing with the harmonics of a particular barrel. Realistically, when you're testing that wide variety of charge weights, what you're looking for is the most repeatable set of harmonics for that barrel. Sometimes you may find a load that works well in several different barrels, but more often than not, you'll find each gun has its preferences.

Looking at target rifles and match ammo, you may find that the barrel will change over time as it wears, or it may provide the best accuracy when dirty or vice versa. The testing and load development for target ammunition will be somewhat different from that of hunting loads. Hunting ammo must perform at shorter distances.

Many of the high ballistic coefficient bullets commonly used in long-range cartridges need time (read distance) to settle down into gyroscopic stability. Group size at 100 yards (where the bullet hasn't had enough time to stabilize) may not indicate how well that bullet will perform at 300, 500, or even 1,000 yards. When you build a house, you want a robust, square, and level foundation, and so with long-range shooting, you'll need all your components and assembly techniques to be as consistent as possible — these are your cartridge's foundation. Slight variations in seating depth of primers and bullets, variations in charge weight or case volume, or differences in the conformation (or shape) of your case dimensions can

Hornady 135-grain A-TIP Match bullets handloaded in the 6.5 Creedmoor.

all affect the accuracy of your handloads.

Couple those factors with the ever-changing winds, and you can understand why extreme long-range shooting is so challenging. Developing a proper long-range handload will take some time. You'll need to test ammo at various distances and measure the muzzle velocities to best predict the long-range trajectory in your atmospheric conditions.

While I've stressed throughout this book the importance of being consistent in all of your reloading parameters to provide the best downrange results, a friend called me on the phone the other day with a rather eye-opening tale. We decided to replicate it several times to see what was going on. Chris Sells, President of Heym USA, was doing some load

development on one of his company's precision rifles chambered in .300 Winchester Magnum and found an accurate load using a 200-grain polymer-tipped boattail bullet. He'd loaded up about 30 rounds and had finished loading one box of projectiles. Upon opening a different lot of the same brand and weight bullet, he noticed a seating depth difference of about 0.030 inch. Now that's quite a bit for any bullet. He and I agreed that because the difference from bullet base to ogive was different, there would be a considerable accuracy difference or at least the point of impact. We were wrong. The two loads printed three-shot groups of 1/2 MOA and an aggregate group of about 3/4 MOA. We batted the ideas back and forth, and we concluded that there is an excellent probability that though the seating depth was different, the barrel harmonics were aligning correctly. Those harmonics may have more of an effect on accuracy than we ever thought possible. The moral of the story? Find the proper harmonic node for your barrel, and you're in business.

CHOOSING THE RIGHT BULLET

The choice of bullet in today's market, where there are more specialty designs than ever before, can be confusing. Also, there is much overlap and design features that may or may not help your cause. When I learned to reload, the whitetail deer was the primary target. Our handloaded ammo was not only functional but integral to the fall family ritual. At that time, my Dad and I were both shooting .308 Winchesters, so we shared the same load, and it was a ton of fun to make hunting ammo with him (we're also business partners and have subsequently hunted around the world together).

The first load we hunted with used the 165-grain Hornady spire point over a load of IMR 4064, and it worked perfectly, especially since my father is a strong proponent of the 165-grain bullets in the .308 Winchester over IMR 4064 powder. Within a few years, we switched to the 165-grain Nosler Ballistic Tip and

Sierra GameKing hollowpoint, as we had begun to experiment with varying brands and shapes of bullets and saw an improvement in velocity (though that Hornady bullet can be wonderfully accurate). But it was the preparation for a moose hunt in Quebec that changed the game, for me at least, as it led to a passionate study of bullet performance.

The .308 Winchester was the only serious big game rifle I owned at the time. I had never seen a moose, and so I did my best to find a load suitable for the big animals at ranges from up-close-and-personal to across-the-lake. Dad and I looked up and down the spectrum, and we settled on the 200-grain Nosler Partition. We did call in one bull on that hunt, and though I got nothing more than a brief glimpse of him through the willow thicket, the hook was firmly set, and the study of ballistics would consume a healthy portion of my life.

While preparing to reload, keep your end goal in mind. Demands placed on the cartridge system directly influence bullet choice. A deer hunter needs a different bullet than an elk hunter. A varmint hunter will want a completely different type of projectile than a hunter preparing for a dangerous game safari. The competition handgunner will probably want a wadcutter to poke neat, easily scoreable holes. And a person handloading for self-defense will emphasize terminal performance to stop bad guys fast.

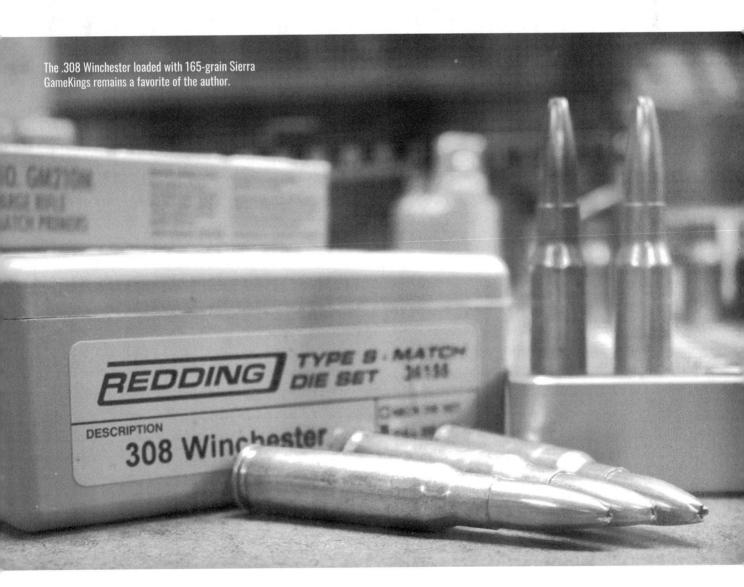

The .308 Winchester loaded with 165-grain Sierra GameKings remains a favorite of the author.

The .30-caliber 150-grain Federal FUSION bullet is devastating on deer and similar-sized game.

Though I've outlined various bullet types in previous chapters, it is here where we will make a conscious choice about what kind of bullet will be employed. Invariably, if you hunt enough different game species, you'll end up with several loads for each rifle. Using the whitetail deer as an example — as it is probably the most prolific game species across North America — you'll find a large number of different projectiles recommended by many reputable sources. Though that may seem contradictory at first, the whitetail isn't exactly difficult to kill. Of course, the bullet will need to strike the vital organs, and no amount of muzzle energy or velocity will make up for a misplaced shot.

For deer, I like a relatively soft bullet that will

expand on impact yet will have enough sectional density (SD) to ensure penetration through the entire animal from almost any angle. (Wikipedia defines sectional density as "the ratio of an object's mass to its cross-sectional area with respect to a given axis. It conveys how well an object's mass is distributed to overcome resistance along that axis.") Again, a deer isn't tough to kill, providing you use common sense. I know several successful hunters who use the .22-caliber centerfires, such as the .223 Remington and .22-250 Remington. I've also seen the frangible varmint-style bullets in those cartridges result in superficial wounds and lost deer, and that's never a good thing. You'll surely want to make a wise choice of cartridge and bullet weight within the given caliber. For deer, antelope, and other similarly thin-skinned species, pick something in the middle weight range. Consider the 120- and 140-grain 6.5mms, the 140- and 150-grain 7mms, and the 150- and 165-grain .30-caliber bullets. There are times when I may go heavier or use a bonded-core or monometal bullet if I'm hunting deer in bear country — which I often do in the Catskills and Adirondacks of New York — but if it's a deer-only menu, the lighter bullets will suffice.

The premium bullets start to shine for the game species such as elk, moose, or any of the larger cervids. The Nosler Accubond and Partition, Swift A-Frame and Scirocco II, Federal Trophy Bonded Tip and Terminal Ascent, Barnes TSX and TTSX, and Norma EcoStrike and BondStrike all can turn your 'run-of-the-mill' .30-06 Springfield into something special. Of course, there are cup-and-core bullets suitable for these jobs as well. Check out the heavier Sierra GameKings and ProHunters with thicker jackets designed to give controlled expansion, as well as Hornady's heavy-for-caliber ELD X bullet. And there are no flies on the classic Speer GrandSlam.

Many of these choices will also work wonderfully for African plains game and the exotic species available in Texas. When you get into the big bears of Alaska, or

The Speer Grand Slam is an often-overlooked bullet for big game, and deserves more respect than it gets.

The Swift A-Frame is one of the toughest soft-point bullets on the market and is a superb choice for dangerous game.

the dangerous game species of Africa, the controlled expansion bullets will get the job done. The Barnes TSX, Woodleigh Weldcore, Swift A-Frame, Peregrine BushMaster, and other 'super premiums' expand reliably on the thick-skinned heavyweights, retaining over 90 percent of their original weight as they deliver deep penetration.

So, as you start shopping around for a bullet for your reloading session, do your best to choose the one best suited to the game you expect to hunt. There are superb bullets for many hunting situations, from rabbits to rhinos, so it shouldn't be hard to tailor your bullet choice to the job at hand. Consult the manufacturer's website for some guidance: Nosler will honestly tell you its Ballistic Tip bullet is a good choice for deer, but the Partition or AccuBond is better for elk and moose.

LOADING FOR SELF DEFENSE

Using handloads in a self-defense gun is a sticky topic filled with legal consequences and wrought with complications. There can be an issue in court should you be forced to use handloaded ammunition to defend your life. Attorneys have accused handloaders of building ammunition "with the express purpose of killing" or "which equates to excessive force." Not unlike the phrase 'hot loads' (oh, you reload? Cool, make me some *hot loads…*), this concept grates on me, as it makes several assumptions that are illogical and downright wrong. First of all, if you've made the conscious decision to use a firearm to defend your life, I'd certainly hope you'd be firmly in the right. I live in the State of New York, where prosecutors scrutinize the use of force more than other states. If I were to defend my life with deadly force of any kind, I'd have to do so knowing prosecutors will turn the microscope on me. But in my mind, the means of that force takes a back seat to the conscious decision to use it, so whether it's a handgun with factory loaded ammo or my handloads, or a shotgun, or a baseball bat, golf club or shingling hammer, my actions should be what matter most. But, some advise firmly against the use of handloaded ammunition to avoid the premeditation accusation.

Secondly, some argue that forensics can accurately determine the distance between shooter and target by examining bullet impact and expansion. As an example, let's assume that a 185-grain Federal Hydra-Shok in the .45 ACP, in factory form, gives a specific performance at 3 yards, which is definitely within life-threatening distances. If you were to develop a 'hot load,' which would increase the velocity, you could expect the same performance from a greater distance, where the bullet had time to slow down. The point? Prosecutors have argued that the shooter fired from a distance where life wasn't in imminent danger, and the shooting was unwarranted.

Forget the fact that varying barrel dimensions can result in velocity discrepancies. And the variations within the ammunition itself. Then please forget that even the best bullets — and the Hydra-Shok ranks among the best designs — will display different characteristics dependent upon the materials they encounter on their journey. There are a considerable number of variables in the equation. I am by no means an attorney nor a court-approved expert witness. Even so, I've seen enough variations in velocity due to dimensional variations and other factors to reliably say that there may not be the ability to perfectly correlate the conformation of an upset bullet to the distance from which it was fired.

Like handloading for dangerous game, I can give defensive ammo the utmost attention. Similarly, I can inspect each element, discarding anything that looks suspect or doesn't meet my standards. The option to have the most reliability when creating ammo designed to save my bacon supersedes the threat of legal ramifications after the fact; put bluntly, I want to live through the experience to argue the ballistic points. And much like the factory ammunition for dangerous game, the defensive ammunition is the best we've ever had. Still, I like to be in control of as many parameters of my ammo as possible.

If you're concerned about the legality of handloads in your self-defense guns or concealed carry handguns, consult a qualified attorney for legal advice. Me, I carry handloaded defensive ammo with little concern. |||

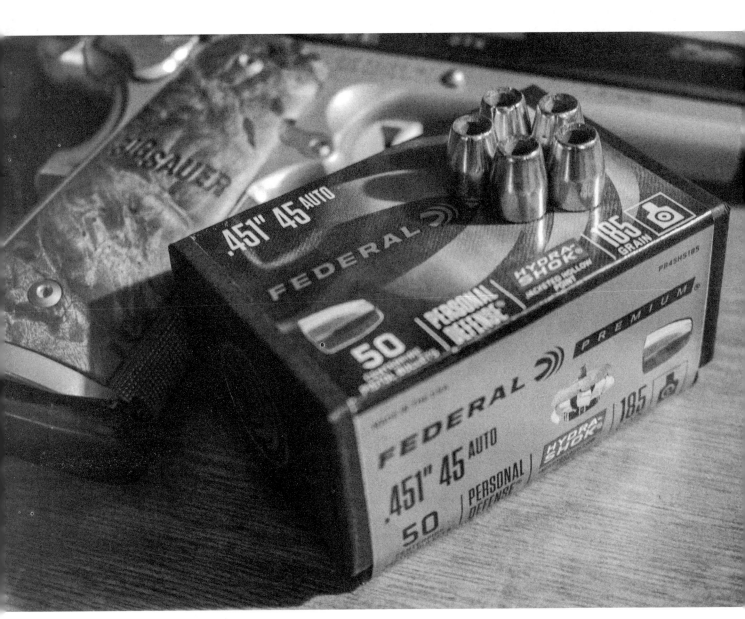

The Federal Hydra-Shok ranks among the best defensive bullets on the market.

Using a chronograph to measure the velocity of rifle cartridges.

Using the chronograph to verify handgun ammunition velocities. Yes, this chronograph data is essential for handgun ammo as well as rifle loads.

Chronographs and Reloading
Measuring bullet velocity is paramount to optimal load development

We handloaders, especially those of us who play the benchrest rifle game or enjoy long-range shooting, strive for the utmost accuracy. We weigh our bullets, cases, and powder charges, hem and haw over 3/4 vs. 1/2 MOA accuracy, yet you'd be shocked to find out how many people don't own or use a chronograph.

While the reloading manuals strive to report the factual data on bullet/powder/cartridge combinations, there are parameters involved in arriving at those velocity values. Knowing your rifle's actual muzzle velocity is paramount — not just an approximation, but the exact number. All the accuracy in the world won't help you when you don't know the proper amount of holdover or dial-up because you're basing your trajectory curve on false information. Even worse, I've seen those who have gone to the trouble of purchasing a custom turret for their riflescope (calibrated for bullet drop at certain distances) and complain that they don't hit where they are supposed to hit.

Some gun competitions require a minimum energy/velocity combination for your handgun ammunition to make 'major.' The only way to ensure you comply with these rules is to chronograph your loads.

You can alleviate problems with the purchase of a good chronograph. They come in many shapes and sizes and a wide variety

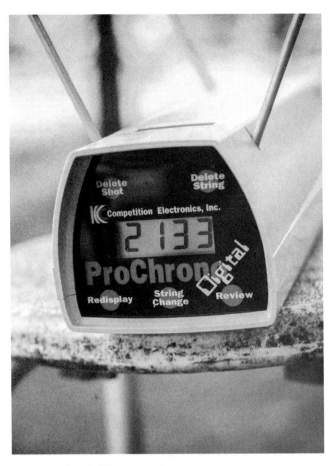

This poor chronograph fell victim to the muzzle blast of a .505 Gibbs!

The author considers the Oehler 35P to be one of the finest chronographs on the market.

of price ranges. The first one I owned was a Competition Electronics ProChrono Digital, and it served me well for years, handily measuring the velocities of rifle and pistol loads alike. That is until my good friend Dr. Mike McNulty and I tried to chronograph his prized .505 Gibbs and cooked the electronics from the pressure of the muzzle blast. I replaced it with an Oehler Model 35P. This amazing machine gives you a cash register-like printout of the string of shots, with an averaged velocity, along with high and low shots and standard deviation, printed out nicely so you can keep a detailed record of your rifle or pistol velocity.

How Chronographs Work

Here's how the most popular models work: a pair or a trio of electronic sensors, directly below the opaque skyscreens, diffuse the light. These sensors are very sensitive, and measure the time difference, right down to a gnat's whisker, that it takes the bullet to cross each sensor. That time, divided by the distance between the sensors, gives you the speed in feet per second (fps). My Competition Electronics ProChrono Digital had two screens, about 18 inches apart, but my Oehler 35P (which I refer to as "The Cadillac of chronys") has three screens. It is about four feet long and measures the time difference between screens one and two, and the difference between screens one and three to record a more precise average and minimize the false readings. When the two readings concur, it is pretty difficult to argue with them. The display gives you all sorts of data to work with and prints them on

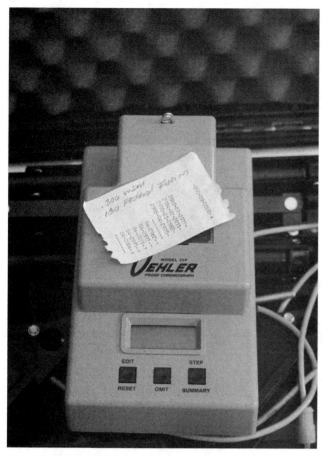

Keep the printed data from the Oehler 35P with your other load data records.

The LabRadar system uses Doppler radar to measure bullet velocity.

adding machine paper so you can save the data in your records. Because the Oehler unit has the 'brains' of the unit removed from exposure to muzzle blast (the 'eyes' of the device have three 20-foot cables to feed the data to the 'brain'), there is no concern with muzzle blast posing an issue.

The 35P displays and prints each shot's velocity in the string, highest velocity, lowest velocity, extreme velocity spread, the average velocity for that group or string, and the standard deviation for that group. It comes in a convenient case and sets up quickly and easily once you get the hang of it. It's available directly from Oehler for just under $600 at the time of this writing.

Of late, the technology for measuring speed has expanded beyond the traditional style of chronograph. The LabRadar system uses Doppler radar to determine the speed of your projectile. Unlike a conventional chronograph, it doesn't need the bullet or shot to pass over it; you place it next to the shooter, aim it at the target, and record the velocity. It doesn't even require a light source (even my Oehler 35P can get funky in low light conditions) and runs on six AA batteries. The LabRadar costs $560; the tripod is an additional $45.

The MagnetoSpeed chronograph uses a sensor mounted to the end of your rifle or revolver's barrel to measure muzzle velocity. It's an accurate device, providing the same type of information as the Oehler. My buddy Mike Buser is a fan of this chrony. However, we've found it will change the point of impact and group size of your ammunition. So, do your accuracy work first, and then use the

The MagnetoSpeed mounted under a rifle barrel.

Mike Buser's MagnetoSpeed, set up to measure the velocity of his .204 Ruger handloads.

The MagnetoSpeed V3 comes in a hard case, with an advanced display unit.

MagnetoSpeed to measure velocities. There are two models: the MagnetoSpeed Sporter and the MagnetoSpeed V3. The Sporter is the simpler and more affordable of the two, with a price tag of $189. It will handle 1/2- to 1-inch barrels, making it an ideal choice for sporter-weight rifle barrels and revolvers with longer barrels. The V3 works with barrels up to 2 inches in diameter, with an extended inch of clearance for dealing with longer muzzle brakes or flash suppressors. It stores data on a microSD card, and you can update its firmware via download. The V3 sells for $399 and is the more rugged of the two.

When using a scope with bullet drop compensated (BDC) reticle, you must ensure that your rifle's trajectory coincides with the BDC's calibration. BDCs operate with certain bullets at specific velocities. While no system is perfect, a glance at a trajectory chart for the bullet you've chosen, at the speed you've measured, will allow you to interpolate the slight differences between the actual trajectory and holdover and the trajectory to which you've calibrated the reticle. Quite obviously, the long-range shooter who needs to develop a dope chart for his or her rifle will need an accurate means of observing the muzzle velocity of their chosen load. Without this piece of vital information, you may as well be guessing at the necessary amount of elevation adjustment.

Leupold offers a CDS (Custom Dial System) turret for its riflescopes. You provide Leupold with the ballistic parameters of your load, and they send you a custom turret. The CDS gives you the ability to dial directly for yardage instead of calculating the necessary minutes of angle or milliradians to adjust. As you can imagine, the CDS turret's accuracy will depend as much upon

The MagnetoSpeed Sporter is the simpler of the two models yet provides all the essential data you'll need.

truthful muzzle velocity as the ballistic coefficient of the projectile. You could be the best shot on the planet, but if you don't have accurate data to feed into the ballistic calculator, you're not going to get good results out of it.

Practical Chronograph Use

A quick example of some chrono observations that have saved my pride and prevented some missed shots: my 6.5-284 Norma gave velocities very close to those advertised in the reloading manual when using flat-based bullets. However, with boattails, the velocities were 150 fps lower than expected. I'd have missed, or worse, wounded a game animal at longer distances had I not put the ammunition through my chronograph and adjusted my trajectory data accordingly. This point became glaringly apparent when I took that rifle and load to the FTW Ranch in Barksdale, Texas, where we shot steel out to 1,800 yards. A chronograph also showed me that a load I'd developed for a customer's 7mm Remington Magnum, which showed terrific accuracy, was running way too slow for that cartridge's potential. Despite the tight groups, we reworked the load to deliver the long-range trajectory the customer needed.

I also used my chronograph extensively when developing a handload for my Heym .470 Nitro Express double rifle. The side-by-side barrels are regulated to deliver a bullet of a particular weight at a specific muzzle velocity, and the bullet paths cross at a set distance, usually 75 yards. If I want to use anything other than the factory load, I need to match the bullet weight/velocity combination. I did just that, experimenting with varying loads and powders until I found the muzzle velocity I needed. The target

The results of diligent handloading in conjunction with an Oehler 35P chronograph: two 500-grain Trophy Bonded Sledgehammer solids at 100 yards.

velocity was 2,150 fps with a 500-grain bullet. I found better accuracy with my handloads, which leave those barrels at 2,160 fps. Three Cape buffalo in Chirisa, Zimbabwe, did not appreciate my efforts.

You'll end up using your chronograph often, so do some homework and find one within your budget. It's a necessary tool for the serious reloader and shooter. Usually, you get what you pay for, and the inexpensive models aren't as reliable as the premium ones. My Custom Electronics model lasted for quite some time until it met that fateful .505 Gibbs, and many models that cost less than $200 will suffice to the recreational shooter. If you typically shoot within 200 yards (the most common zero distance for hunting cartridges), the chronograph's role won't be as important to you as it would be to a long-range shooter. Even so, it's essential to know the velocities you're generating, as it will correlate to the amount of kinetic energy you're generating (hunters will want to know this). The chronograph is not only valuable to handloaded ammunition; you might be surprised to see how much variation you'll find in factory loads as well. All barrels are unique and will generate different pressures and velocities. Knowing is half the battle.

RELOADING SAFETY

There is no question that reloading, when done correctly, is no more dangerous than cooking on your kitchen stove. However, it can be hazardous when done incorrectly, resulting in broken stocks, burst barrels, cracked cylinders, injury, and even death. Safety is, was, and always shall be the priority.

If at any point in time, you find yourself unsure of what you're doing, or if you feel something isn't correct, stop and start over, or consult a competent reloader to verify things. You will see many tools designed to save time — and they will do just that — but don't focus on time or be in a rush. Complacency in reloading or handling a firearm is never safe.

This .270 Winchester was loaded too hot and blew the primer out of the pocket. *No bueno.*

Whether your goal is to make ammunition at the top of the pressure/velocity range for your chosen cartridge or to load practice ammo, follow the same safety procedures outlined in this book and the various reloading manuals. Blindly jumping in at the maximum powder charge or heedlessly substituting primers can result in trouble, just as using loads designed for modern firearms in a vintage gun — where the metallurgy wasn't as consistent as today's — can be disastrous.

I don't want to insinuate that you should operate in a constant state of worry, but you should treat the science and art of reloading with respect. I have written about my preference to handload for dangerous game hunting and defensive handguns, primarily because I can control and inspect the components and assembly of the loads, where I cannot do so when it comes to factory ammunition. That principle doesn't only apply to those two circumstances. As a reloader, I've developed the habit (perhaps annoyingly, but I would rather err on the side of caution) of devoting the same level of attention to any cartridge I reload. Is that helping my cartridge per hour production rate? Certainly not, but I'm okay with that, as I can sleep soundly knowing that I haven't cut any corners that may result in danger to myself or those around me.

Assume nothing. Even in reloading manuals, there is the possibility for typographical errors, though I've only found a few over the years. Check and double-check the data you're using, making sure you didn't misread the chart or inadvertently skip a line when looking

Keeping a detailed record of your reloading activities, including all the components used and the amounts thereof, will help keep you safe, as well as preserving those loads that shoot the best.

IMR 4350 has a different burn rate than Hodgdon H4350 or Accurate 4350. They are not interchangeable.

at the powder charge weights. Be sure you have the bullet weight correct and that you are looking at the correct cartridge — I've always been amazed at how a page can get flipped without my noticing. Picking out your powder type/charge weight combination and writing it down clearly in your notebook helps keep things straight.

Though I have a more extensive operation than the average reloader, I keep only one powder (the one for the project I'm working on) on the bench at any given time. The same goes for primers and bullets. This attention to detail may sound a bit OCD, but it's not hard to have things go pear-shaped if there are multiple components on your bench. I'm too familiar with Mr. Murphy and his Law to take a chance. Also, be sure of the powder brand, as many have the same numerical designation with a different prefix. For example, there is IMR 4350, H4350 from Hodgdon, and AA4350 from Accurate Arms. All use different data and burn rates and are not interchangeable.

DRINKIN' AND SMOKIN'

When I think back to my childhood — where all my relatives smoked like chimneys everywhere they went — it's a wonder that they didn't incinerate everything in their path. Here's one point about smoking that is irrefutable: smoking around gun powder is not smart. I think back to how many times somebody was smoking at the reloading bench, and I thank my lucky stars that there was no tragedy. If you've ever seen a large amount of powder ignited, you know how scary that can be. Powder burns fast, and powder burns hot. Keep sparks and embers far away from full dispensers or cans of powder. If you're a smoker (and I don't judge), take a break and go outside for your cigarette.

Alcohol impairs coordination and clouds your brain's ability to process information. Reloading requires your full, undivided attention, and while few people enjoy a fine cocktail more than I do, I wait until I've stored the reloading tools and components. I don't mean to sound like Nancy Reagan, but I've seen guys grab

Alcohol and reloading DO NOT MIX. Save the cocktails for after you put the dies and powder away.

Lead bullets are an economical choice and great to practice with but will assuredly get on your skin during the reloading process. When you finish, be sure to wash your hands thoroughly.

the wrong powder, primers, bullets, and more when partaking. I can't prove a negative and say they wouldn't have done that if they hadn't been drinking, but I hope you'll agree it's a bad idea to consume alcohol while playing with explosives.

ENVIRONMENTAL CONDITIONS

Depending on where you set up your reloading equipment, there may be environmental conditions that can compromise your safety or loaded ammunition's integrity. Certain types of carpeting can cause static electricity and sparks, which, as we've discussed, is never a good thing around powder. Heating and cooling vents can move a considerable amount of air, affecting electronic and even some balance beam scales. Keep them and their location in mind when setting up your equipment. Depending on where you intend to load, be wary about the means of heating and cooling. If you use a garage, shed, or other outbuilding, space heaters can be convenient but can be knocked over. Open flames or heating elements don't mix well with gun powder.

Also, direct sunlight is not a good thing, as it can shorten canister-grade powder's life. If you have considerable direct sunlight in your reloading room, keep the powder in a dark corner, preferably in a wooden box that will shield it from the sun. As mentioned previously in this book, it bears repeating: Never keep powder canisters in an airtight container. Any accidental ignition should be allowed to burn *openly* — keeping the ignition airtight and under pressure will immediately turn it into a bomb.

CLEANLINESS MATTERS

I'm not the neatest guy in the world, but I strive to keep my bench organized. Having primers rolling all over the place or powder granules all over the bench is poor practice. Primers fall and powder spills, but you'll need to keep things clean.

Primers have a flammable compound located within the cup. There are times when small bits of that compound can come loose, and if that stuff builds up in the wrong places — such as your primer tray, internal mechanisms of a hand primer, or the priming tube of a progressive press — trouble can follow. To reduce residue and prevent primers from spilling all over the room, don't dispense more than 20 at a time. Take a small brush and wipe out the primer trays regularly to prevent any buildup of primer residue.

If you have rugs, occasionally shake them outdoors, so you don't accidentally send a live primer through your vacuum cleaner. There are numerous debates about the dangers of using a vacuum to clean up a powder spill. I've done it and lived to tell the tale, but I usually pick up as much as I can with a broom and dustpan first.

LEAD EXPOSURE

Unless you load nothing but lead-free monometal bullets or lead-free shot, you're going to be exposed to lead if you reload. You'll expose yourself if you cast bullets (casting requires a particular procedure and extra attention to adequate ventilation). Still, even if you load lead-core bullets, you'll have a decent amount of lead exposure. Additionally, the tools used to load those bullets can build up a considerable amount of lead shavings and residue. You can absorb lead through your skin, so washing your hands vigorously after a reloading session is critical. Some reloaders use the thin latex gloves common to hospitals and the medical field; I don't wear them, but I wash my hands to minimize the lead absorption in my skin and keep my hands and fingers out of my mouth, eyes, and off my face while reloading.

Lead buildup on your tools is a definite concern, and copper, lead, and brass bits, flakes, and shavings will be the primary pollutants on the bench. Clean your dies, seating stems, and other frequently exposed areas to minimize lead dust inhalation. Lead absorption and inhalation are probably the most significant cause for concern to the reloader unless you make a habit of chewing on semi-wadcutters, which I don't recommend at all.

RELOADING FOR OLDER FIREARMS

Reloading for the old antique guns can be a dangerous proposition, as there are firearms on the market with metallurgic qualities that can't handle the same pressures as modern reproductions, though they may look the same. For example, certain U.S. Army Springfield rifles were heat-treated to varying levels of hardness. Where rifles with specific serial numbers are fully capable of handling normal pressures, others are brittle and cannot handle the same pressures. Likewise, firearm metallurgy underwent several changes as the shooting world went through the transition from blackpowder to smokeless powder. It's essential to know the limits of your firearm. You don't want to stuff 3-inch magnum steel shot into a vintage shotgun that can't handle it.

If you're unsure of the vintage or the pressure capabilities of any firearm, consult a competent gunsmith who can identify the gun and determine whether or not it's safe and in proper working order. Don't make assumptions. Doing so can cost someone their life. If you have a re-barreled rifle — like so many Mausers reworked after the end of World War II — and aren't sure of the chambering, have a gunsmith cast the chamber and slug the bore to determine the correct cartridge. I've seen shooters assume that a rifle was a 'stock 7x57 Mauser,' when in fact, it was re-barreled to .270 Winchester. You don't want to be the person

The Speer Hot-Cor and Sierra GameKing are both jacketed rifle bullets; though most of the bullet has a copper jacket, the exposed nose can transfer lead to your skin. Be sure to wash your hands thoroughly after loading.

pulling the trigger when a .284-inch bullet is driven down a .277-inch barrel.

While the Internet can be a fantastic resource, there are times when you should consult an expert. I've seen too many instances where the firearm in question was 'beyond a doubt' firearm X — based on the criteria found on (*fill-in-the-blank-dot-com*), only to find another 'exception to the rule.' Rather than take a chance by assuming what you've got in your hands, err on the side of caution and be sure before you proceed. |||

10

HANDLOADING ECONOMICS

I got into reloading for a couple of reasons: first, it was something I wanted to do with my Dad, as it kept us shooting together in the offseason; second, it allowed me to build premium ammunition at a lower cost than I could buy it. I'm not sure that is true any longer, but it warrants taking a detailed look at the cost breakdown of what it takes to make a box of cartridges compared to what it would cost to buy factory loaded stuff. And, never forget, your time is worth something, even if you spend it performing a labor of love.

The volume of ammo you expend will affect the numbers game, as you'll need to purchase the same tools to make one box of ammunition as you'll need to load twenty. And it'll also depend on the cartridge you're shooting; the cost ratio of reloading to factory ammo is going to be much different for the 9mm Luger, .45 ACP, .223 Remington, and .30-06 Springfield than it will be for the .455 Webley, .318 Westley Richards, .333 Jeffery, and .350 Rigby Magnum. Then there is the ability to load for rifles and pistols that have no factory ammunition option. You can then only place the value

Brands such as American Eagle offer an incredible value. When you consider the cost of the investment in reloading tools and components, plus your valuable time, bulk factory ammo may be the better value (only if you can get it).

on the ability to shoot that gun, making the cost of reloading irrelevant as it's the only option you've got.

Couple these ideas with the ammunition drought of 2013–2014 and the incredible increase in sales of both firearms and ammunition in the madness that began in 2020, and you'd have to add some value to having the ability to reload when there is almost nothing available on store shelves. No matter what the usual market price of your favorite factory ammo, when it's unavailable, you'll pay a premium. The value of handloads increases accordingly.

WHAT'S THE REAL COST?

Let's use the universal and popular .30-06 Springfield as an example for cost analysis, assuming you're a new reloader and starting with no more gear other than a heaping pile of once-fired brass you've saved in a shoebox over the years. Looking at the big picture, at a bare minimum, you'll need a reloading press, a set of dies, a scale, trimming capabilities, measuring tools, case lube, reloading manual, and other accouterments. Let's say you jump into the pool with one of the reloading kits, such as the Rock Chucker Supreme Master Reloading Kit, which has a street price of $400. I'd add to that a trimmer, say an RCBS for $135, and a set of standard dies at $40. Before you buy a single component, you're now $475 in the hole. You'll need a pound of powder for roughly $30 and a box of 100 large rifle primers for $4. Let's use a standard deer hunting bullet such as the Sierra GameKing 165-grain spitzer boattail at $30 per box of 100. You've invested $539 and have the capability of loading five boxes of ammo. That works out to $107.80 per box of 20, but that's not realistic because you can use the tools for decades.

Suppose you take care of your reloading tools, and they last you a lifetime. Further, to simplify the analysis, let's remove the equipment's initial cost from the equation. To be conservative, let's throw in 100 brass

Factory ammunition for a standard chambering such as the .30-06 Springfield is generally available and affordable, but once you experience the freedom of handloading, you may never look back.

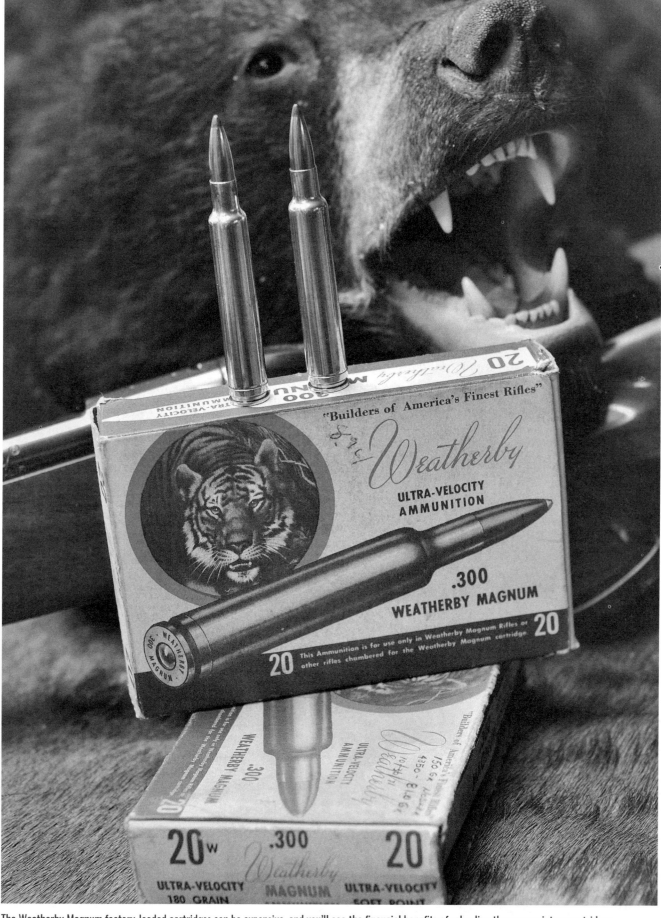

The Weatherby Magnum factory-loaded cartridges can be expensive, and you'll see the financial benefits of reloading these proprietary cartridges.

cases from Federal at $62/100. Our components for 100 newly loaded .30-06 rounds would come to about $126, or $1.26/round. By comparison, a 20-round box of Federal Premium with that same Sierra 165-grain GameKing bullet fetches $30-$37 — or $1.50-$1.85/round. So, yes, you can handload these rounds for a $.24-$.59 cent per round savings. Not only that, as I write this, there is a run on ammo, and you can't find that Federal factory load in stock. If you have the components on hand, you can always load some up.

If you're a one-deer-a-year consumer who generally confirms zero on Ol' Besty and heads afield, perhaps the factory ammunition is the way for you to go. But if you enjoy recreational shooting and the benefits of routine practice with your big game rifle, you can see how the investment in reloading tools can pay for itself in a short amount of time. If you get a couple of buddies together to share the tools' cost, you can see a return on your investment even sooner.

Compare this idea to a cartridge such as the .300 Weatherby Magnum, where factory ammunition runs from $40 to $90 per box. Suddenly, your investment in tools seems much more worthwhile. Should you shoot multiple calibers — both rifle and pistol — you will see how reloading gear can quickly provide a return on your money. I've also experienced the frustration of finding a factory load that a rifle loves, only to have the factory change the recipe (whether intentional or not, I cannot answer), resulting in ruined accuracy and me scratching my head wondering what happened to the rifle. What's more, experimenting with different factory loads can be a hefty investment, especially if you're shooting a rare and costly cartridge. The initial investment of the reloading tools, and the cost of components, coupled with the time spent developing a load, are all well worth it to me. I can grab primer X, charge the case with my known charge of powder Y, and seat bullet Z on top to arrive at the load that will serve for the rifle's life.

I gave the example of purchasing a reloading kit, and that is certainly a sound idea, but you could also buy your tools individually. Depending on your budget, you can make the tool list as expensive or inexpensive as you choose. One benefit of reloading: dies and presses are interchangeable — should you choose a Redding press, you could easily use a Hornady resizing die, an RCBS seating die and a Lee crimp die, or just about any combination. You can buy as you go, keeping your eyes open for specials and deals on reloading gear to keep costs to a minimum.

Online shopping has become popular, and that applies to reloading as well. But primers and powder require a Hazardous Materials fee on shipping. This fee can add a considerable amount of money to your components' cost, so keep that in mind and try and order in bulk, even if you have to combine orders with a friend or two. I recommend combining primers and powder on the same order under the same HazMat fee.

For the high-volume handgun shooter, there are many quality, inexpensive projectiles available that will keep the cost of ammunition down. Federal's SynTech is a great example. It's a synthetic-coated lead bullet, perfect for the indoor ranges, which cost between $23 and $27 per box of 100, or roughly 2/3rds the cost of Federal's premium handgun bullets. It runs clean and is accurate for practice. If you don't mind scrubbing lead from your bore, companies such as Meister Bullets offer hardcast lead bullets in bulk that can be as cheap as $0.07 per bullet for the classic 230-grain round-nose .45 ACP bullet if you buy them by the 1,000 count. Berry's Bullets offers plated projectiles for both rifles and pistols at an affordable rate; they are accurate, and you can use them in an indoor range.

AVAILABILITY IS PRICELESS

Whether or not you intend to handload for hunting, target shooting, self-defense, or competition, reloading can make the difference between having any ammo or none at all. At the risk of sounding like an alarmist, 2020 has shown that the ammunition shelves can

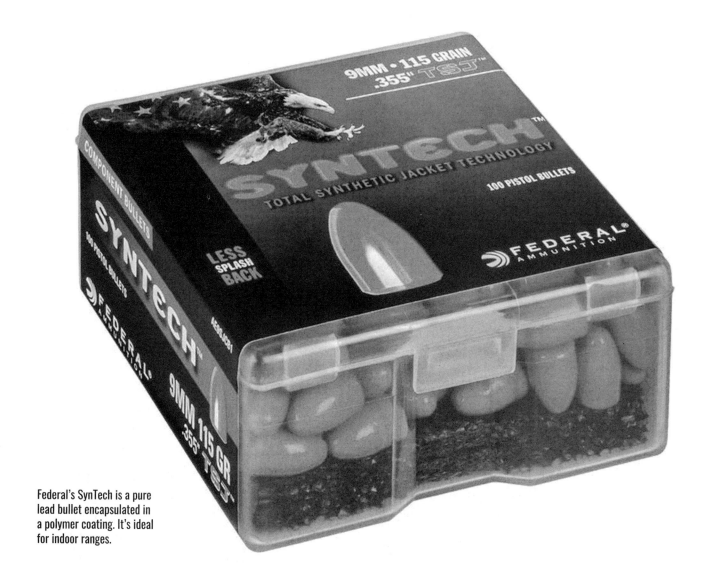

Federal's SynTech is a pure lead bullet encapsulated in a polymer coating. It's ideal for indoor ranges.

go bare in less than a fortnight. If you've purchased this book, and especially if you've read to this point, you possess a desire to reload. Let me say this: just as you've learned how to safely store, handle and shoot a firearm, learning how to reload may save someone's life, especially when there is a shortage of factory-loaded ammo.

Whether it's hunting for meat to fill the freezer for the winter or defending your loved ones from a riotous mob, a firearm without ammunition is no more effective than a club. The components need to be on hand, and the primers are the one part that cannot be reused or created, and therefore must be purchased. In a pinch, you can make crude blackpowder, and you can cast bullets from lead, but you must stockpile the primers.

Lead has become more difficult to source in recent years, though you can still hit the junkyards to procure material for pouring bullets. Working as a surveyor, I've picked up wheel weights on the side of the road, but there are too many varieties of metals in wheel weights these days to bother with them. Linotype alloy ingots can be purchased from the reloading supply shops and mixed with lead to achieve appropriate hardness. RCBS has long made a line of bullet molds for both rifle and pistol, and though sales are assuredly down, there is a small but enthusiastic group of cast bullet fans who keep the flame alight.

KEEPING THE CLASSICS ALIVE

A group of us, cartridge nerds, enjoy shooting and hunting with cartridges that are less-than-popular. We recognize, and use, some of the more common ones such as the .30-06 Springfield, 7mm-08 Remington, .300 Winchester Magnum, .22-250 Remington, 6.5 Creedmoor, and .375 H&H Magnum, yet also enjoy the early 20th-century British safari cartridges including the .318 Westley Richards, .300 H&H Magnum, .350 Rigby Magnum, .350 Remington Magnum and more. Many tragically overlook these latter-mentioned rarities to one degree or another, and components, cases, and bullets may present unique challenges to the shooter who is enamored with them. Factory ammunition is most prevalent for the .350 Remington Magnum and .300 H&H Magnum but is limited at best. The other two are limited to the odd run of Kynoch ammunition (which, in my honest opinion, is equally overpriced and overrated, with the bullets giving an erratic terminal performance and the cost running as much as $10 per round), and that stuff has seen better days. My best option for all of these cartridges is to handload them and keep them running with the limited list of components and tools available. RCBS once made dies for both the

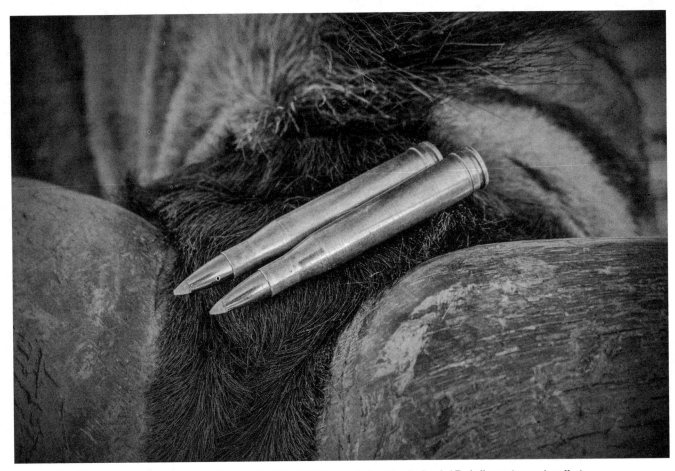

The .300 Holland & Holland Magnum on safari. The author handloaded 180-grain Federal Trophy Bonded Tip bullets to impressive effect.

.318 Westley Richards and .350 Rigby Magnum, but the Huntington Dies Specialties custom die shop was closed in 2019. Even so, there are alternate custom die options. Also, you can form the .318 Westley Richards case from ultra-common .30-06 Springfield brass. But the .350 Rigby Magnum — which predates its more popular and larger sibling, the .416 Rigby, by a few years — is a unique design, and you can't fashion its cases from any other cartridge.

To handload the .350 Rigby Magnum, you'll either have to source some of the Kynoch spent cases or rely on a custom cartridge company to make some new brass for you. When I was building a .350 Rigby Magnum rifle, I relied on component cases from Roberson Cartridge Company in Texas to produce new brass for me. Were their cases inexpensive? No, but you get what you pay for, and the Roberson stuff is uber-consistent and lasts considerably longer than the cheaper stuff. Roberson cuts its brass instead of drawing it, and the molecular structure is both unique and unparalleled. Bottom line, you're going to have to handload for the latter two cartridges if you

Between dies from RCBS, cases from Bertram and Roberson Cartridge Company, and bullets from Woodleigh and Peregrine, handloading keeps the .318 Westley Richards alive.

want reliable ammo. The .350 Rigby Magnum uses the lineup of .358-inch-diameter bullets common to the .35 Whelen, .358 Winchester, .358 STA, and .358 Norma — as does the .350 Remington Magnum — so there is no lack of component bullets. My rifle likes the 250-grain Nosler Partition and Hornady Interlock. At the same time, Dave deMoulpied's Remington 700 Classic in .350 Remington Magnum prefers the shorter bullets, such as the 220-grain Speer Hot-Cor, 200-grain Hornady InterLock, and 200-grain North Fork. |||

The .350 Remington Magnum works best with shorter bullets, like these Hornady InterLock round-nose projectiles.

11

PROBLEM SOLVING

Most of your reloading sessions will go smoothly. However, I'll wager that sooner or later, you'll need to employ some of the ideas and techniques outlined here to prevent or solve potential reloading problems.

STUCK CASES

A stuck case in a resizing die may not happen often, but when it does, it can be a session ender unless you've got the proper tools. A stuck case can result from not having enough lubricant on the outside of the case, so when you attempt to extract it from the die body, you'll rip a good portion of the rim off the case. Stuck cases also result from accidentally grabbing the wrong shell holder. I once inadvertently used an RCBS #4 — designed for the H&H Magnum cartridge family — while loading for the .30-'06 Springfield, which requires an RCBS #3. It went into the resizing die smoothly, but there was no contact on the rim when I tried to remove the case — it remained stuck

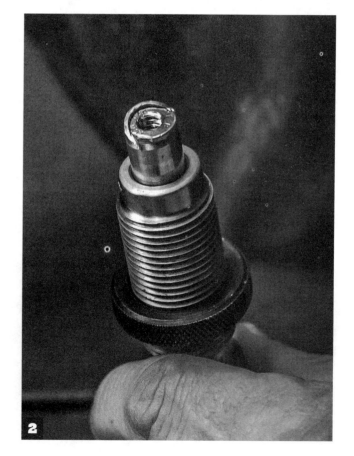

Drill a hole through the stuck case webbing with the provided drill bit.

as I lowered the press handle.

Regardless of how it happens, you'll need a stuck case remover tool kit designed to — wait for it — remove the stuck case. The tool kit is simple and requires only a power drill. It includes a drill bit of proper diameter, a tap to thread the hole, an Allen-head bolt, and a spacer cup to cover the case's rim and make contact with the bottom of the die body. Here's the process in a nutshell: with the provided drill bit, drill a hole through the case's web, centered on the flash hole. Next, use the tap (you'll need a tap wrench) to thread the drilled hole. Slip the steel cup over the base of the die, aligning it with the die body, and start the Allen-head bolt into the threaded hole. Using the Allen key, screw the bolt into the threaded hole in the case, which will back the case out of the die body.

Here are some pointers to help you avoid destroying your resizing die. First, back the expander ball as far

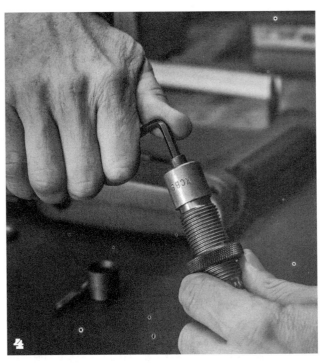

Place the steel cup over the base of the stuck case and against the mouth of the die body, and screw the Allen-head bolt into the threaded hole.

The kit contains a tap so you can thread the drilled hole.

The bolt will work the stuck case out of the die. Be sure to clean the die thoroughly to remove brass shavings.

The RCBS polymer inertia hammer uses collets to hold the cartridge in place. Smacking it against a block of wood pulls the bullet out of the case.

out from the base of the die and cartridge case as possible, though it probably won't make it out of the neck (assuming you've stuck a bottleneck case). Second, go easy with the drill, as when you finally make your way through the web of the case (the thickest part of the brass), the drill bit may jump forward into the decapping pin and expander ball. I can attest to the damage a drill bit can cause to the inside of a resizing die. It's not a pretty scene.

Once you get that case out of the resizing die, you'll find brass flakes and shavings inside the die. Give your resizing die a careful cleaning, preferably in an ultrasonic cleaner. Should you have had the misfortune of damaging the decapping pin and expander ball, you'll need to replace them, and this is why I try to keep replacement parts on hand.

PULLING BULLETS

There are times when you'll need to pull bullets out of loaded cartridges, either because you've made some mistake — perhaps you've seated the bullets too deep, or you've used the wrong powder charge — or

you may need to use the factory-loaded cases for your handloads. The latter situation has come up when I've needed to handload for a rare cartridge. You may have ancient factory ammunition or a supply of loads with a bullet you don't want to use for your application. Perhaps you want to use the projectiles for a different cartridge. No matter the cause, you'll need to be able to disassemble a cartridge safely.

I use two tools, and both are equally effective, so it'll depend on your choice. The first is a simple inertia hammer. The inertia hammer is made of heavy-duty molded plastic and looks much like an ordinary hammer, but with a threaded cap on the rear. It uses collets designed to fit different rim diameters. You insert the cartridge into the hammer's body, screw the threaded cap over the base to keep things firmly in place, and much like a hammer, strike the front against a hard surface (I use a block of wood). Depending on the cartridge you're disassembling, it can take multiple hits to work the projectile free, and if you go too hard, you can damage the bullet when it comes out and hits the front of the hammer's chamber. I often use a small piece of foam in front of the cartridge to protect the bullet.

I also use an older RCBS Collet Bullet Puller. Using the standard 7/8-14 threaded die body, it also employs a collet to grab your cartridge. You install the die into the press, raise the cartridge into the die body (where the bullet will run up into the collet), tighten the collet with the handle on the top of the unit. When you lower the ram, the bullet and case will pull apart, leaving the components intact for reuse. If you exert too much force on the collet, though, you can disfigure the bullet, so use only as much force as needed. RCBS sells it without collets, so you can choose the bullet diameters you need as you go, buying them individually.

Both tools are useful during load development. You'll invariably end up with some oddball cartridges that didn't give the desired result or that half-box of unidentifiable handloads of suspect origin. You can pull the cartridges apart and start over.

REMOVING LIVE PRIMERS

Removing live primers is a touchy situation. That's because you have a live component, which most definitely reacts to pressure, pressed tightly into the primer pocket. You've got one of two choices: either use the decapping pin of your resizing die or a universal decapping die to remove them carefully while still live, or take the primed cases to a safe location, preferably the range, and fire the primers.

If you choose to remove them at the reloading bench, use a smooth, even stroke to drive the primers out; don't slam or jerk the ram, or you risk detonating the primer.

The RCBS Collet Bullet Puller uses a collet of specific diameter and the power of the reloading press to pull bullets from cases.

I've removed hundreds of live primers without issue. Just be careful to go as slowly and evenly as possible, keep all powder off your bench, and wear safety glasses should you ignite a primer.

EXCESSIVE ROLL CRIMP

There are a few times where a roll crimp is necessary, and while I've detailed the process of applying the proper roll crimp, as you start reloading, the untrained eye may not see a potential problem. You can crumple the case wall of a straight-walled case or roll the mouth over so much that it will be difficult to chamber the cartridge in a bolt-action rifle, and any autoloader will lock tightly.

Trimming your cases to a uniform length is as important as having the proper seating depth. Doing so keeps the cannelure (crimping groove) in the right location, and you can crimp it without stressing the projectile. Spend the time to learn how a proper roll crimp feels, both when loading the ammunition and feeding the ammo into the firearm. To me, a properly roll-crimped cartridge is a thing of beauty and can stabilize muzzle velocities.

RESIZING PROCESS IRREGULARITIES

You may find that your resizing die's feel has changed, giving more resistance when drawing the case downward over the expander ball. You may hear a squawking noise or feel a chatter when you open the case neck. These signals could be the result of several different issues. The expander ball could be too rough at the top, creating an excess drag on the downstroke. A light polishing — just enough to smooth it out, but not so much to change the ball's diameter — will do the trick. I've also had excess gunk — mostly a mixture of tiny brass bits, burnt powder, and case lube — build up on the top of the expander ball, resulting in some difficulty on the downstroke.

Another possibility is that your case's neck or wall is dirty, and the residue is causing friction when being drawn over the top of the expander ball. A good case brush and some elbow grease can get that stuff out of there.

Brass cases that are polished to a high sheen tend to stick more than rougher ones. You should clean your brass cases before resizing them, but save the polishing process until the cases are all resized. Nickel-plated cases can leave little nickel chips — a much harder metal than brass — and scratch the inside of your resizing die, though that may reduce the chances of a stuck case.

SEATING DIE ISSUES

The science of the projectile is evolving at an ever-increasing rate, especially as the long-range shooting market continues to expand, and the distances to the target continue to increase. Our projectiles' ballistic coefficient becomes more favorable, but at the cost of long, tapered ogives and severe boattails. These factors can influence the tools you use to handload. Many tools have been developed (or modified) to handle the VLD (very low drag) bullets. They include chamfer tools that put a too uniform bevel on the inside of the case mouth but at a degree more favorable to the VLD projectiles and seating stems that are compatible with these uniquely shaped bullets.

Most of the reloading die manufacturers offer a VLD-style seating stem as either an option in the die set or an aftermarket piece you can use with your existing dies. One thing is for sure: if you're loading bullets with a modern ogive (either the secant curve profile or the hybrid tangent/secant hybrid), your bullet's seating depth will be much more uniform when using the proper seating stem. A consistent seating depth is an integral part of the accuracy potential of such a bullet design.

There are also specialty seating stems that you could use in the big-bore cartridges, which often use spitzer and round-nose bullets. For example, cartridges such as the .375 H&H Magnum, .375 Ruger, .416

Remington Magnum, .416 Rigby, and .404 Jeffery all readily use a mixture of round-nose and spitzer soft point (expanding) bullets as well as round- and flat-nose solids (non-expanding). A round-nose bullet can easily wedge itself in a seating stem designed for spitzer bullets, so there are die sets for this cartridge class with seating stems for various nose profiles. I learned this lesson the hard way, with a used set of .375 H&H dies and a round-nose soft-point wedged so hard into the seating cup that it wouldn't seat in the case.

Using the proper seating stem makes life much easier and will alleviate many problems on the shooting and reloading bench. In some instances, I keep two different seating dies — each with specific seating stems — for particular cartridges, such as the .375 H&H.

Also, pistol dies often have different seating stems for loading a variety of bullet shapes. Quite apparently, the round-nose bullets require a different seater than the semi-wadcutter or wadcutter profile to give optimum consistency.

CASE CAPACITY ISSUES

Case capacity won't be an issue with pistol cartridges, but specific rifle cartridges can be challenging. The .308 Winchester is an example of one of these cartridges, especially when dealing with the longer, monometal bullets. I like a powder charge that comes close to filling the case, but not an overly compressed charge. I don't like to break the grain structure because that can directly affect pressures and velocity. For such situations, check out the ball powders.

Extruded stick powders vastly outnumber the available ball powder choices, but a ball powder takes up less volume when you need to maximize space. Ball powder works very well with automated dispensers and meters superbly in the mechanical powder throwers. Some classics such as Hodgdon's H380 have worked well in the .22-250 Remington (named for Bruce Hodgdon's .22-250 38.0-grain load with a 55-grain bullet), .308 Winchester, .375 H&H Magnum, and .375 Ruger.

My long-time hunting buddy Dave deMoulpied has had a deep love for the obscure .350 Remington

This .270 WSM cartridge's bullet shows the seating stem's mark; note the ring on the ogive of the bullet where the seater plug made contact. Use a VLD-style seating stem to prevent this issue.

This spherical powder is ideal for use with the calibers listed below. More data is available from our basic manual or at our website – http://www.hodgdon.com

CALIBER	CHARGE	BULLET		CASE	PRIMER	C.O.L.	VELOCITY
22-250 Rem.	46.0 gr.	52 gr.	HDY A-MAX	Win.	Win. LR	2.350"	3692 fps
220 Swift	44.0 gr.	55 gr.	HDY SP	Win.	Win. LR	2.680"	3833 fps
243 Win.	40.0 gr.	100 gr.	SPR BTSP	Win.	Win. LR	2.650"	2963 fps
6mm Rem.	44.0 gr.	95 gr.	NOS BT	Win.	Rem 9-1/2	2.825"	3117 fps
30-06	55.5 gr.	180 gr.	SIE BTSP	Win.	Win. LR	3.300"	2743 fps
338 Win. MAG	72.0 gr.	160 gr.	BAR XFB	Win.	Win. LRM	3.280"	3143 fps

MAXIMUM LOADS – DO NOT EXCEED – REDUCE BY 10% TO START

DANGER FLAMMABLE EXPLOSIVE • SEE PRECAUTION ON SIDES

MADE IN USA

Ball powder can be a lifesaver when case capacity poses a challenge, as it takes up less volume than stick powder.

Magnum for decades — another fine example of a cartridge with limited capacity. Couple the lack of real estate in a short-action magazine — where the overall length is also limited, and you can't load many of the spitzer bullets without the case mouth falling on the bullet ogive — and you've got a real specialty case on your hands. Dave and I have found a half-dozen bullets that work well with the case, and as it likes medium-burning powders, we've had great results using Winchester's 748 ball powder, as it gives the velocity we wanted while not being overly compressed.

The .458 Winchester Magnum, long criticized for its lack of case capacity, was designed to replicate the ballistics of the classic .450 3-1/4-inch Nitro Express. Whereas the .450 used a 480-grain bullet at a muzzle velocity of 2,150 fps, the .458 Winchester Magnum launched a 500-grain bullet, making matters worse. The ammo produced in the late 1950s and early 1960s never achieved the advertised velocities. Modern powders have solved the problem, but when my Dad — Ol' Grumpy Pants — and I booked a Cape buffalo hunt to Tanzania, he wanted to use the A-Square duo of Dead Tough soft points and monolithic solids, which meant handloading. I had some trouble attaining the velocity and accuracy figures I was after but finally found what I sought with a stout load of Hodgdon's H335, getting three-shots groups just under 1-1/4 MOA, with a muzzle velocity of 2,080 fps out of a 22-inch-barreled Winchester Model 70. (We attained the Winchester figure with a longer barrel.)

Even the magnum cartridges can benefit from the ball powders. I've used Alliant Power-Pro 4000 MR and Hodgdon's H414 in the .300 Winchester Magnum, the 7mm Remington Magnum, and the .300 Winchester Short Magnum. Of the three, the .300 Winchester is often criticized (though I feel it is unwarranted) for the fact that the bullet's base will extend below the neck/shoulder joint. Because of the cartridge's short neck (it measures just 0.264 inch), this will happen with nearly all the bullets used. Even the long monometal bullets, such as the 200-grain Barnes TSX, can extend into the case considerably. Yes, stick powders work well, but the ball powders really perform in the .300 Win. Mag's case. Also, H414 has a burn rate just a tad faster than the classic H4350 and IMR 4350, which makes it perfectly suited to the three cartridges I've mentioned. Alliant's Power-Pro 4000MR is considerably slower than H414, being more in line with IMR 7828, and is not only applicable to the three cartridges but works well with the larger cases used in the .300 Remington Ultra Magnum. It also performs in standard cases such as the .243 Winchester, .280 Remington, and .30-06 Springfield.

I'm not saying that ball powders are superior in performance to the extruded stick types, but they can be a problem solver in specific applications. |||

SHOTSHELL RELOADING

By David C. deMoulpied

Author's note: While I've loaded my fair share of shotshells over the years, my buddy Dave deMoulpied loads them much more than I do. When we grab our shotguns and head out for pheasants and partridge, it's Dave who usually brings the shotshells, and they're more often than not his handloaded stuff. I'm confident he can best walk you through the steps of reloading shotgun ammo.

If you're a beginner interested in reloading shotgun shotshells, the obvious question is, why reload them at all? With 12-gauge reloads, you'd save less than $1 per box of 25 shells. If you're shooting some of the less popular gauges, such as 28 gauge and .410 bore, then reloading makes obvious sense. After all, ammo availability for the smaller gauges can be hit or miss, and it can be economically advantageous to load them yourself. But what about reloading the big 12-gauge shells? The main benefit is total control.

You want to control the performance of the shells produced by using quality components. And as that may seem a little odd to some, think about this: There is a huge market for premium rifle projectiles right now. Many whitetail hunters, myself included, are spending money and time developing loads for the premium bullets that will not only penetrate a deer from stem to stern but hammer bears and some large African critters as well. I would be willing to bet that hunters kill more deer with old cup-and-core bullets than with all of the newer bullets combined. But for some reason, I can't bring myself to buy off-the-shelf

cartridges — the vanilla-grade ammo with which my father and his generation hunted so successfully. It's the whole "what if" question that drives reloaders. Remember this: everyone who loads their ammo has an opinion, and usually a strong one.

This chapter will discuss shotshell reloading based on my own experience — my likes and dislikes. You should experiment with the published data and find

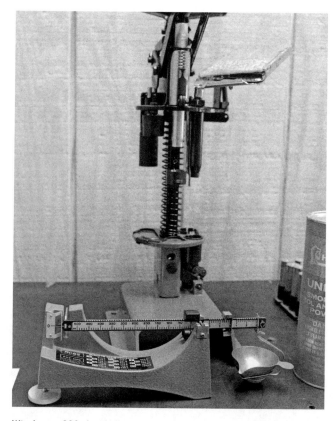

Winchester 209 shotshell primers loaded into a standard shotshell reloading press. You should always use a beam scale to double check powder charge weights when using a progressive press.

Empty hulls ready for reloading.

out what works for you and what shoots well out of your shotgun. So, let's break down a shotshell, looking at its components, and talk about each of them.

HULLS

The quality of the shotshell hulls you start with will dictate how many times you can reload them. Don't skimp on these! My two favorite hulls are the Remington STS and the venerable Winchester AA. I've been able to get up to 10 reloads out of the STSs, but that's pushing the envelope. Hulls "go bad" for two reasons: the first is cracking of the hull walls, and the other is the inability to get a tight crimp on a completed shell. It's important to visually inspect each of the hulls before putting them into your reloading queue. An inspection doesn't take long, and it'll save you headaches when pellets start

Winchester 209 shotshell primers.

falling out of an open, poorly crimped shell. I know because I've had it happen to me.

If you're just starting, you have a few options in obtaining your hulls. You can buy new components or save a few dollars and purchase once-fired hulls. At my local sporting clays club, we pick up hulls from around the course and give them away for free. So, if you're pinching your pennies, you could quickly pick up a few boxes of once-fired shells for nothing. Just remember to stick with the hulls I mentioned earlier.

POWDER

Veteran reloaders have their favorite powders. As someone new to reloading, choosing a powder can be overwhelming. Alliant, for example, offers 14 different powder choices for shotshell reloading alone. I recommend you go online to Alliant's or Hodgdon's websites and research their loading data. I use Alliant Reloader's Guide. Load data is up to date and laid out clearly for the novice or expert alike. If you shoot skeet, trap or clays, and are a club member, find out who

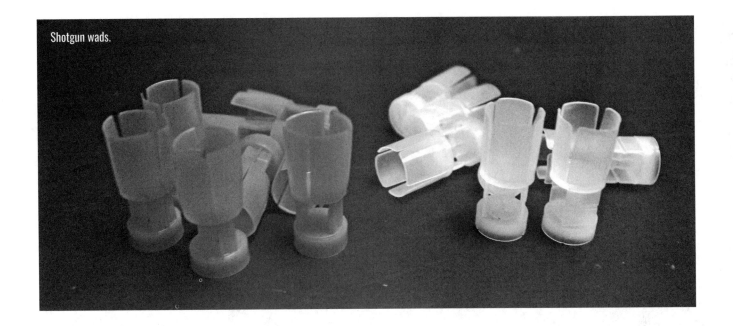
Shotgun wads.

reloads, and talk to them about what powder they use. There's no sense reinventing the wheel here. Getting a good starting point on what powder to use for busting clays will not only put your mind at ease but will give you confidence as you delve into your new hobby.

I use a starting point of 1,150 to 1,200 fps, essentially 2 3/4- and 3-dram equivalents. SAAMI says that a 2 3/4-dram equivalent load with 1 1/8 oz. of shot will travel approximately 1,150 fps, while 3 drams with 1 1/8 oz. will do 1,200 fps. You can't go wrong with either of these velocities. Indeed, 2 3/4-dram shells will break any clay you can hit. For longer crossing shots on the clays field, 3-dram shells will give you that little extra zing you're looking for on those types of shots. If I were beginning, I'd pick one of the popular powders such as Green Dot, start with a velocity of 1,200 fps, then see how it feels to shoot. Remember, firing 100 rounds on a Saturday afternoon with an over/under shotgun, running 3-dram/1-1/8 oz. loads can be tough on your shoulder. You can always go down to 2 3/4 dram/1 oz. loads, and not give much away. There isn't a target out there that 1 oz. of #8 shot at 1,200 fps won't pulverize. Find what you are comfortable with, and then pattern your gun on paper with your loads.

PRIMERS

Primers are the little caps in the base of shotshells struck by the shotgun's firing pin, thus igniting the powder. Important note: Not all 209 primers are the same. Some burn hotter than others, and you must be careful when putting together a reloading recipe. Pay close attention to the primer brand. Don't assume 209 means Remington, Winchester, or CCI. Loading data tables are very specific about which brand primer to use in any given recipe, so pay close attention. Also, make sure to put leftover primers from your loading session back into their original labeled box.

WADS

Wads are what hold the shot in the shell and cushion it from the exploding powder. This cushioning prevents deformed pellets, meaning fewer "flyers" and tighter, more consistent shot patterns. If you think one size fits all for wad selection, you're sorely mistaken. Go to any of the websites of big companies such as Remington or Winchester, and you'll see specific wads for different shooting applications, be it hunting or clays. They are probably the most overlooked component in shotshell reloading, but there is a lot of science behind every design out there. You can save money buying wads

A finished shell loaded with quality components will instill you with confidence. That quality should help your wingshooting, which is mostly a psychological game.

that are clones of the ones made by the big brands. Companies such as Claybuster and Downrange are two fine examples. If you look at the Alliant Reloader's Guide, you'll see wads from these companies suggested in many of the shotshell recipes for clays shooting.

SHOT

There's more to shot than size alone. The basic rule of thumb: For target shooting, use shot sizes from #7-1/2 to #9. I shoot skeet with #9 shot. For sporting clays and trap, I'll use #7 1/2s. Consider pellet hardness. Antimony added to lead shot makes the pellets harder. The hardened shot breaks clays easier and has less pellet deformation, fewer flyers, tighter shot strings, and more uniform patterns. These attributes are essential for clay busters and bird hunters alike. Chilled lead shot is slightly softer

than magnum lead shot alloyed with higher antimony concentrations. Many shooters prefer hardened magnum shot for its ability to retain its spherical form.

Conversely, chilled lead shot contains lower antimony concentrations and is lighter than lead (though slightly denser than magnum shot). There's also copper- and nickel-coated shot to consider. I've gone to the sporting goods store to pick up four boxes of shells to shoot clays when there was no time to reload, and there were no target loads available. My only choice was the bargain Dove and Quail-type loads. It must be psychological, but my confidence in that round was low, and my shooting suffered. I was shooting soft lead and crummy wads, and it got in my head. Don't settle for low-grade shells with cheap components. Buy hard (magnum) shot for clays and bird shooting.

Now that we've looked at what goes into a shotshell, here are the types of presses you'll need and how to set them up.

TYPES OF SHOTSHELL RELOADING PRESSES

There are two types of shotshell reloading presses: single-stage and progressive. A single-stage press requires you to work the press handle while manually moving the shotshell through the different stages. Progressive presses allow you to work on multiple shells simultaneously using features such as auto-priming. The progressive types turn out large volumes of shells quickly. Check shells periodically to ensure charge weights and crimps. A repetitive quality control process is always paramount to production volume. Note that progressive presses take longer to set up and can be finicky at times compared to the more straightforward, single-stage press.

MOUNTING THE PRESS TO THE BENCH

Ideally, if you have the available space, you should bolt your loading press securely to a benchtop. If you don't have that luxury, then you can mount it to a piece of 3/4-inch plywood. Make sure to measure approximately 4 to 5 inches wider than the loader's base and about 7 to 8 inches longer. This extra space will give you the room you need to clamp it to your work surface properly. Make sure to use a large, wide-mouthed C-clamp to hold your press securely in place. After mounting, work the loader's handle up and down a few strokes to confirm it travels freely. This arrangement allows people with limited space to use their loader when needed and then have the space available for other projects when done reloading.

SETTING UP YOUR PRESS

Now that your loading press is securely mounted, the next step is setting up the charge bar. Most loaders come with multiple bushings that allow you to charge different weights of the powder and shot. (MEC, or Mayville Engineering Company, makes an adjustable

The MEC Sizemaster shotshell reloading press, assembled and mounted on the bench.

Charge bar showing that it's for a single-stage press (#302) and that it delivers 1-1/8 oz. of shot (118).

"universal" charge bar that will enable you to create any size powder/shot load combination. I've used one on my MEC Sizemaster and MEC 650 for years.) Once your charge bar has the correct bushing in place, fill and attach the powder and shot bottles to the unit.

Once you've filled the powder and shot bottles, make sure that you label each one with what's inside. For instance, if you're using Green Dot powder, write it on a label and put it on the powder bottle. This attention to detail will be invaluable as you acquire different powders and sizes of shot. I purchase the extra powder and shot bottles for each type/size that I'm going to use. When not in use, they are capped tightly and kept on a shelf, ready to go when I need them. At this point, I like to take an empty hull with a used primer in the bottom to throw powder charges to weigh for accuracy. Never trust what's written on the bushings for charge weights.

Two types of charge bars: One uses interchangeable bushings for different weight powder charges, and a MEC Universal Charge Bar.

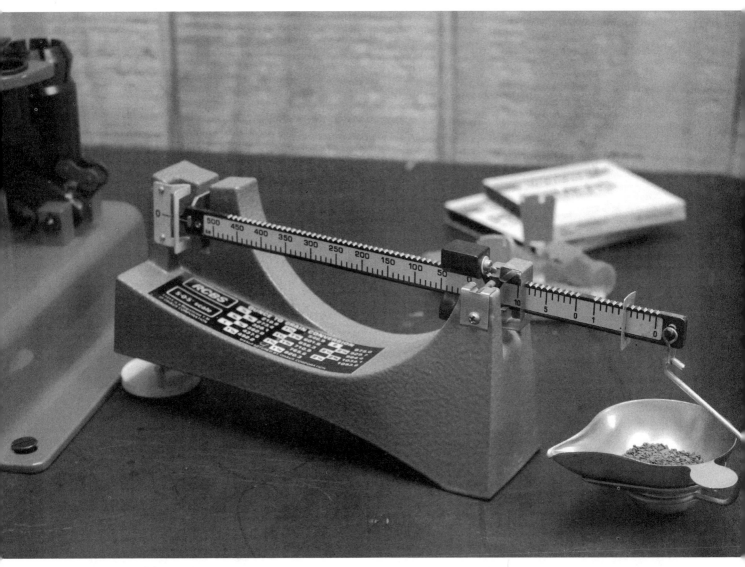

Weighing powder charges before reloading begins.

Environmental conditions like humidity, or a nearly empty powder bottle, will give you different weights per charge volume. Invest in a quality balance scale. (I use the same scale that I use for rifle reloading — my trusty RCBS 505.) Throw at least four or five powder charges (the first charge always being culled from the group), record the weights to make sure they are close to the desired weight. Tweak the adjustable bar until it delivers the charge you need. Reloading is all about R+R: Repeatability and Reproducibility. And that's why, after you've verified your charge weights, check a sample every 6 to 8 rounds to make sure things are staying the same and that the crimps are looking good.

Date and document your load in a notebook. Detail the type and weight of powder and shot you are charging into your hull. Also, note hull make, primer type, and wad information. Make sure you write down the bushing numbers or charge bar settings as well. This attention to detail sounds like a lot to do, but if you walk away from your reloader for several weeks and sit down and try to remember what you loaded last on it from memory, you'll be lost. Another critical point: Always keep your reloading components such as primers and wads in their original container. You don't want to mix up primers, which is easy to do since they all look the same. Attention to the smallest details, and reloading without distractions, are essential to safe shotshell reloading.

To start the reloading process, insert an empty hull into your press. Pull down on the handle to remove the old primer. This action will simultaneously press a new primer into the primer pocket at the base of the hull. Note: With progressive loaders (and certain single-stages), you fill an auto-feed tray with primers and attach it to the reloader. Primers are then automatically dispensed as each shell rotates through the machine.

The second stage requires you to slide the charge

Powder and shot in bottles. Be sure to label these, so you always know what you're working with.

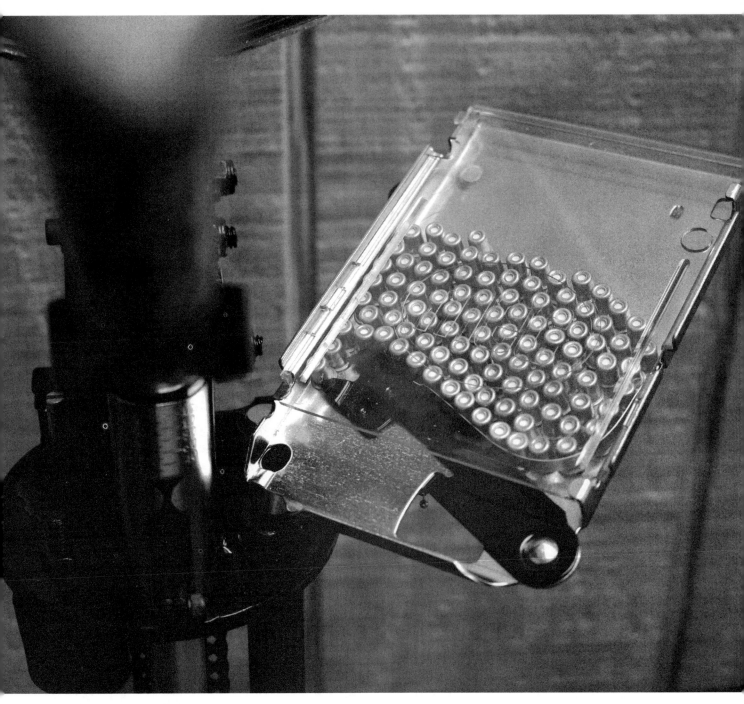

Auto primer tray filled and set in place.

bar to one side to dispense the powder charge into the hull. You then press a wad into the shell. With the handle still down, slide the charge bar to the opposite side. The shot charge should drop into the wad. The press advances the shell to the next station where the first crimp is started, and finally, the last station where the final crimp is applied.

If you shoot autoloading or pump shotguns, it makes sense to add the extra step of resizing. To resize, after the final crimp, shells are collected, and then a resizing die is installed. (Some loading presses resize the brass and remove the old primers simultaneously). You pull the handle downward, resizing the brass base and adding a slight taper at the end of the shell. The taper allows for smooth feeding into the chambers of autoloading and pump shotguns.

The good thing about some progressive loaders, such as the MEC 650, is that you can use it as a single-stage press. Just unhook the auto primer feed, and you're all set. This double-duty capability is good for someone just starting who wants to get the feel of each reloading stage. Once comfortable, you can easily convert to the progressive setup and start cranking out high volumes of loaded shells fast!

FAVORITE LOADS

Stage 1- Deprime and resize the shell.

Stage 2- Prime the shell.

Stage 3a - Charge powder into the shell.

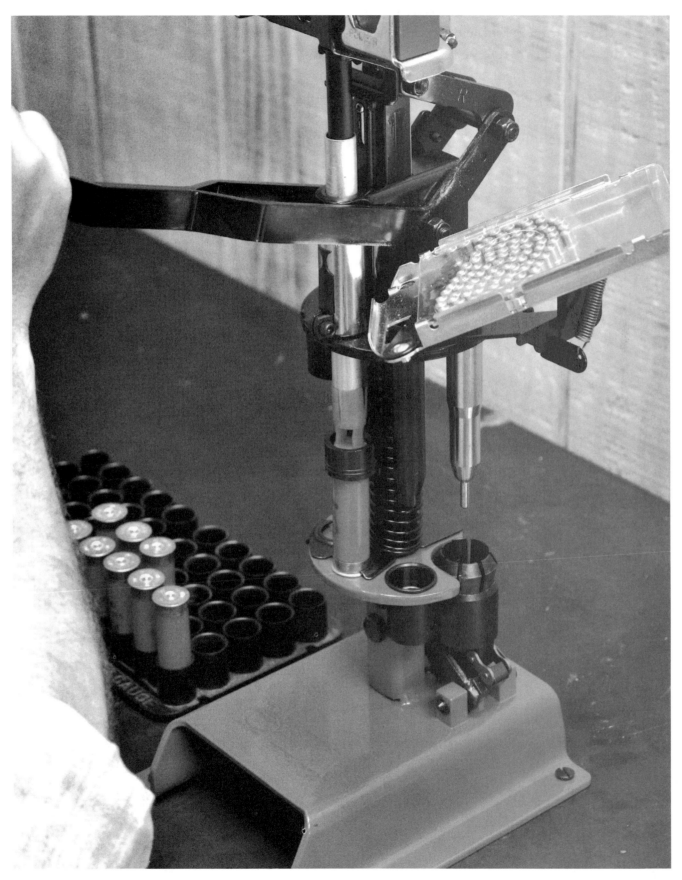

Stage 3b - Insert the wad into the shell.

I find that the loads I've developed for clay shooting translate very well to the upland hunting fields here in the Northeast. Our quarry runs from the diminutive woodcock (aka Timberdoodle) to the elusive ruffed grouse and the hearty pheasant. Early season hunts for grouse and woodcock take place when foliage clings to trees and brush. In my 12-gauge Browning Superposed, I'll have the first barrel choked Skeet with 1-1/8 oz. of #7 1/2s and the second barrel choked Improved Cylinder with 1-1/8 oz. of #6s. Since I hunt over a pointing dog, my opportunity for a close first shot is good. But partridge are often unpredictable and will bust before the dog locks on point. With the #7

Stage 3c – Charge shot into the shell.

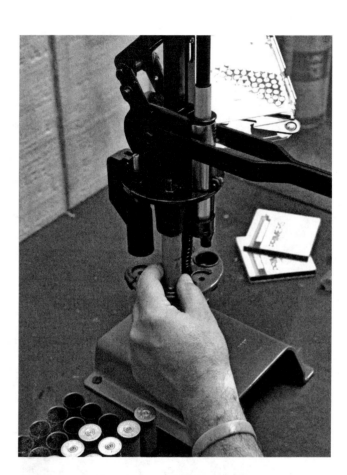

Stage 4 – Apply the first crimp on the shell.]

Stage 5 – Finished crimp applied.

1/2s and an open choke, I have my best opportunity of hitting the bird. If I've missed, which is a good possibility, I have the larger shot size of the #6s, with more retained energy to get through the foliage and drop the bird.

On the other hand, Pheasants are a tough, unpredictable bird that will run one day and hold tight the next. I've taken them with shells from size #7 1/2 down to #4s. My preference, though, is for 1-1/4 oz. of #5s at 1,300 to 1,350 fps, especially in the second barrel when the bird turns on the afterburners after you've missed that easy first shot. I've found that #5s give you a little more oomph on the longer 35- to 40-yard shots than the same load of #6s, and there are more pellets in that charge as in the equivalent load of #4s. So to me, it's the best of both worlds.

Depending on what type of clay busting I'm doing, I have a few pet loads that have served me well over the years. For skeet, I'm a #9 shot guy, shooting 1-1/8 oz. at 1,200 fps all day long in my old Remington 1100. I know many shotgunners who swear by #8s. Either is fine; it's a matter of personal preference. While I don't shoot a lot of trap, my friends who do say 1-1/8 oz. of #7 1/2s is the ticket. For sporting clays, I'll bring a mix of #7 1/2s (1 oz. and 1-1/8 oz.) and #9s. For longer-distance targets, and when I'm shooting a fixed choke — say Improved Cylinder — I like the extra pellets in the heavier #7 1/2 load for good shot density at those longer pokes.

NON-TOXIC ALTERNATIVES TO LEAD SHOT

Lead poisoning of waterfowl became a significant issue in the late 1970s after a federal study showed that more than two million birds died each year from ingesting lead pellets. In 1987 and becoming nationwide in 1991, the U.S. Fish and Wildlife Service (USFWS) imposed a ban on lead shot for waterfowl hunting. The push for non-toxic alternatives to lead shot continues today. On July 1, 2019, California banned all lead projectiles — bullets or shot — from all hunting use.

Throughout this article, I compare alternate shot type densities to lead shot. That's because lead is the "gold standard" at a little more than 11g/cc and is safe to shoot in nitro-proofed shotgun barrels.

Here are a few of the most popular non-toxic alternatives to lead shot for reloaders, which currently meet the USFWS's requirement. I'll also touch on typical reloading components such as wads and powders typically used with each of these different shot types: Steel, Bismuth, HEVI-shot, and ITX.

STEEL SHOT – DENSITY 8.0G/CC

Steel shot was the first non-toxic alternative to lead and is attractive due to its low cost. Today, you can expect to pay approximately $20/10 lbs. (By comparison, 10 lbs. of HEVI-shot will set you back close to $400.) For the reloader who does a lot of waterfowl hunting, this is an attractive alternative. But as in life, everything is a give and take, so what you make up in price, you pay for in terminal performance. Here are some of the pros and cons of steel shot:

Given that steel shot's density is about 30 percent less than lead's, you can expect to need more pellets per ounce relative to a comparable lead load. Steel yields higher velocities than lead as well yet doesn't retain speed or energy like lead shot. The standard rule of thumb has been to go down two sizes from your typical lead shot to even the playing field. If you shoot #4 lead for ducks, you should move down to #2 steel to see similar results. Steel shot hardness means your patterns will be tighter due to lack of pellet deformation. While you won't suffer as much from pellet deformity/irregular pattern, the steel shot will lose momentum at longer distances and retain less energy than lead.

There are some safety aspects of shooting steel you should understand. You need to ensure that your load of pellets sits entirely within the wad of your hull. The wad protects your barrel from being scored as the shot speeds down the bore after you shoot. Another characteristic of steel shot is that it doesn't deform when fired, so more pressure is generated. Firing a larger steel shot through an older, "softer" steel shotgun barrel can lead to pressure issues and a potentially dangerous situation. Always shoot steel shot through a newer shotgun made for waterfowl hunting, or use an appropriate stainless steel choke tube, no tighter than Modified. (I recommend you use mica when reloading different types of shot. Add a teaspoon or so of Mica Wad Slick to a bag of wads and shake it up. Mica slicks things up, especially when you're dealing with compacted loads.)

Regarding powders used in steel shotshell reloading, one of the most popular is Alliant Steel. This powder is a slow-burning propellant that achieves high speeds with lower pressure. It's a fluffy and low bulk density propellant, which means it does not meter accurately

Alliant Steel is a slow-burning shotshell powder that scoots your loads along at high velocity and minimizes pressure.

Fiber spacers (left) and wads (below) specially designed for steel shot.

or repeatedly through reloading bushings. The volume-to-weight ratio does not make getting a reproducible and accurate charge attainable. So, Alliant suggests that you weigh charges manually on your reloading scale and then add them to your shells, one load at a time.

Wads for steel shot tend to be thicker than ones used with lead. The thicker wads protect your barrel as the shot passes through the bore. There are also fiber spacers of various thicknesses, from 1/4 to 3/8 inch, that you can place at the bottom of your wad to fill out your shot cup (depending on your payload size), thus allowing a better-finished crimp on your shells.

Three popular steel shot wads come from Reloading Specialties, makers of "SAM" wads, Ballistics Products, and Precision Reloading. There are many from which to choose. Refer to your favorite reloading manual and follow its suggestions.

BISMUTH – DENSITY 9.8G/CC

Bismuth introduced its shot as a non-toxic alternative to steel, with more of lead's desired characteristics. It is softer than steel, denser, does not need filler wads, and you can use it in older, non-choke tube guns without fear of damaging the barrel. The biggest downside is its cost. Currently, it costs about $150/10 lbs.

Reloading bismuth shells is very similar to standard lead loads. Just be aware of the density difference, so you don't overcharge your shot size; there will be more volume of bismuth shot vs. lead for the same charge

Note the "belly band" around the ITX shot pellets.

weight of the shot. You can go up one bushing size or, better yet, use a universal charge bar and dial in your shot payload. Always verify shot charge using your balance scale before you begin mass production. If you're loading larger shot sizes for waterfowl, consider replacing your standard shot drop tube with a larger volume one made for the larger shot. This tip will prevent you from binding the shot in the drop tube.

For typical field use, I recommend Hodgdon 800X or Winchester WSF powders.

HEVI-SHOT – DENSITY 12G/CC

HEVI-shot uses a high-density Tungsten alloy blend. With a density greater than lead, this would seem to be the ultimate answer for non-toxic lead substitutes. But it has its issues, the first being its cost. HEVI-shot is priced some 20 times that of steel, at $400/10 lbs.

A blend of Tungsten alloy, nickel, and iron, HEVI-shot is extremely hard, and with that brings similar problems to steel shot in your barrel. You'll need to fully contain the shot in a non-toxic shot cup so it doesn't score your barrel. As with steel, you'll need to run a stainless steel choke tube or use a newer model shotgun made with barrel steel that can handle the punishment this stuff dishes out. As a minimum, you'll need a Modified choke when using HEVI-shot, preferably even something more open such as IC or Skeet.

Examples of shot cups (wads) made for this rigorous application is Ballistics Products, Inc (BPI) TPS line of wads. As with steel, you may need to place 1/8-inch fiber or felt spacers in the bottom of the wad to fill out the payload and improve your crimps.

Once again, Alliant Steel is a great powder loading HEVI-shot. Also, try Alliant Blue Dot, a very slow-burning powder ideal for magnum 12-gauge loads in the 1-1/4 to 2-oz. range.

ITX – DENSITY 10G/CC

ITX shot is a blend of powdered Tungsten mixed with iron and a proprietary binder. At 10g/cc, its density is slightly less than lead, making it a safe choice to shoot in older shotguns. Its most notable feature is a "belly band" that goes around the middle of each pellet.

There are several varieties of ITX shot available, but I recommend starting with ITX Original-10, which uses 10g/cc density pellets. ITX also makes a denser Tungsten blend of shot claiming 13g/cc densities, ITX Extreme -13 Shot, and these should be a great asset to turkey hunters using sub-12-gauge loads and smaller shot, while delivering more pellets on target downrange.

The manufacturer states that this pellet provides more lethality through larger wound channels and energy transfer when striking a bird. The close-to-lead density should also provide downrange performance, something missing from steel shot. The shot's ductility also minimizes pellet fracture during ignition, sometimes seen with more hardened, more brittle pellets. The cost of ITX shot is between steel and HEVI-shot, at about $200/10 lbs.

Once again, due to the unique pellet geometry of ITX-10, be careful you don't plug up your drop tube when using larger-sized pellets. You may want to weigh out the shot by hand on your balance beam scale and charge your shells manually, just to be on the safe side.

I've seen the gamut of powders suggested for use with ITX-10, from Hodgdon 800X, Universal, and Longshot. Get one or two reloading manuals, and read up on some of these powders to give yourself a good, safe starting point.

As you can see, there are many options for reloading non-toxic shotshells. While less straightforward than lead, the process is similar. Do your research, check your pocketbook, and decide what you think will work for your type of shotgun shooting.

Once you finish loading your first box of shotshells, you'll realize how fun and easy it is to do. So get yourself a press, a reloading guide or two, and start cooking up some great loads for yourself! |||

13

HANDLOADING FOR LONG-RANGE SHOOTING

The long-range shooting market has never been bigger. More rifles, optics, cartridges, and projectiles exist for this task than we've ever had. And as I've said before, we may be living in the Golden Age of factory ammunition. It's better than it has ever been, with a wide array of choices. But, and it's a big but, there are times when handloads will outshine the factory stuff, and that's usually beyond 1,000 yards. Let's look at what it takes to produce the best ammunition for extreme long-range shooting.

Loading for long-range shooting requires specialized tools.

In the world of extreme distance shooting, precision components, and adherence to ultra-tight tolerances are paramount. When you're taking shots out to the one-mile mark or more, every little variation can have a significant effect. The high ballistic coefficient bullets will retain their energy best and offer superior resistance to wind deflection. Handloading allows you to use such bullets in your loads.

BALLISTIC COEFFICIENT

The bullet manufacturers' ballistic coefficient values are expressed in either the G1 or G7 model to represent how the projectile resists atmospheric drag. The B.C. values are unitless and are fluid, changing as the bullet's velocity varies. The manufacturers will give their bullets an average, but it isn't a wise choice to accept that value as gospel, as many atmospheric conditions will change the bullet's flight.

The bullets with optimal B.C. have a gently tapering ogive on the front, in addition to a severe boattail on the back. These bullets have unique characteristics, taking time in flight to 'settle down' and stabilize. They may not show their best accuracy potential at 100 yards and often exhibit optimal accuracy at 300 yards and beyond — as the bullets stabilize gyroscopically. Think of a spinning top: the initial force that imparts the spin causes it to wobble, slightly off-center, but as the spin continues, it becomes much more uniform (stable), appearing to stand still. The same thing happens with a bullet. It takes time to become stable in flight.

Now here's where things can get strange: flat-base bullets stabilize earlier than boattails, which is why boattail bullets may 'shoot better' at 300 yards than they do at 100 yards, and why flat-base ones can be more accurate on a closer 100-yard target. Some bullet manufacturers recommend flat-base bullets if your shots stay inside of 300 yards (as most hunters do).

For long-range ammunition, you'll want bullets with high B.C. Look at the success of the 6.5 Creedmoor. Though it doesn't have the highest muzzle velocity, it excels as a 1,500-yard cartridge. It will beat the .308 Winchester past 1,000 yards, despite similar muzzle velocities and case capacity. Its B.C. values are what set the 6.5 Creedmoor apart. The 6.5mm 140-grain ELD Match bullet — perhaps the most popular factory combination for this cartridge — has a G1 B.C. value of .646 — a very good figure. To match that in .30 caliber, you'd have to reach for the 212-grain ELD Match, and

the .308 Winchester can't come anywhere close to the 2,700 fps muzzle velocity of the Creedmoor. This illustration is one reason why the 6.5 Creedmoor has been so successful and why the bullet's B.C. value is so critical. If you bump up the muzzle velocities with a high B.C. bullet, the downrange performance only gets better, though it comes at the cost of additional recoil, muzzle blast, and barrel and throat wear. If you're okay with these things, you'll enjoy the flatter trajectory and improved wind deflection values.

SPECIALIZED TOOLS

The B.C. of your chosen bullet is dependent on the shape and consistency of the meplat (meplat, as a reminder, is the technical term for the bullet's flat or nose). It's such an essential point that Hornady put

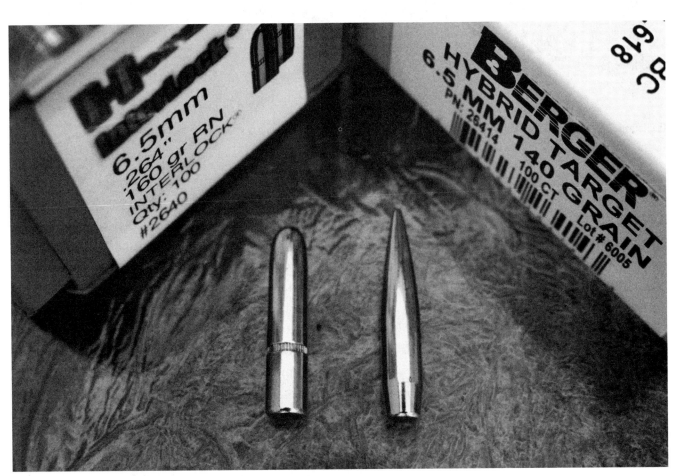

The 160-grain round-nose bullet will settle before the 140-grain boattail bullet, but the 140-grain bullet's higher Ballistic Coefficient makes it a much better choice for long ranges.

The Hornady 6.5mm 140-grain ELD Match (shown here loaded in the 6.5-284 Norma) has a high B.C. value well-suited to long-range shooting.

an awful lot of time and effort into its Heat Shield Tip, constructed of a new polymer, which reportedly doesn't melt or deform from the heat of atmospheric drag. Other bullets use a small hollowpoint, formed by the jacket's terminus at the meplat, such as the Sierra MatchKing and Berger VLDs. And then there are others, such as the Hornady A-TIP Match, which use a machine-turned aluminum tip to not only keep the meplat consistent but to locate the bullet's center of gravity properly.

For any of these bullets, if you alter the conformation of the meplat, you change the B.C. When it comes to long-range shooting, that is not a good thing, So, the use of a VLD seating stem, specifically designed to work with very low drag bullets, will keep the meplat intact during the bullet seating process.

When loading ammo for long-range shooting, you can get as nerdy and meticulous as you want. Examples include VLD chamfer tools that cut a steep angle on the inside of the case mouth to avoid marring the bullet in any way during the seating process. Micrometer-adjustable seating dies. Or even Redding's Instant Indicator Headspace and Bullet Comparator — coupled with Redding's Competition Shellholders. Redding's Slant Bed Concentricity Gauge allows you to observe the runout of your loaded cartridges and make sure bullets aren't seated cockeyed.

Your handload precision will improve from the meticulous weighing of each powder charge, and you should upgrade to match primers such as the Federal Gold Medal Match or CCI Bench Rest. I also recommend starting with the best brass you can afford.

The Redding Slat Bed Concentricity Gauge enables you to ascertain bullet runout and works equally well on handloaded and factory ammunition.

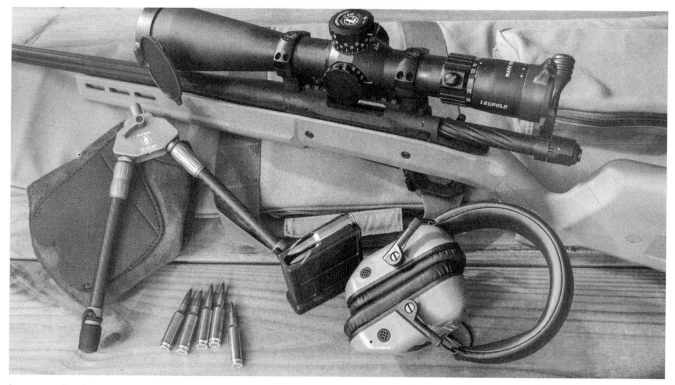

Long-range shooting requires a specific set of quality tools, as well as shooting skills, but it all depends on high-quality ammunition.

I've long been a fan of Norma, Lapua, and Nosler brass cases. Bushing dies will extend the life of your cases by working the necks only as much as is needed and preserving the malleability of the brass.

The chronograph is essential in the pursuit of good dope. Knowing the precise muzzle velocity of your load is vital for predicting your trajectory. However, atmospheric conditions will dictate the trajectory more than the combination of muzzle velocity and stated B.C. Truing the rifle (see sidebar) is the best method of achieving the proper trajectory, but during the load development process, measure your load's performance with a chronograph.

SPLITTING HAIRS

For those who become enamored (some may use the word obsessed) with accuracy — and it very well may happen to you along the way — here are some ideas that will help achieve your goals. Accuracy (actually 'precision' is the proper term) is the result of consistency. While this book doesn't concern itself with firearms or shooting technique, per se, the ammunition is our concern and can make a big difference in your target results.

While the acceptable accuracy level for a hunter is one issue, the precision expected by a serious target shooter will undoubtedly exceed the former. I'm not saying that hunting ammunition should lack attention. However, long-range shooters hold the components used for target loads to higher scrutiny than the hunting stuff.

To construct the best target loads, start with the highest quality components you can obtain. I suggest Norma, Lapua, or Roberson brass, match primers (I have a penchant for Federal Gold Medal Match), temperature-resistant powders, and specialty bullets. Even among the premium cases, you want the optimum consistency. Once your cases are resized and trimmed to a uniform length, weigh them. Assuming that you resized the outside dimension into a consistent conformation, any weight changes would indicate a wall thickness variation. Therefore, that would mean a difference in the volume of the inside of the case.

You could see a variation of pressure and velocity, directly affecting the loads' consistency. Weed out brass showing considerable deviation from the mean — depending on the case or the brand, try to stay within 2 or 3 grains — using only the most consistent cases for the load.

The same goes for the bullets: You want the most consistent of the chosen lot. Since you have no control over the bullets' dimensions (unlike cases, you're unable to adjust the projectiles' size or shape), you can only choose the most consistent ones. Keep bullets within 0.3 to 0.4 grain of the intended weight, and limit component variation. Weigh each powder charge on a trusted scale. You want the charges to be spot on. Work diligently during load development to find a powder charge that exhibits the best blend of velocity consistency and accuracy for your cartridge.

Bullet seating depth can be crucial to attaining that last bit of accuracy and can make a difference in downrange performance. The bullet will have some amount of jump or freebore (the distance between the bullet's resting place within the cartridge to the point where it engages the rifling). When that dimension is changed, it can affect (sometimes drastically) the group size.

Generally speaking, the longer the cartridge's overall length (and the shorter the freebore), the higher the velocities will be, and vice versa. Seat the bullet deeper, and you'll see a *reduction* in muzzle velocity. However, the group size may open or shrink depending on that seating depth. When it comes to target loads, I'll sacrifice speed to improve accuracy.

I recommend using the Redding Slant Bed Concentricity Gauge to weed out less-than-desirable

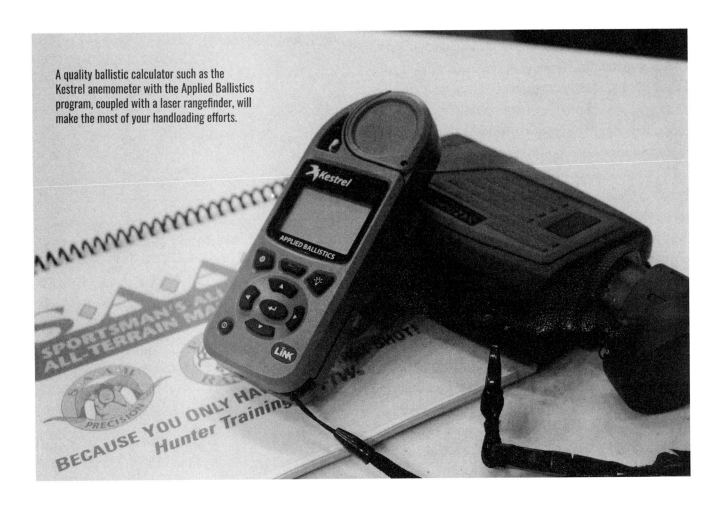

A quality ballistic calculator such as the Kestrel anemometer with the Applied Ballistics program, coupled with a laser rangefinder, will make the most of your handloading efforts.

cartridges after they are loaded: You roll your loaded cartridges on the stainless steel bearings. Simultaneously, a stud and a dial indicator show you any runout or "wobble" in the bullet. (I recommend setting it at a 30-degree angle to avoid any off-center readings.) This handy device works for factory loaded ammunition so that you can separate it into lots. You can also use it to assess your brass cases, separating any that don't meet your concentricity expectations.

CONSISTENCY IS THE KEY

Long-range shooting will magnify any inconsistencies in your loads, so you'll want to keep things as consistent as possible. Consider the temperature-insensitive powders to combat temperature swings. Always avoid fighting environmental conditions when you can. Your chronograph will be a huge help again, telling you which loads offer the most consistency, i.e., the lowest velocity spreads.

You'll need a ballistic calculator to input changing environmental conditions. For example, the day's heat can raise the density altitude, the winds are always changing, and humidity can pose an issue. But like any calculation, you'll get out what you put in, and inconsistent ammunition will not help your efforts.

Your shooting techniques need to be on point, and you've got to have a good rifle, mounts, and scope, but the bullet is what is going to do the work and is the only part of the system that touches the target. Think of your handloaded ammunition as equally important as the other hardware; just as you'd never make a scope adjustment that is 'good enough,' you should never load target ammo that is anything less than the best you can make.

Taking time to experiment with different bullet seating depths, powder types and charge weights, primer types, and cartridge case brands can be a labor of love, but the rewards can be incredible. Once you find that magic formula for your rifle, you can rely on that level of accuracy for years to come. |||

When you measure your shooting distances in miles, you'll want the best ammo you can get, and that quite often means handloading it yourself.

The author spotting for a shooter who is engaging a 1,500-yard target. These shooting situations require ultra-precise ammunition.

Truing your rifle involves shooting at a long-distant target (700+ yards preferably) and recording the actual amount of bullet drop. You then input that 'real-world' figure into your ballistic software to "true" the data.

Truing the Rifle

You'll see a particular ballistic coefficient (BC) listed for each bullet as you study ballistics. This unitless figure describes the way a bullet will slip through the atmosphere. While manufacturers attempt to provide an accurate figure for each bullet, that number represents an average since the BC will change as the bullet's velocity varies. One quick look at the Sierra website will prove the point, as it lists varying BC values for each bullet, based on the velocity range. Why is this figure useful? You'll use it to estimate your bullet's trajectory and wind deflection values. You can say the same for chronographs — they are more accurate than they've ever been, but sometimes the numbers observed don't agree with the trajectory, especially at long ranges.

The best means of obtaining accurate trajectory data is to 'true' the rifle, which means shooting it at a long distance to record its true trajectory, rather than projecting an estimated trajectory using calculated data.

Zero your rifle at 100 yards, then shoot a target at the longest distance possible. Record the amount of holdover needed to hit the target at that distance and compare it to the data provided by your ballistic calculator. You may find a significant discrepancy, but you'll have to trust the real-world data—what the bullet is doing downrange at the target. Most of these programs will allow you to input the real data, adjusting the trajectory accordingly. The farther you can shoot to observe real-world performance, the more precise the projected trajectory will be at all distances. The calculated BC value can be considerably different from the one provided by the manufacturer. That discrepancy is no fault of the manufacturer but results from environmental changes that affect the bullet's flight.

Bottom line: the more real-world data you can obtain at longer distances, the better any trajectory projections will be, and you'll see a definite increase in long-range hits on your targets.

14

ADVANCED IDEAS

While this book's premise is basic reloading, I would like to share some advanced ideas you should be aware of as you progress as a reloader. These may inspire you to continue to learn as time goes on.

MAKING THE CASE

As I've stated throughout this book, the overall benefits of reloading are two-fold: The ability to customize ammunition, thereby freeing you from the bonds of factory loads, and to be able to load ammo for those situations when you can't purchase it. It's also often the only way to get ammo for the obsolete cartridges. For example, the .318 Westley Richards is a British cartridge that was highly popular in British East Africa and India in the early parts of the 20th century. It was considered an all-around big game hunting cartridge. It uses a .330-inch-diameter bullet and has a case head diameter slightly smaller than the 7x57 Mauser and .30-06 Springfield (though the

The author used information gleaned from *The Handloader's Manual of Cartridge Conversions* by John J. Donnelly to create brass for his .318 Westley Richards.

.473-inch Mauser/Springfield case head works in the Westley Richards bolt face). I have a custom .318 Westley Richards rifle built on a 1916 Gewehr 98 Mauser, and several friends have rifles of varying pedigrees. Factory ammunition for this obsolete cartridge is as rare as hen's teeth — being made in limited runs by Kynoch, with projectiles of questionable reliability — though cases are available from Bertram Brass, Quality Cartridge, and, new to the scene, Roberson Cartridge Company.

The first two companies have limited availability, and Roberson's stuff is excellent — they machine it on a CNC lathe — but it can be costly. Before discovering those companies, I made my brass using a set of RCBS dies and some good old .30-06 Springfield cases. I consulted a book that I feel is an essential volume for any reloader's shelf: John J. Donnelly's *The Handloader's Manual of Cartridge Conversions*. This book will help you make cases for rare cartridges from some of the more popular and available cartridges, with varying degrees of complexity. For the .318 Westley Richards, it is relatively simple. The first step is to cut the case down to proper length, from the 2.4940-inch length of the .30-06 to the .318's 2.400 inches (note: there are different sources that list the case length for the .318 as 2.368 or 2.380 inches, but all the examples I have seen, including many lots of vintage Kynoch ammunition, measure 2.400 inches). Once you've trimmed, chamfered and de-burred the brass, run the cases through the resizing die, where one pass will open the case neck from .308 inch to slightly less than .330 inch for proper neck tension. Recheck the case length to make sure it didn't stretch beyond spec during the sizing process. Since

The author proudly took this good Zimbabwean kudu bull using his .318 Westley Richards rifle handloaded with 250-grain Woodleigh Weldcore bullets.

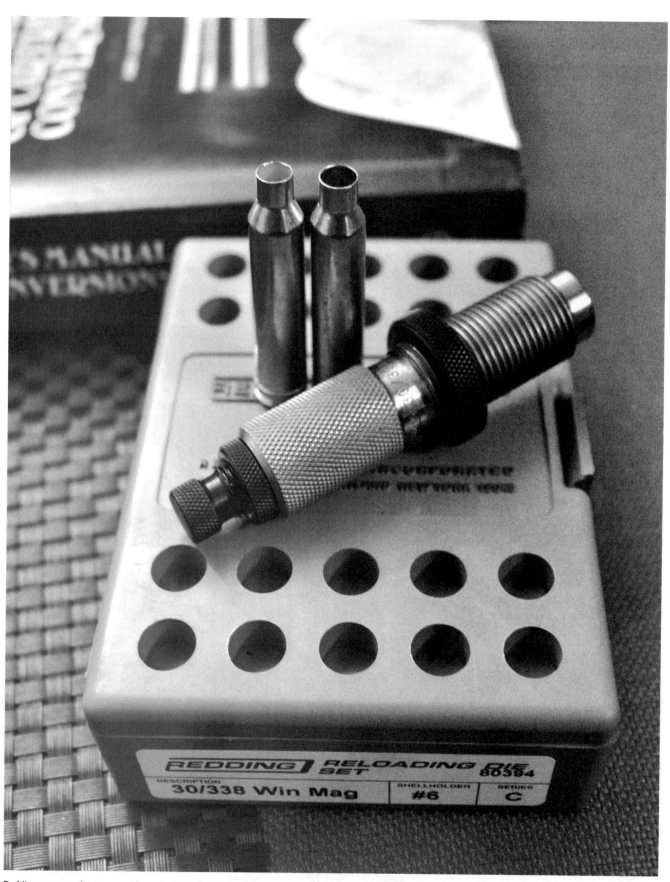

Redding came to the rescue with a set of dies for the .30-338 wildcat. One pass turned 7mm Remington Magnum brass into the correct size for the wildcat.

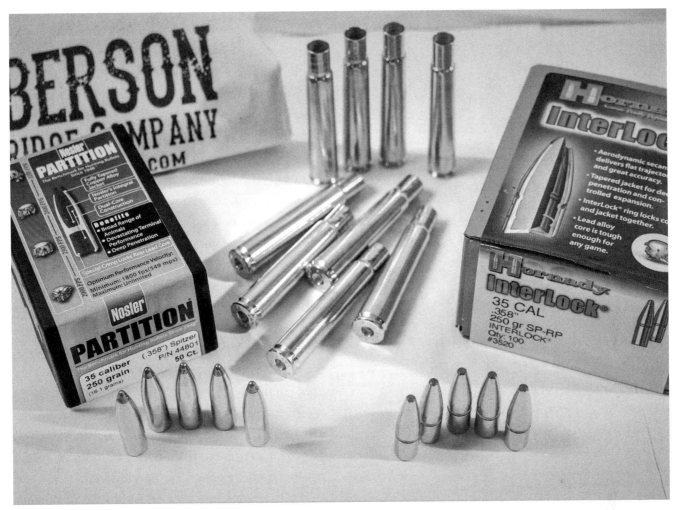

Roberson Cartridge Company provides lathe-turned brass cases for just about any cartridge you can imagine. It was a lifesaver for the author's .350 Rigby Magnum project.

the datum line — the distance from base to shoulder — of the two cartridges is close (1.948 inches for an unfired Springfield case, which has usually stretched during firing, versus 1.972 inches for the .318 Westley Richards), you can load the case without worry. It's a quick process, and the ammunition produced has been wonderfully accurate, giving sub-MOA accuracy with several different projectiles, including the classic 250-grain Woodleigh Weldcore, the 225-grain Peregrine BushMaster, and the Hornady 205-grain InterLock spitzer usually used for the 8x56R cartridge, which shares the same .330-inch-diameter. I've taken the .318 Westley Richards to Zimbabwe for kudu and zebra and on deer hunts here in the States, and I enjoy using the classic cartridge.

I've also converted cases to solve a head-scratcher for my buddy and world-renowned writer, Craig Boddington, when he obtained a rifle of unknown chambering. It was a late 1950s/early 1960s .30-caliber rifle, chambered for a magnum case with the H&H belt. While the signs pointed to the .308 Norma Magnum (released in 1960), Craig said the Norma ammo he had wouldn't completely chamber; the bolt wouldn't close. Digging through the archives and speaking with a few knowledgeable gunsmiths, we ascertained someone chambered the rifle for the .30-338 Magnum wildcat (the .338 Winchester Magnum necked down to hold .308-inch-diameter bullets). The .30-338 Magnum was the precursor to the .308 Norma and .300 Winchester Magnum and is slightly shorter than the .308 Norma

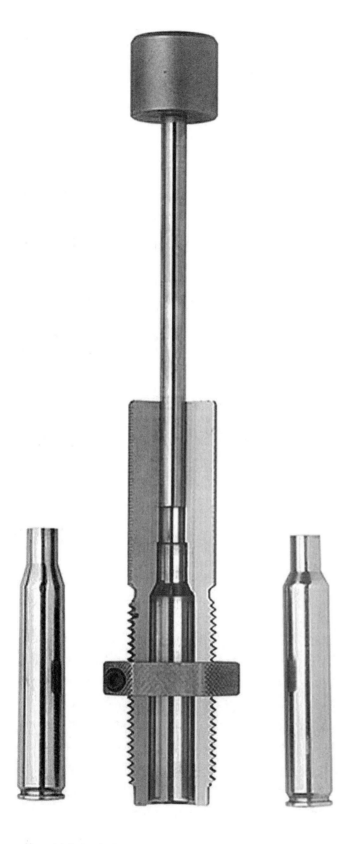

Hornady's hydraulic die-forming system.

Magnum (hence the bolt wouldn't close). The next steps were the easiest.

I hunted up a set of Redding dies for the .30-338 wildcat and decided to use 7mm Remington Magnum cases to form the brass, as the .284-inch neck was closer to .308 inch than the .338-inch stuff. Plus, I knew that the ammo wouldn't chamber in a 7mm Remington Magnum, even though that's what its headstamp indicated; however, it would chamber in the .338 Winchester Magnum. Once formed in the resizing die (the shoulder angle is the same as the 7mm Remington Magnum), we were good to go, and Craig printed three-shot groups of just over 1 MOA.

In both instances, the transition wasn't a difficult one, just some trimming and basic resizing. You may have to turn a brass belt off of an H&H case or fireform the cases in some instances. (When fireforming, use lighter powder charges to shoot the parent case in the rifle you're loading for, with the resultant firing expanding the case to the proper dimension.) Or, you can use a step-die to open up a case neck in stages. Again, Donnelly's book can be a lifesaver.

The Roberson Cartridge Company (RCC) is a unique outfit, which the fan of rare cartridges should keep in their contacts list. RCC offers a unique product. It employs a proprietary formula for brass and then creates cases by turning them on a lathe rather than drawing them from a cup. The result is an incredibly consistent brass case, which lasts longer than the typical drawn type.

The Roberson turned cases tend to be thicker than drawn ones, so I recommend that you start at the minimum charge for your cartridge when using this brass. You'll also use unique data for Roberson cases. Since they're tougher than standard brass, you'll achieve higher velocities with less powder than reloading manuals will indicate. Roberson can make any design you'd like, though it can be costly. They've come to the rescue for me with properly headstamped .318 Westley Richards brass, and more recently with the

.350 Rigby Magnum, I'm having built by Hillbilly Custom Rifles. The .350 Rigby Magnum predates the famous .416 Rigby by three years (being released in 1908), and like its more popular younger brother, is a proprietary design with no parent case. There are very few ammunition or component brass sources — even Kynoch has discontinued its costly ammo. Bertram offers a limited run occasionally yet is currently unavailable. Roberson fills a void for the more obscure cartridges, and in this instance, there was no other option for component brass.

DIES FOR THE RARITIES

While dies for most of the popular cartridges are readily available from the major players such as RCBS, Hornady, Redding, Lee, and Lyman, there are times when you'll have to dig deeper to procure dies for rare cartridges. RCBS used to offer dies for oddities such as the .318 Westley Richards dies I use so often, but the sister company that made those dies, Hunting's Die Service, is no longer in business. (Fred Huntington was a major player in RCBS. The Huntington's Sportsman's Store and wildlife museum are next to the RCBS factory in Oroville, California.)

There are other options, though, including custom die companies. Hornady offers a custom option, where you provide the vital information, including fired cases, a chamber reamer drawing, proper dimensions,

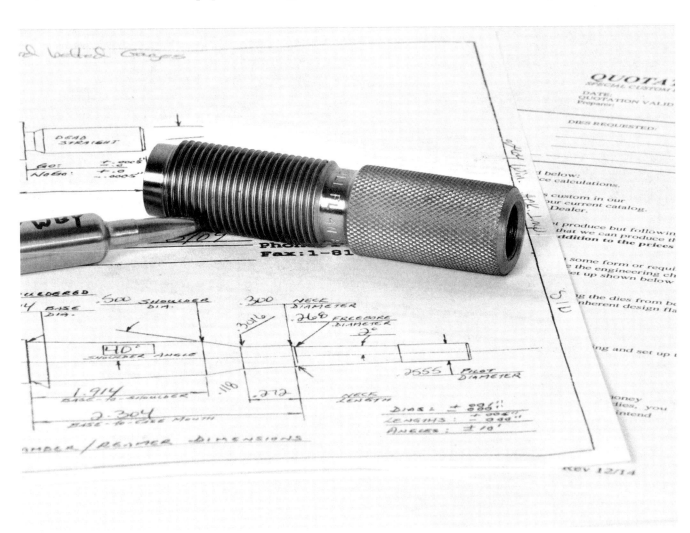

Redding offers a custom die service, which can be a considerable aid to the wildcatter.

and the cartridge name. It's a lengthy process and can be costly, but the price is worthwhile if you want to shoot an obscure cartridge. Hornady even offers a hydraulic forming die, which uses water pressure to form a cartridge case from one shape to another. Imagine you wanted something obscure such as the .257 Roberts Ackley Improved, and you needed to make cases for the rifle. You could fireform .257 Roberts cases in the Ackley Improved rifle, or you could use Hornady's ingenious system, which puts the hydraulic pressure of water to good use. It's a neat solution.

Redding is currently offering a service like Hornady's, so if your cartridge isn't on the long list of dies it regularly produces, they can make custom ones for you. Some companies, such as Whidden Gun Works and CH4D, specialize in custom die work that can help the reloader looking for a means to reload rare cartridges.

The process of having custom dies made is a lengthy one, sometimes taking several months, and it can be pricey. Still, it's not supposed to be cost-effective or economical. The objective is to produce ammunition — irrespective of cost — and that can sometimes be priceless if you want to shoot a rare gun badly enough.

REDUCED RECOIL LOADS

I have a couple of friends who cannot handle high

You can use Accurate 5744 powder to develop reduced recoil loads.

recoil levels due to multiple shoulder injuries and resulting surgeries. Accordingly, they must use specialty gear if they wish to shoot without making a quick trip to the chiropractor. I've made many reduced velocity, reduced recoil loads for these and other people over the years. I've also loaded lower velocity practice rounds for those entering the world of big-bore rifles. And for people new to shooting a handgun who want ammunition that is comfortable to shoot before moving up to full-house loads.

Several methods exist for ramping down the recoil of a particular cartridge through handloading. Still, it comes with a warning: *An underloaded cartridge can generate a pressure spike that is just as dangerous as an overloaded cartridge, so don't go below the minimums listed in the reloading manuals.* I remember a Ruger No. 1 in .300 Winchester Magnum, which, when loaded with the minimum charge weight of IMR 4320 listed in a reloading manual from 1971, produced some of the most hellacious recoil ever experienced. While counterintuitive, increasing the powder charge and velocity brought the recoil back into the realms of sanity.

Depending on the shooter and their recoil tolerance, you may be able to use lighter bullets at a reduced velocity to alleviate the problem. I've got a buddy with shoulder issues who loves his Winchester Model

Trail Boss powder has a 'Cheerio'-like structure and is perfect for low-recoil loads used to train new shooters.

Reloder 15 and a Kynoch wad took substantial recoil out of the .470 Nitro Express.

70 Featherweight chambered in .30-06 Springfield. However, factory loads are too painful for him to shoot accurately. They caused a wicked flinch, which only extensive range work with a .22 Long Rifle could cure. So that he could hunt deer, we loaded 125-grain Nosler Ballistic Tip bullets — assuredly light for caliber — to a muzzle velocity of 2,650 fps using Accurate 5744 powder. Yes, he must pick his shots, and yes, that combination is more along the lines of the .300 Savage, but he shoots it accurately, and he's hunting with a favorite rifle rather than sitting home.

For radical reductions in recoil, there are a few tricks the reloader can use to help new shooters learn how to handle their rifle or handgun properly. Accurate 5744 powder is one such tool that will do just that, and I've used it in several loads for the big safari cartridges to help shooters acclimate to their rifles. Loaded with 5744, the .416 Rigby and .416 Remington Magnum will push the 400-grain bullets, which are typically launched at a muzzle velocity of 2,400 fps, as slowly as 1,600 fps. While energy drops off as well, this load is suitable for hunting deer and feral hogs inside of 100 yards, in addition to practicing all the aspects of marksmanship and the fundamentals of quickly loading the rifle without taking your eyes off the target.

Trail Boss is another powder to use for safely reducing

The mighty .505 Gibbs had the same recoil reduction as the .470 NE when using Reloder 15 and a foam wad to compress the load.

the muzzle velocity of a cartridge. Trail Boss can bring the muzzle velocity of those .416s with 350-grain bullets into the range of 950 fps to 1,140 fps. With a load like that, you could easily send 50 rounds downrange in a single session without pounding the hell out of your shoulder. The .300 magnums will hover between 1,400 and 1,700 fps with a Trail Boss load under a 150-grain bullet. Even the .243 Winchester — a cartridge potent enough for the largest deer — can be dropped down to 1,400 or 1,500 fps, and I can think of no better tool to

teach a new shooter or a youngster the fundamentals of marksmanship at the shooting bench. The quieter report and relative lack of recoil make shooting what is typically known as a speedy cartridge an absolute joy to shoot, and with the 100-grain bullets, you can use it to take deer, hogs, and coyotes at close ranges. If you need to reduce muzzle velocities, these powders will get the job done. There are useful data from multiple sources, and you'll be doing yourself a favor by trying them.

You can purchase match bullets such as the Sierra Tipped MatchKing in large lots to keep things consistent.

TAKE OUT THE STING

I learned a few good things about the genuine big-bore cartridges while loading ammunition for a Zimbabwean safari my buddy Mike McNulty and I did for Cape buffalo and plains game. Mike shoots a Heym Express in .505 Gibbs, which can generate hellacious recoil. I was loading for my .470 NE double rifle, which is no slouch.

These cartridges can use many different powders, from the medium-burning stuff such as IMR 4064, Varget, and Reloder 15, up through the faster-burning powders such as H4895 and Reloder 25. Mike could easily dial in his bolt gun to varying points of impact. However, my double rifle required a specific velocity for proper regulation — 2,150 fps, to be precise — and I needed to adhere to that speed. I was chatting with Chris Sells, the President of Heym USA, about loading for the double rifle, and he shared his insights. "Look to Reloder 15, and compress the load with a Kynoch No. 2 wad; the velocity will be there, and the recoil will

The lighter-colored area below the shoulder to the case mouth is clear evidence of an annealed case. Annealing softens the brass, prevents cracking, and increases case life.

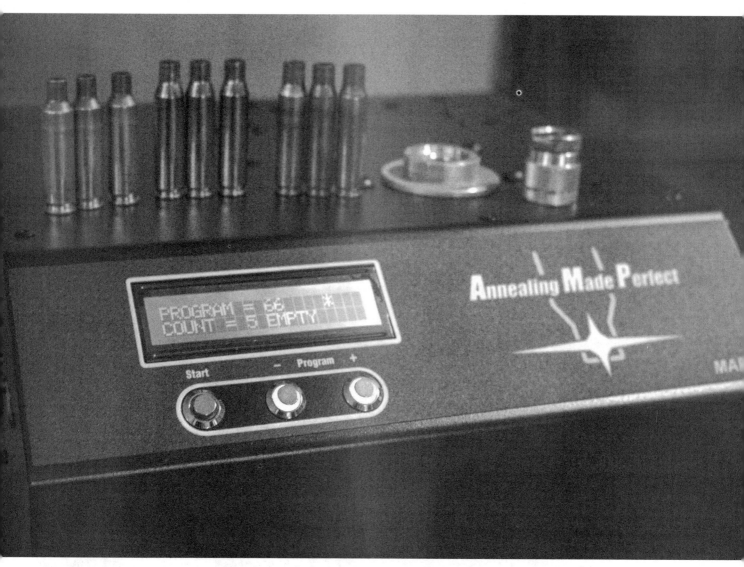

Annealing Made Perfect makes a unit — while expensive — that will increase the number of times you can reload your brass cases.

For both common and obscure cartridge cases, Roberson Cartridge Company is a great source. Shown here are their lathe-turned cases, L-R .300 PRC, .318 Westley Richards, .425 Westley Richards, .277 Fury, and .333 Jeffery.

With a good set of dies and some quality information, you can feed an obscure rifle for a lifetime; if you enjoy spending time with the oddballs, reloading is the way to go.

drop off by 15 percent or so." He had my attention, as the .470 Nitro isn't terrible to shoot (especially in my 12-pound Heym double), but if I could shave off any of that recoil and get back on target quicker for the follow-up shot, I'd take it.

Load data for Reloder 15 suggests between 87.0 and 90.0 grains for 26-inch barrels to hit that velocity. Compare that to about 115 grains of Reloder 25, and you can understand the need for that Kynoch foam wad to keep the powder charge compressed against the primer for consistent ignition and velocity. Sells was correct. The recoil dropped off considerably, and I found the best accuracy with a load of 88.0 grains of Reloder 15 at 2,165 fps. I took three buffalo on that safari.

I then had the idea that we could apply the same concept to Mike's big .505. He was immediately interested in the same recoil reduction once he tried my double. Long story short: it worked. The difference between Reloder 22 and Reloder 15 when using the 525-grain Barnes TSX bullets was remarkable.

The Kynoch wad provides consistent velocities, and there was no problem with the ammunition in any environment. Not only could you feel it immediately when shooting that big stick, but you could also see it when watching Mike shoot it off the bench. Here, the moral of the story is that there are means of reducing felt recoil in several different cartridges with some judicious experimentation. While I'm not particularly recoil sensitive, I do have my limits and will not subject myself to unnecessary punishment.

CHASING THE FACTORY

I had a buddy call me the other day, wondering if we could reverse-engineer a factory load that shot particularly well in his rifle. I explained that trying to identify powder by sight is a terrible idea. There are times when the factory might use a blend of powders (something reloaders should never attempt), and that there are so many powders that look alike that you could quickly create a dangerous situation. Instead,

I suggested an alternative approach, one much safer than playing "guess-that-powder."

When it came to this particular situation, we knew what the bullet was — both model and weight — so I recommended that he use his chronograph to measure the muzzle velocity of the factory load and use that as the goal to aim for to reproduce the harmonics of that particular barrel. You see, barrel harmonics, or how a barrel responds to the vibrations caused by the bullet traveling through it, is an integral part of the accuracy equation. When you find a velocity node that the barrel likes, you're in business.

Some barrels may seem to be somewhat 'finicky,' in that they may not like a particular load that other rifles of the same cartridge shoot well. Assuming there are no other mechanical or human malfunctions, it could very well be the harmonics in that particular barrel. Often, the art of handloading and load development is simply the hunt for the proper barrel harmonics.

Often this happens at a particular velocity. I've seen quite a few .300 Winchester Magnums that came to life with a 180-grain spitzer bullet at about 2,950 fps. It's a strange thing, and I've seen it in other cartridges and velocity combinations as well. The .22-250 Remington with 55-grain bullets at 3,700 fps, the .375 H&H with 300-grain bullets at 2,500 fps, the .338 Winchester Magnum with 250-grain bullets at 2,550 fps. If you find a factory load your rifle likes, try using your chronograph to replicate the velocity, and hopefully, the harmonics.

COMPONENT CONSISTENCY

Once you've found a recipe that works for your gun — be it a small-bore rifle, big-bore safari gun, revolver, or deer rifle — you want to maintain that consistency. Nothing can be more frustrating than assembling a new lot of ammunition, which you know has worked well for you for some time, only to look at the target and wonder just what the hell went wrong. I've often sat there wondering if it was me having a

bad day shooting or if my gun had been knocked or damaged in some way.

The truth is that the components may not be as consistent from lot to lot as we'd like to believe. And when you're loading for accuracy, small variations can rear their ugly head on the target board. Buying in bulk is one way to avoid the lot-to-lot variations. It's convenient to purchase powder in 1-pound canisters, replacing it when you're out, but to keep things as consistent as possible, try an 8-pound canister or a case of ten 1-pound canisters with the same lot number. The same for primers: order them by the box of 1,000 for consistency's sake.

Projectiles can be a problem in that not all the makes and models are available in bulk. Some of the match bullets — Sierra's MatchKing (both standard and Tipped), and Hornady's ELD Match and A-TIP Match come quickly to mind — come in lots of 500, but the hunting bullets rarely do. Try to purchase bullets of a standard lot number to minimize variations. I recommend purchasing brass cases in bulk lots.

Consistency in the handgun cartridge components is important, but because the pressures and velocities are lower than rifle rounds, the slight variations won't have as dramatic an effect. Even so, you should still keep your components as uniform as possible.

ANNEALING BRASS CASES

Annealed cases last longer, as the process keeps the brass softer and malleable, avoiding splits and cracks. If you've ever noticed your brass cases have a rainbow tinge to them, especially on the case neck and mouth, someone has annealed them. In annealing, you heat the cases to a specific temperature to soften the brass (unlike steel, which you harden by heating). You can anneal your cases in a few different ways, from a blow torch to high-tech machines such as the Annealeeze or the Annealing Made Perfect unit. These machines are not inexpensive, but they are effective. Annealing preserves the hard work you invested during case preparation, especially if you have any custom dimensions for your cases, such as neck-sized brass or a specific shoulder dimension suited for your rifle. It's also an excellent means of getting the most out of those hard-to-find cases, or for wildcat brass you've meticulously prepared.

I've spent some time with the Annealing Made Perfect machine, and though it's costly, you could split that cost with a few reloading buddies, and all of you could extend brass life. Such efficiency is vital in these trying times when component brass isn't available. Keep the case neck and mouth soft, and you will see a marked difference in case life. |||

15

CASTING LEAD BULLETS

Bullet casting has been a part of shooting nearly as long as men have ignited gun powder. The earliest firearm projectiles were pure lead round balls, which our forebears shot from smoothbore muskets. As technology advanced and the modern metallic cartridge came onto the scene and took root, the ability to reload those cartridges was paramount — especially on the frontier, where supplies of loaded ammunition were scarce, if they existed at all. Winchester often included reloading tools and a bullet mold with its rifles, so the shooter equipped with a supply of primers and powder had the capability of pouring their bullets.

BULLET MOLDS

A bullet mold consists of two cast-iron, steel, or aluminum blocks, each of which contains an impression of one-half of the bullet and comes together to form a

Casting bullets has been a part of shooting since the advent of firearms.

cavity the exact shape of the bullet or ball. The mold blocks are usually held in a set of wooden handles, operating much like pliers. The concept of cast bullets isn't very complicated. For the most basic bullets, one pours molten lead through the sprue (the hole in the mold, where you pour the lead) into the mold's cavity and allows it to cool. The sprue cutter shaves off the excess lead from the bullet or ball, flowing up the sprue hole. Of course, there's more to it, but that is the basic concept.

My first experiences with bullet casting involved pouring round balls for muzzleloading rifles and cap-and-ball pistols with my Dad. We'd melt lead fishing sinkers in an old cast-iron pan over a fire and have at it. We had a single-cavity mold at first, but we decided a four-cavity mold would serve us much better as we began sending more of those little round wonders downrange. Keeping the balls' sprue toward the center of the bore (to avoid throwing lead knuckleballs), that replica 1851 Colt Navy revolver gave hours of fun. We then graduated to pouring bullets (as opposed to round balls) for the .54-caliber muzzleloaders we used for deer hunting, and I must admit I was surprised at how accurate a patched bullet could be at 75 yards. Terminally speaking, the 300-grain bullets handled whitetail deer just fine.

For generations, casting lead handgun bullets was an economical means of feeding those guns and was a hobby unto itself. This book may not be the proper place to debate the merits of using lead ammunition, but some hazards are involved with lead, especially with molten lead. The vapors produced from melting lead can be harmful to you — extremely toxic in high doses — so cast your bullets in a well-ventilated area,

RCBS mold blocks and handles. This model is a two-cavity mold.

Lyman's Orange Magic bullet lube is readily available from most shooting supply houses.

preferably outside. Though that old cast-iron pan we repurposed for our casting duties worked, there are much better means of safely melting lead. I ended up with an electronic melting pot, which uses an element to melt lead. Lead melts at 621.5 degrees Fahrenheit, so it doesn't take a crazy amount of heat to get there. Like a hot water heater, the electric element provides a sufficient temperature to melt lead quickly without overheating things.

Pure lead bullets are the simplest to cast, as you're just melting the ingot and pouring from there, though you should use some material to flux the lead, meaning you skim the impurities off the top. However, pure lead bullets can make a mess of the bore of your barrel. "Leading" is the condition where the barrel's bore becomes overly fouled with lead deposits because of the bullet traveling through it. Leading can drastically affect the accuracy and can be a real chore to clean up. For the muzzleloading pistols and rifles where a fabric patch is employed or the few folks who still paper-patch their bullets, this is no big deal, as the bullet has a buffer between it and the barrel.

BULLET LUBE

Lubricating a lead bullet helps reduce the amount of lead fouling in your barrel, and cast bullets will feature a groove or series of grooves to hold the lubricant. You can buy pre-made lubricants, such as Lyman's Orange

Magic, Alox or Super Moly, RCBS bullet lubricant, or Saeco Green Bullet Lube, or make your own. Many recipes are available, such as the classic NRA lube formula of beeswax and Alox2138F grease in a 1:1 ratio or some variation of a tallow/paraffin/beeswax mixture. There are plenty of books, websites, and forums that delve deeply into the experimentation of different formulae, which can be made at home and will save you money.

LEAD ALLOYS

You can also vary your bullets' composition by adding specific amounts of tin and antimony to the mix. A 'hardcast' lead bullet will not foul a bore as quickly as a softer full lead one, and you'll enhance its terminal performance. A hardcast lead bullet in a classic lever-action cartridge is suitable for nearly any game animal. Wheel weights — at least the older style that crimped onto wheel rims — are generally comprised of 95 percent lead, 3 percent tin, and a bit of antimony. These offer a hardness well-suited to general shooting with a Brinell Hardness of 12.

This formula allows the bullet base to upset just enough to seal the hot, expanding gases behind it, yet it will not make a mess of your bore. Linotype, the metal used in the old linotype machines used for printing newspapers until the 1980s, makes excellent bullet material and offers a harder alloy than wheel

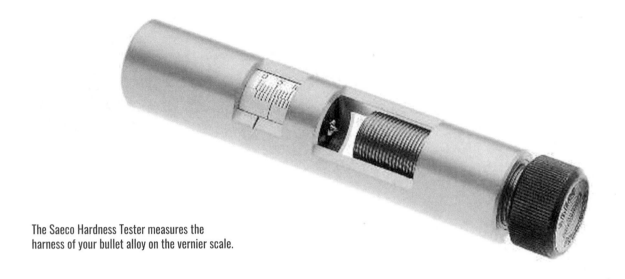

The Saeco Hardness Tester measures the harness of your bullet alloy on the vernier scale.

Hornady sells its gas checks in boxes of 1,000.

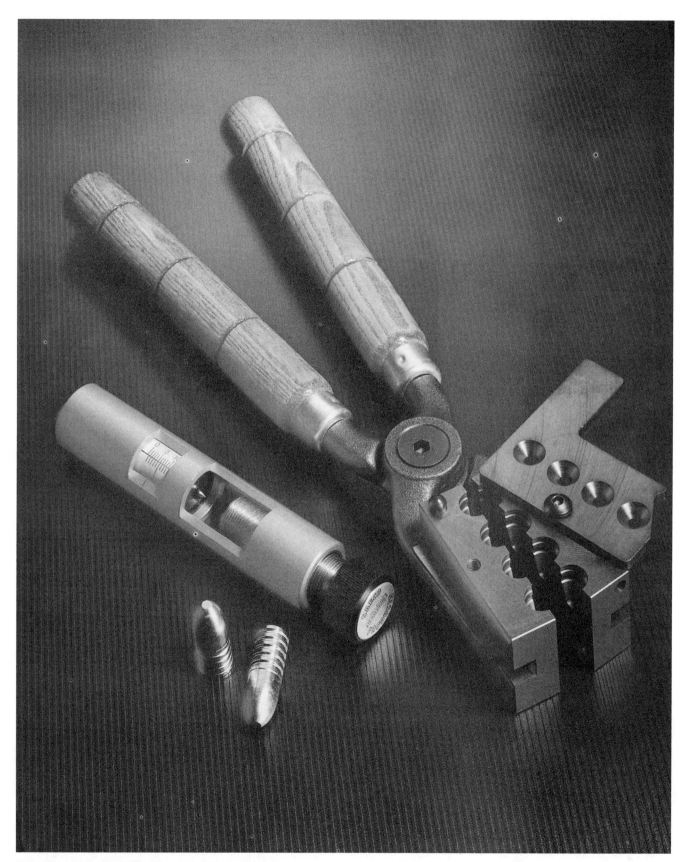

Saeco bullet molds and handles are among the best available.

weights, better suited to hunting applications. You can purchase alloys of varying composition in ingot form from most reputable reloading supply companies, from which you can cast consistent bullets. Bullets made of a lead/tin/antimony alloy will take some time to reach maximum hardness, sometimes taking as long as a month to cure completely. Saeco makes a lead hardness tester you can use to measure the hardness of your cast bullets.

GAS CHECKS

Gas checks are small copper cups that are crimped onto the base of cast bullets to seal the gasses behind the bullet and protect the base's shape when you touch off the charge. They are diameter specific. Cast bullets designed for gas checks feature a recess at the bullet base where you crimp the gas check during the bullet sizing process. They aren't expensive — running about $0.05/piece — and are readily available from Hornady and Lyman, sold in boxes of 1,000.

Lyman's Mag 25 Digital Furnace is a sound investment for the shooter who is serious about casting lead.

The RCBS Lube-A-Matic 2 is an efficient means of lubricating cast bullets.

Not all bullet molds are created equal. A mold with blocks that don't mate perfectly can cause issues with your bullets, such as projectiles being out of round. Small burrs can keep a set of blocks from closing completely, and under rigorous inspection, you will see light between the two halves if they don't close completely. Polish those burrs carefully away to let the two halves sit perfectly together. Alignment pins with excessive movement can also be a culprit, as can an over-tightened sprue cutter. Sometimes even flecks of molten lead can adhere to the mold walls, preventing a tight seal.

There can be too much of a good thing in casting bullets when it comes to heat. If you're using an electric pot with an adjustable temperature dial, somewhere between 700 and 750 degrees should be the sweet spot where you'll get the best castings. The mold blocks will need a chance to warm up to give the best results. Quite often, the first dozen bullets will be tossed back into the lead pot to be re-melted. You'll use these for bringing your molds up to temperature. You can also preheat your molds by placing them on top of the electric pot while waiting for the lead to melt.

Should you raise your alloy's temperature too high while melting it, you run the risk of the tin oxidizing. This oxidization is another reason I recommend electronic lead furnaces. Lyman's Mag 25 is a digital melting unit with the bottom pour spigot capable of holding up to 25 pounds of lead, which will create a much more consistent temperature for longer. Plus, the bottom spout feature keeps the impurities that float on the top out of the bullet mold.

THE PROPER POUR

When you pour the lead into the sprue hole, give your bullet a chance to cool. You want to pour enough lead to fill the entire cavity, with a slight excess on top of the mold, to ensure that there are no air voids in your bullet. When the lead on the top of the mold appears to have hardened entirely, use the sprue cutter to shave the bullet's base (on base-pour molds) or on the nose of the bullet (with a nose-pour mold). Give the sprue cutter a good whack with a piece of wood (never strike your blocks with anything metal). You can use a wooden dowel or an old wooden hammer handle, and some like to wrap it with rawhide or leather to protect their blocks further. With the lead properly melted and your mold blocks raised to a uniform temperature, your bullet should have an even shine to lightly-frosted appearance, with square grooves that have sharp edges. If the bullet appears heavily frosted, the mold block was too hot; allow more time between pours. An old towel can serve as a landing pad for the freshly made projectiles. Once cooled, knock the bullets out of the mold onto the towel so you don't mar or ding them.

BULLET SIZING AND LUBRICATION

In addition to lubrication, you'll want to size your cast bullets to a uniform dimension, and you can tailor the diameter of your bullets to optimize performance. The sizing process may first require 'slugging' the bore of your firearm to observe and obtain the actual bore dimensions. Slugging involves ramming a soft lead bullet or fishing sinker through your bore and then measuring its outside diameter with a micrometer. The popular .45-caliber pistol cartridges use a jacketed bullet diameter of 0.452 inch (some specify 0.4515 inch). Yet, an old worn .45 Colt may show a preference for bullets

Saeco's Lubrisizer will quickly and efficiently lubricate your bullets.

Lee's Alox liquid lubricant is quick and easy.

as large as 0.454 inch. It's easy to cast your bullets and use a sizing die to produce bullets of a diameter that will work best in your rifle or pistol.

There are numerous sources for sizing dies to even out your cast bullets. Lyman, Lee, and RCBS are among the most popular. In essence, the sizing die swages the bullet to the desired diameter. A top punch of the proper ogive, which pushes down on the bullet's nose, is a necessary item to avoid deforming the meplat. Lee offers a bullet-sizing die that works with any standard reloading press (based on the 7/8-14 die body).

You can lubricate and size in one step with a 'lubrisizer' such as the Lyman 4500 Lube Sizer, RCBS Lube-A-Matic-2, and Saeco Lubrisizer. These look like miniature reloading presses and not only size the bullet to the proper diameter but apply the lube as well. The lube is sold in sticks, a hollow cylinder that you load into the lube magazine and hydraulically apply to the

Semi-wadcutter bullets for the .38 Special, those on the left have gas checks affixed.

bullet during the sizing process.

There are other techniques for lubricating bullets, such as the pan method and the tumbling method, which are simple to use. The tumble method uses a liquid lubricant — Lee's Alox is a popular choice — to coat the bullets. Like those made by Tupperware, a small plastic container, or an empty margarine tub, can be used to apply the lube. Put your bullets in the container, squirt a small amount of the liquid lube, and tumble the bullets around until the lubricant is evenly applied.

The pan method is slightly more complicated, though you can easily do it on your kitchen stove. You'll need three pans: fill one with water, another to melt the lubricant, and the third to hold the bullets. What you're making is a double boiler — you don't want to melt your lubricant directly over a flame as you can scorch it, so you'll instead put the pan with the lubricant inside

These cast semi-wadcutters are an excellent choice for the mild-recoiling .38 Special.

For the shooter who wants to create a large volume of ammunition, cast lead bullets are an affordable and attractive projectile choice.

the pan with the boiling water. This method gives a nice, even melt with no risk of damaging the lube. In the third pan, you want to stand your bullets nose up, leaving at least 3/4 inch of space between them. Once you've melted the lubricant, carefully pour it around the bullets until all the grooves are covered. Once the lubricant has cooled, remove the bullets from the hardened lubricant. Here's a cool trick I learned from Larry Potterfield of Midway USA: once you've removed the first run of bullets from the hardened lube, you can put the next set of bullets into the holes where the first batch was and place the whole pan with bullets and lubricant back in the double boiler. The lubricant will melt again – and you can add more lube if necessary to bring it back to the proper level. Repeat the process until all your bullets are lubricated.

A LABOR OF LOVE

Casting bullets is an economical way to shoot more often, provided you're willing to provide the labor.

In this crazy, hectic world — where time is money — you'll have to look at cast bullets as a hobby and a dedicated pastime. Back when Elmer Keith was developing his famous No. 429421 255-grain semi-wadcutter for the .44 Magnum, casting bullets was as much a necessity as it was economical. In today's environment of overnight shipping and next-day orders, you can have anything you want in a timeframe that would have been inconceivable just 50 years ago.

Casting gives you the freedom to produce ammunition when factory ammo or component bullets are simply unavailable. And while a cast bullet isn't as complicated as our premium jacketed designs, a cast bullet is undoubtedly better than no bullet. However, they are labor-intensive, but then again, so is reloading, and if you want a means of spending time doing something shooting related, casting bullets can be rewarding. It's a fun way of spending time with buddies and a fantastic way to get a kid involved in reloading. |||

16

PROGRESSIVE PRESSES

Thus far, we've concentrated on single-stage loading for metallic cartridges. However, single-stage presses can be tedious and time-consuming, and as each phase of the operation requires undivided attention, it can take time to accumulate a pile of ammo. To significantly increase your ammunition production, a progressive press is one way to crank out the cartridges. But it comes at a price. I look at it this way: when you're loading single-stage, you are the musician, playing all the notes on the instrument and concentrating on your particular piece of music; on a progressive press, you are the conductor of the orchestra, keeping all the moving parts well-organized.

HOW PROGRESSIVE PRESSES WORK

While a single-stage press performs just one operation at a time, every crank of the progressive press handle — both up and down — completes multiple processes, and you must use a very uniform stroke to ensure consistency in each simultaneous operation. The progressive uses a

The nucleus of the progressive press, the rotating shellplate.

rotating shellplate instead of a shellholder, with several cartridge slots matching the press stations. As you work the handle, the shellplate rotates so that the brass case passes through each operation phase. The first station resizes the case and drives the spent primer out on the upstroke while pressing in a new primer on the downstroke. The case mouth pushes on the powder dispenser on the next upstroke, charging the case with powder. Once charged, the powder check die indicates the proper charge in the case. The next station flares the case. Next, the upstroke seats the bullet. You may have enough stations to add crimp in a separate procedure. If not, the press will eject the completed cartridge on the downstroke.

You'll store primers in a tube or plastic strip, depending on the model of press, and there may be the option of automatic case feeders and automatic bullet feeders. You can also opt to feed the cases and bullets by hand. By the time you have every station set up, you'll be loading a case and a bullet on each pull of

An RCBS shellplate, with five stations machined into the rim.

The RCBS Pro2000 progressive press. Note the APS priming strip in the lower right corner.

the handle. When all the stations are full, each time you work the handle, one of these processes will be happening; and this is why I use the 'conductor' analogy. The uniform up and down stroke ensures the primers are seated to a uniform depth, the bullet is seated, the powder dispenser dumps a charge, and the cartridge receives a crimp. The process can be remarkably consistent, but it will take some patience to get things rolling correctly.

Study your progressive press closely. Become familiar with the setup, design, and working mechanics. Unlike the simple, efficient design of the single-stage press, which you can screw to the bench and pretty much forget about, the progressive will require cleaning and lubrication. Powder granules, spent primer anvils, brass, and copper shavings can fall into the indexing mechanism and gum up the works. You'll need to be fully able to disassemble, clean, and reassemble the unit periodically.

SAFE OPERATING PRACTICES

Always consider safety. First, you've got a tube or strip full of live primers, sitting right next to a dispenser filled with gun powder. Should one of those primers accidentally detonate — which is a rarity but can happen — you run the risk of setting the entire tube or strip off, or even worse, you can ignite the powder dispenser. So, keep an eye on the way the primers are feeding. If anything feels strange on that downstroke, stop immediately, and rectify the problem. Second, should you run out of primers in the tube or strip, you run the risk of charging a case with a hole in it and possibly having powder leak into the workings of your press, which is not a good thing. Count the number of cartridges made to ensure you've got some primers left in the tube, and top the tube off when needed. Third, watch your powder dispenser to make sure you don't run out. The larger pistol and rifle cases use a substantial amount of powder, and as you get cranking, the powder

The Hornady Lock-N-Load ammo plant, shown here in its simplest form.

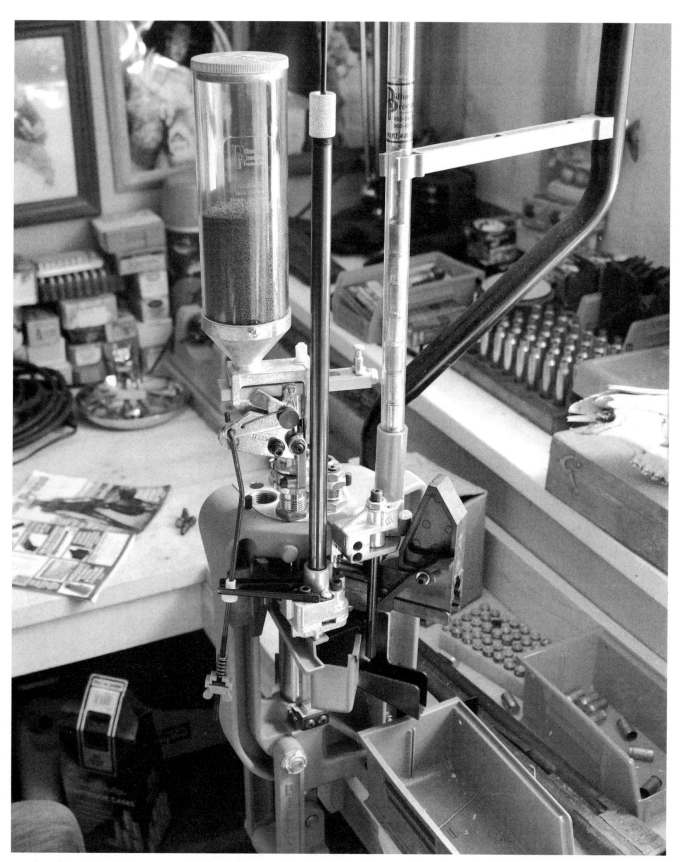

The Dillon XL650 is the author's favorite progressive press.

can run low faster than you'd think. If you don't run a powder check die or a powder lockout die, you can create a squib load, which may lead to a bullet wedging itself in your barrel on one shot, which becomes an obstruction for the subsequent shot. That's not good.

It may seem like a lot is going on, and it should. While I want to enlighten you about the possible dangers, I don't want to scare you away from progressive presses.

If you thoroughly understand each of the processes and can walk and chew gum at the same time, you should be able to run a progressive safely. Take the time to learn the press's feel and deal with a repetitive, monotonous operation patiently. It will also require constant self-evaluation during the reloading process: If you suspect something is wrong, immediately disassemble loaded cartridges from that session to avoid any tragedies.

Dillon offers a dual-sided bullet seater for various bullet profiles, easily changed with the pull of a cotter pin.

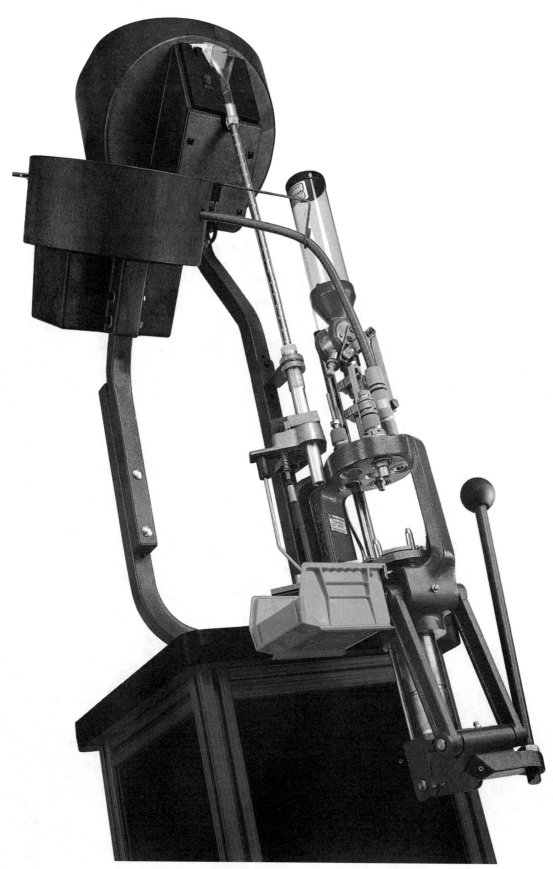

The Hornady Lock-N-Load Ammo Plant in full regalia, with case and bullet feeders.

The RCBS Pro2000. Note the removable die plate, simplifying cartridge swaps.

Unlike single-stage reloading, if a primer were to be installed incorrectly (sometimes they can flip in some inexplicable manner), you probably wouldn't see it until the assembled cartridge is kicked loose from the shellplate.

While a single primer won't cause you to cease operations and recall a session's worth of ammo, a powder measure out of adjustment is another story. I use a handful of spent cartridges to check the powder weights before starting the reloading process. Check charges on a trusted balance beam scale to ensure that nothing has come out of adjustment. Remember, the powder dispenser used in the progressive press is a mechanical device, using springs for consistent tension. As any tool can, it will wear, move, and need occasional adjustment. Checking the dispenser and adjusting it when necessary — especially when switching cartridges or bullets — is something you should become proficient at if you want to run a progressive press0

RIFLE CARTRIDGE LOADING

Most folks assume the progressive presses are for the pistol cartridges only. While progressive-loaded pistol rounds are assuredly most popular among high-volume handgunners, many people rely on their progressive press for handloading large quantities of .223 Remington/5.56mm NATO, .308 Winchester, and other popular rifle cartridges. The rifle cases require more force on a progressive press, mostly to keep things uniform, and their larger volume will eat up much more powder per case, so you'll be refilling the hopper more often than you will with the pistol cases. I don't think the rifle ammunition created on a progressive press is as precise or consistent as the stuff made on a single-stage, but ultra-precision isn't the goal here. Quite often, folks are perfectly content to create 'plinking' ammo for use in AR-15s and military-style replicas, and the progressive press is perfect for this application.

BRANDS AND MODELS

Shopping for a progressive press is much like shopping for a vehicle: you can go with a simple, no-frills model, or you can splurge on a luxury model, will all the bells and whistles. And much like a vehicle, either choice will get you down the road; it merely depends on what level of style and comfort you can afford. Most of the companies that manufacture reloading gear offer a progressive press. Hornady, Lee, Lyman, RCBS, and Dillon all offer sound designs. The only exception is Redding.

I've spent most of my time behind four different progressive presses: An RCBS Pro2000 Auto Index, an RCBS Pro-Chucker 7, a Hornady Lock-N-Load Ammo Plant, and a Dillon XL650. All have different

The RCBS Pro-Chucker 7, a well-designed progressive press capable of cranking out a healthy amount of ammunition.

strengths and weaknesses, and each has a different feel, but Dillon specializes in progressive presses, and you can tell when you operate one. To me, the Dillon represents the best value in a progressive press. It's a smart, ergonomic design that produces a consistent result. Dillon dies are designed to match its progressive presses and have many features that enhance performance. The Dillon dies' internal mechanisms are easily removed with a simple cotter key — allowing you to clean them often. This feature is convenient when loading a considerable number of lead bullets. (Also, you can quickly flip over the two-sided bullet seaters if you're changing bullet profiles.)

I like the Dillon powder dispenser (using all-steel linkage) and the quick-change tool head, making changing calibers a simple matter of pulling two pins and swapping the tool head and the shellplate if necessary. The Dillon machines are stoutly built and offer useful upgrades that are a great value: the automatic case feeder is a worthy purchase, and I like the roller handle, too, especially for long loading sessions. Dillon also offers a "No B.S." lifetime warranty, which indicates how well they stand behind their product.

Hornady's Lock-N-Load Ammo Plant is a tall machine that can take up a considerable amount of room but quickly makes quality ammunition. The automated case feeder and bullet feeder speed the process up, though the plastic hoppers can be noisy. I found the Hornady machine's setup was a tad tricky, but it was a pleasure to use once assembled. The press has a huge, 2-inch ram with zerk fittings to keep parts well-lubricated and also features the Hornady Lock-N-Load die bushings, making the chore of switching out reloading dies a pleasure. These bushings allow you to remove the die body with just a quarter turn and return it to the place you set it. Hornady's shellplates and metal parts are beefy (you could say over-designed), and if you

properly assembly the Ammo Plant, it will give a lifetime of good service.

The RCBS machines I've used have been, for the most part, good choices. The older Pro2000 Auto Index was a reliable progressive press, but instead of a primer tube, it used the plastic APS primer strips. They look like a plastic strip with teeth on the sides and advance the primer strip through the press. While this system correctly positions the primer most of the time, it went terribly wrong when it went wrong, often putting the primer in an offset position. This hiccup would result in a bent primer cup and shave off a crescent moon-shaped plastic piece. You would then need to clean that mess, clear the case of the bent primer and plastic, and you'd have to reset the strip, and get it moving at the proper increments. Long story short: the Pro2000 is a good machine if you convert the APS priming setup to the tube-fed system.

I had much better results with the RCBS Pro-Chucker 7, as it has the tube-fed primer system, and the seven-station head allows for much more flexibility for those who like the powder lockout die, separate crimping die, or bullet feeder. Equipped with zerk fittings for proper lubrication, the Pro-Chucker 7 is simple to set up and just as easy to use. The die plate is quickly changed when switching cartridges, and I recommend using multiple die plates if you intend to load more than one cartridge. The powder measure has a quick drain feature to efficiently empty one powder to allow you to replace it with another.

Each of these machines advertises a specific round-per-hour capability, and that may influence your choice. Be honest with yourself about the amount of ammo you need to generate, as the larger machines, with their automated feeders and hoppers, can take up a lot of room on your bench. I don't burn through a ton of ammunition, as I'm much more of a hunter than a shooter, so a progressive with fewer accouterments suits me just fine. If you shoot IDPA or similar competition or train hard with your AR-style rifle, the ability to quickly produce large quantities of ammunition might be your thing. If so, take full advantage of the bullet feeders, case feeders, and any other gadget that will enhance your production.

ARE PROGRESSIVES FOR YOU?

The progressive presses are a boon to those who can run them confidently, knowing when to stop the process and recalibrate things, so all the ammunition is safe. I do not feel they are an appropriate choice for novice reloaders or even for those intermediate handloaders who feel more comfortable taking their time with a single-stage. However, for the experienced reloader who can tell either by feel or visual inspection that something is wrong, the progressive press can be a definite asset, creating the large quantity of ammunition they need.

Only you can determine what level of control you want and how that will offset the amount of ammunition you want to create. I enjoy the monotony of single-stage loading, and for the volumes of ammo I require, a quality turret press like the Redding T7 serves my purposes well. I prefer the control of seeing each stage's results to be certain that everything is in order. I don't shoot competitively, and most of my focus is on hunting rifles, so I'm not what you'd call a high-volume shooter. I have several close friends who shoot pistol and rifle competitions and are self-defense instructors, so they need a considerable amount of ammo. Their use of progressive presses makes all the sense in the world. ▌▌▌

For those who wish to load different cartridges on the same progressive, RCBS offers additional die plates for its Pro2000 press. You leave the dies set up in the plates and switch the entire plate.

The Dillon 650 progressive press ready for action. Dillon makes what the author considers to be the best progressive on the market.

APPENDIX: RELOADING RESOURCES

Hodgdon Powder
www.hodgdon.com
913-362-9455

IMR Powder
www.imrpowder.com
913-362-9455

Winchester Powder
www.wwpowder.com
913-362-9455

Alliant Powder
www.alliantpowder.com
800-256-8685

Ramshot Powder
www.ramshot.com
406-234-0422

Accurate Powder
www.accuratepowder.com
406-234-0422

Vihtavuori Powder
www.Vihtavuori-lapua.com
800-683-0464

American Pioneer Powder
www.americanpioneerpowder.com
888-756-7693

Precision Ballistics
www.precisionballisticsllc.com
702-331-1337

MTM Molded Products
www.mtmcase.gard.com
937-890-7461

CCI Primers
www.cci-ammunition.com
800-256-8685

Rainier Ballistics
www.rainierballistics.com
800-638-8722

Cutting Edge Bullets
www.sitecuttingedgebullets.com
814-345-6690

Berger Bullets
www.bergerbullets.com
714-441-7200

Lee Precision
www.leeprecision.com
262-673-3075

Hornady
www.hornady.com
800-338-3220

Lyman Products
www.lymanproducts.com
800-22LYMAN

RCBS
www.rcbs.com
800-533-5000

Redding Reloading
www.redding-reloading.com
607-753-3331

Whidden Gun Works
www.whiddengunworks.net
229-686-1911

Forster Products
www.forsterproducts.com
815-493-6360

Dillon Precision Products
www.dillonprecision.com
800-762-3845

Swift Bullet Company
www.swiftbullets.com
785-754-3959

Barnes Bullets
www.barnesbullets.com
435-856-1000

Sierra Bullets
www.sierrabullets.com
888-223-3006

North Fork Technologies
www.northforkbullets.com
541-929-4424

Nosler Bullets
www.nosler.com
800-285-3701

Speer Bullets
www.speer-bullets.com
800-256-8685

Remington Reloading Components
www.remington.com
800-243-9700

Downrange Manufacturing
www.downrangemfg.com
402-463-3415

Winchester
www.winchester.com

Woodleigh Bullets
www.woodleighbullets.com.au
+61 3 5457 2226

Federal Premium
www.federalpremium.com
800-379-1732

Norma USA
www.norma-usa.com

Lapua
www.lapua.com
800-683-0464

Lazzeroni Arms
www.lazzeroni.com
888-492-7247

TulAmmo
www.tulammousa.com
888-317-5810

MagTech Ammunition
www.magtechammunition.com
800-466-7191

Fiocchi
www.fiocchiusa.com

Bullseye Camera Systems, LLC
www.bullseyecamera.com
541-357-7035

Lawrence Brand Lead Shot
www.lawrencebrandshot.com
866-618-7468

MEC (Mayville Engineering Company, Inc.)
www.mecshootingsports.com
800-797-4632

Quality Cartridge
www.qual-cart.com
301-373-3719

Jamison International
www.custombrassandbullets.com
928-387-2222

Buffalo Arms
www.buffaloarms.com
208-263-6953

Starline
www.starlinebrass.com
800-280-6660

Falcon Bullets
www.falconbullets.com
931-339-7010

Berry's Manufacturing
www.berrysmfg.com
800-269-7373

Oregon Trail Bullet Company
www.oregontrailbullet.com
800-811-0548

Hawk Precision Bullets
www.hawkbullets.com
856-299-2800

Sinclair International
www.sinclairintl.com
800-741-0015

GLOSSARY:

Ballistic Coefficient (BC): The measure of a bullet's ability to resist the effect of air drag. The number is derived from a complex mathematical formula involving standard deviation (SD). It is a direct comparison of shape to a standard bullet model and is also represented by a three-digit decimal. The higher the BC, the better the bullet can "slip" through the air. BC is a debatable figure and is dependent upon velocity. High BC bullets will resist wind drift better and have a flatter trajectory than low BC bullets.

Brass: a common term for cartridge cases. When someone says, "I picked up some brass for my .45ACP," it means they have acquired cases for the firearm.

C.O.L.: Short for Cartridge Overall Length. It is a standardized measurement of a loaded cartridge's long axis, represented by inches and decimal portions of an inch. There are maximum dimensions allowed by SAAMI, and for the handloader, it is crucial to adhere to these dimensions.

Decapping: The act of removing a primer. Standard primers are a derivation of percussion caps, and the term has carried over.

Feet per second: Abbreviated fps, or FPS, it is a measure of a bullet's velocity. Just like your vehicle's speed in miles per hour, bullet velocities are defined by how many feet the bullet travels per second.

Flash hole: The centrally drilled hole in the case web allows the primer's spark to reach the powder charge.

Grains: A unit of weight used to measure both powder and bullets. There are 7,000 grains in one pound.

Headspace: The distance between the bolt's face, breech or cylinder, and the part of the chamber that stops the forward motion of the cartridge case. For rimmed cartridges such as the .30-30 WCF or .38 Special, the rim serves to headspace the cartridge. In a rimless cartridge, two methods are usually employed: most headspace off the shoulder, such as the .308 Winchester or .223 Remington; and a few headspace off the case mouth, such as the .45 ACP or .450 Bushmaster. In the belted magnum case, the original design used the belt for headspacing. This belted design still holds in the .375 Holland & Holland Magnum and the .300 Holland & Holland Magnum. They have a minimal, sloping shoulder, which is not pronounced enough to use for accurate headspacing. The more modern belted magnums, while still retaining the belt of the H&H cases, can be adjusted to headspace on the shoulder of the case. The .300 Winchester Magnum, 7mm Remington Magnum, and .338 Winchester Magnum are examples of this situation. Headspacing is very important to a firearm. If it is too short, the cartridges will not fit properly. If it is too long, dangerous gases can escape upon firing. There are several useful headspace gauges available, and if there is any question, you should invest in one for your firearm.

Heavy-for-caliber: A term used to describe the longer bullets for a given diameter. The bullet diameter must remain constant in any caliber, so it must be lengthened for a bullet to have more weight.

Meplat: The technical term for the flat or open tip on the nose of a bullet. The shape of the meplat is vital in determining how the bullet moves through the air. The size and shape of the meplat have a significant effect on the ballistic coefficient of a bullet.

MOA: Minute of angle. We define an arc as 1/60th of a degree. Used in shooting terms to represent a group of shots with an extreme spread no greater than the sine of one minute of angle at the particular distance to the target. At 100 yards (a common shooting distance) 1 MOA = 1.04 inches.

Ogive: The curved nose section of a bullet. Some ogives are hemispherical, some based on secant, others on tangent curves. Almost all bullets have some sort of an ogive, save the wadcutters and semi-wadcutters.

Over-bore: ie. Over-bore cartridge. A cartridge that has a large case capacity relative to bullet diameter. We assume that "over-bore cartridges" waste much of the powder, except in the longest of barrels, where the law of diminishing returns does not create more velocity, only additional muzzle blast, and recoil.

SAAMI: The Sporting Arms and Ammunition Manufacturers' Institute, Inc. Since 1926, the national association in the U.S. for firearms and ammunition makers, responsible for setting safety and dimensional standards for cartridges and firearms.

Sectional density (SD): the ratio of a bullet's mass to its cross-sectional area (caliber). Represented by a three-digit decimal, the higher the SD, the heavier the bullet. The number is derived by dividing the bullet weight (in pounds) by the bullet diameter squared. For example, a .375-inch diameter 300-grain bullet will have an SD of 0.304. The calculation: 300 grains/7,000 (the number of grains in a pound) = 0.042857. Square the bullet diameter (0.375 x 0.375) to get 0.140625. Divide the first number (0.042857) by the second (0.140625) to arrive at a Sectional Density of 0.304.

Softpoint: A jacketed bullet with an area of exposed lead at the nose.

Solid: A bullet designed for the largest game animals, designed originally as a copper-clad steel jacketed bullet with a lead core and no exposed lead at the nose. Today they are often constructed as a homogenous metal alloy.

Burn rates of common powders, from fastest to slowest (as provided by the Hodgdon Powder Company)

RELATIVE BURN RATES FROM FASTEST TO SLOWEST

1	Norma R1	51	Accurate Arms No. 7	101	HodgdonVARGET
2	Winchester WAALite	52	Alliant Pro Reach	102	IMR Co IMR 4320
3	Vihtavuori N310	53	Hodgdon LONGSHOT	103	Winchester 748
4	Accurate Arms Nitro 100	54	Alliant 410	104	Hodgdon BL-C(2)
5	Alliant e3	55	Alliant 2400	105	Hodgdon CFE 223
6	Hodgdon TITEWAD	56	Ramshot Enforcer	106	Hodgdon LEVEREVOLUTION
7	Ramshot Competition	57	Accurate Arms No.9	107	Hodgdon H380
8	Alliant Red Dot	58	Accurate Arms 4100	108	IMR Co IMR 4007 SSC
9	Alliant Promo	59	Alliant Steel	109	Ramshot Big Game
10	Hodgdon CLAYS	60	Norma 8123	110	Vihtavuori N540
11	Alliant Clay Dot	61	Vihtavuori N110	111	Winchester 760
12	Hodgdon Hi-Skor 700-X	62	Hodgdon LL GUN	112	Hodgdon H414
13	Alliant Bullseye	63	Hodgdon 110	113	Vihtavuori N150
14	Hodgdon TITEGROUP	64	Winchester 296	114	Accurate Arms 2700
15	Alliant American Select	65	IMR Co IMR 4227	115	IMR Co IMR 4350

16	Accurate Arms Solo 1000	66	Hodgdon H4227	116	IMR Co IMR 4451
17	Alliant Green Dot	67	IMR Co SR 4759	117	Hodgdon H4350
18	Winchester WST	68	Accurate Arms 5744	118	Alliant Reloder 17
19	Hodgdon Trail Boss	69	Accurate Arms 1680	119	Accurate Arms 4350
20	Winchester Super Handicap	70	Norma 200	120	Norma 204
21	Hodgdon INTERNATIONAL	71	Alliant Reloder 7	121	Hodgdon HYBRID 100V
22	Accurate Arms Solo 1250	72	IMR Co IMR 4198	122	Vihtavuori N550
23	Hodgdon PB	73	Hodgdon H4198	123	AliiantReloder 19
24	Vihtavuori N320	74	Vihta Vuori N120	124	IMR Co IMR 4831
25	Accurate Arms No. 2	75	Hodgdon H322	125	Ramshot Hunter
26	Ramshot Zip	76	Accurate Arms 2015BR	126	Accurate Arms 3100
27	IMR Co SR 7625	77	Alliant Reloder 10X	127	Vihtavuori N160
28	Hodgdon HP-38	78	Vihta Vouri N130	128	Hodgdon H4831 & H4831SC
29	Winchester 231	79	IMR Co IMR 3031	129	Hodgdon SUPERFORMANCE
30	Alliant 20/28	80	Vihtavouri N133	130	Winchester Supreme 780
31	Alliant Unique	81	Hodgdon BENCHMARK	131	Norma MRP
32	Hodgdon UNIVERSAL	82	Hodgdon H335	132	Alliant Reloder 22
33	Alliant Power Pistol	83	Ramshot X-Terminator	133	Vihtavuori N560

34	Vihta Vuori N330	84	Accurate Arms 2230	134	Vihtavuori N165
35	Alliant Herco	85	Accurate Arms 2460s	135	IMR Co IMR 7828
36	Winchester WSF	86	IMR Co IMR 8208 XBR	136	Alliant Reloder 25
37	Vihtavuori N340	87	Ramshot TAC	137	Vihtavuori N170
38	Hodgdon Hi-Skor 800-X	88	Hodgdon H4895	138	Accurate Arms Magpro
39	IMR Co SR 4756	89	Vihtavuori N530	139	IMR Co IMR 7977
40	Ramshot True Blue	90	IMR Co IMR 4895	140	Hodgdon H1000
41	Accurate Arms No. 5	91	Vihtavuori N135	141	Ramshot Magnum
42	Hodgdon HS-6	92	Alliant Reloder 12	142	Hodgdon RETUMBO
43	Winchester AutoComp	93	Accurate Arms 24951R	143	Vihtavuori N570
44	Hodgdon CFE Pistol	94	IMR Co IMR 4166	144	Accurate Arms 8700
45	Ramshot Silhouette	95	IMR Co IMR 4064	145	Hodgdon H870
46	Vihtavuori 3N37	96	Norma 202	146	Vihta Vuori 24N41
47	Vihtavuori N350	97	Accurate Arms 4064	147	Hodgdon 50BMG
48	Hodgdon HS-7	98	Accurate Arms 2520	148	Hodgdon US869
49	Vihtavuori 3N318	99	Alliant Reloder 15	149	Vihtavuori 20N29
50		100			

A GUIDE TO CONTEMPORARY POWDERS BY BRAND

HODGDON

Titewad

A flattened spherical shotgun powder. It features low charge weights, mild muzzle report, minimum recoil, and reduced residue for optimum ballistic performance. Designed for 12 gauge only, meters superbly and is ideal for 7/8, 1, and 1-1/18 oz. loads. As the name implies, "a little goes a long way!"

Hi-Skor 700-X

This extruded flake powder is ideal for shotshells in 12 and 16 gauge, where the norms are clay target and light field loads. It doubles as an excellent pistol target powder for cartridges such as the .38 Special and .45 ACP, and many more.

Trail Boss is an excellent choice for reduced velocity loads in pistol and rifle cartridges.

Trail Boss

Trail Boss was designed specifically for low-velocity lead bullets suitable for Cowboy Action Shooting. It is primarily a pistol powder but has some application in rifles. Its technology allows very high loading density, good flow through powder measures, and stability in extreme temperature variation.

Clays

Introduced in January 1992, Clays has "taken the clay target world by storm." It is one of the cleanest burning, most consistent 12-gauge 7/8 oz., 1 oz. and 1-1/8 oz. powders available today. This powder's burning characteristics produce soft, smooth recoil, ultra-clean burning, mild muzzle report, and excellent patterns. These features transfer directly to handgun applications where target shooting is the primary goal. For example, .45 ACP and .38 Special are two of the cartridges in which Clays provides target accuracy.

International

International is the second in the "Clays" series of powders. Its burning speed accommodates 12 gauge, 2-3/4-inch light, medium, and heavy 1-1/8 oz. loads, with some 1 oz. listings. Also, it works well in 20 gauge, 7/8 oz. target and light field loads. As with Clays, clean-burning and flawless functioning are the rules.

A little Titegroup goes a long way and is a perfect choice for all pistol cartridges.

Titegroup

As the name implies, Hodgdon designed this spherical propellant for accuracy. The unique design provides reliable ignition with all types of primers, including the lead-free versions. Unlike pistol powders of the past, powder position in large cases (.45 Colt,

.357 Magnum, and others) has virtually no effect on velocity and performance. Cowboy Action, Bullseye, and Combat Shooters should love this one.

HP38

HP38 is a spherical pistol powder that is great for low velocity and mid-range target loads in .38 Special, .44 Special, and .45 ACP. This high-energy powder provides economy in loading.

Universal

Universal handles the broadest spectrum of cartridges for both pistol and shotgun. From the .25 ACP to the .44 Magnum, Universal provides outstanding performance. It produces excellent performance for shotgun loads in 28 gauge 3/4 oz., 20 gauge 7/8 oz., 16 gauge 1 oz., and even 12 gauge.

CFE Pistol

New in 2014, this excellent spherical pistol propellant utilizes the CFE formula — Copper Fouling Eraser — virtually eliminating copper fouling, plus providing top velocities with clean burning and minimal muzzle flash. For competitive shooters and handloaders seeking the perfect powder for target or self-defense loads, CFE Pistol delivers optimum performance in cartridges such as the 9mm Luger, .38 Super, .40 S&W, .45 ACP, and more.

HS-6

HS-6 is a spherical propellant that has wide application in pistol and shotshell handloading. In pistol, 9mm, .38 Super, .40 S&W, and 10mm Auto are some of the cartridges where HS-6 provides top performance. In shotshells, HS-6 yields excellent heavy field loadings in 10 gauge, 12 gauge, 16 gauge, 20 gauge, and even the efficient and effective 28 gauge.

Longshot

This new spherical shotshell powder might be the most versatile heavy field propellant Hodgdon has ever produced. Loaders can develop excellent field loads in 10 gauge, 12 gauge, 16 gauge, 20 gauge, and 28 gauge. The propellant provides magnum velocities with consistent patterns. Also, Longshot is the best choice for those competitors shooting "race" games such as "Buddy" shoots, "Annie Oakleys," and more.

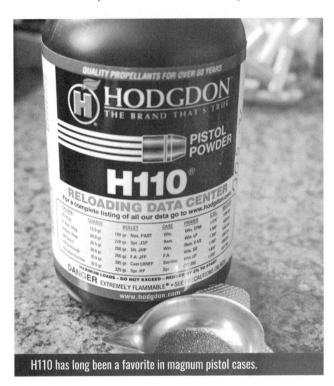
H110 has long been a favorite in magnum pistol cases.

H110

H110 is a spherical powder that delivers top velocities with accuracy in the .44 Magnum, .454 Casull, and .475 Linebaugh. Silhouette shooters claim it is the most accurate .44 powder they have ever used. Also, H110 is a solid choice for the minuscule .410-bore shotgun. It handles all 2-1/2-inch, 1/2 oz. as well as all 11/16 oz. loads for the 3-inch version.

Lil' Gun

The .410 bore has long been difficult to load due to shortcomings in powder fit, metering, and poor burning characteristics. Hodgdon designed Lil' Gun to remedy these issues, with fit, meter, and performance in the 410 bore. Also, Lil' Gun has many magnum pistol applications and is superb in the .22 Hornet.

CFE BLK

This new spherical propellant was designed expressly for the .300 Remington AAC Blackout cartridge. It provides a smooth function in AR-type rifles throughout the bullet weight range and is perfect for those sub-sonic reduced loads. In addition to being outstanding in the .300 Blackout, it performs in many smaller-capacity cartridges, particularly varmint rounds such as the .17 Hornet, .17 Ackley Hornet, .218 Bee, .221 Fireball, and many more. It also yields top performance in the 6.8 Remington SPC and the 7.62X39mm Russian cartridge. This powder meters like a dream, leaves no copper residue, remains accurate during extended shooting periods and makes clean-up quick and easy.

H4198

This extruded propellant has gone through some changes since its inception but maintains its crucial burning speed. Hodgdon shortened the kernels for improved metering and added elements to make it insensitive to hot and cold temperatures. H4198 is outstanding in cartridges such as the .222 Remington, .444 Marlin, and 7.62x39mm.

H322

This powder has won more benchrest matches than all other propellants combined. It provides match-grade accuracy in small- and medium-capacity cartridges such as the .223 Remington, 6mm PPC, and the 7mm TCU. As a fine extruded powder, it flows through powder measures with superb accuracy.

Benchmark

As the name implies, Hodgdon developed this propellant for precision cartridges, such as the 6mm PPC, .22 PPC, 6mm BR, .22 BR, .223 Remington, and .222 Remington. Additionally, it performs superbly in the .308 Winchester with light match bullets in 147 and 155 grains. With small, easy metering granules, reloaders appreciate how it flows through progressive presses.

Hodgdon's H335 is fantastic in both the .223 Remington and .45-70 Government cartridge.

H335

H335 originated as a military powder for the 5.56 NATO or .223 Remington

H4895 is an excellent choice for the .458 Winchester, especially in the heat of the tropics.

H4895

H4895 is a most versatile rifle powder. This member of the Extreme Extruded line is great for .17 Remington, .250-3000 Savage, .308 Winchester, and .458 Winchester, to name just a few. It had its origin in the .30-06 as a military powder and was the first propellant Bruce Hodgdon sold to the loading public.

Varget may be one of the most versatile rifle powders on the market.

Varget

The first of Hodgdon's revolutionary Extreme Extruded powders, Varget features small extruded grains for uniform metering, insensitivity to temperature extremes, and higher energy for improved velocities over other powders in its burning speed class. Reloaders can obtain outstanding performance and velocity in popular cartridges such as the .223 Remington, .22-250 Remington, .308 Winchester, .30-06, .375 H&H, and many more.

BL-C(2)

BL-C(2) is a spherical powder that began as a military propellant used in the 7.62 NATO, commonly known as the .308 Winchester. It instantly succeeded when Hodgdon first introduced it to handloaders, benchrest shooters, and other target competitors. BL-C(2) works exceptionally well in the .223 Remington, .17 Remington,

.22 PPC, and, of course, the .308 Winchester, plus many more.

CFE 223

Introduced in January 2012, this versatile, spherical rifle propellant incorporates CFE, Copper Fouling Eraser, in its formula. This ingredient, originally used in military propellants, deters copper fouling. It contributes to more extended periods of maximum accuracy with less barrel cleaning time. It meters accurately. CFE 223 yields top velocities in many cartridges such as the .204 Ruger, .223 Remington/5.56mm NATO, .22-250 Remington, and the .308 Winchester/7.62mm NATO. Match, varmint, and AR shooters routinely use this one.

LEVERevolution

Hodgdon Powder Company and Hornady Manufacturing teamed together to provide the powder used in Hornady LEVERevolution ammunition for reloaders. Yes, this is the same spherical propellant used in Hornady's high-performance factory ammo. The propellant meters well and makes lever-action cartridges such as the .30-30 Winchester yield velocities more than 100 fps over any published handloads, with even greater gains over factory ammunition. Other cartridges include the .35 Remington, .308 Marlin Express, .338 Marlin Express, and the .25-35 Winchester. The list of cartridges and bullets is limited with this highly specialized powder.

H380

[Ch02-19 H380 is a natural choice for the .22-250 but also works well in the .308 Winchester and .375 Ruger.]

H380 was an unnamed spherical rifle propellant when the late Bruce Hodgdon first used it. When a 38.0-grain charge behind a 52-grain bullet gave one-hole groups from his .22-caliber wildcat (now called .22-250 Remington), he appropriately named the powder H380. H380 is also a superb performer in the .220 Swift, .243 Winchester, .257 Roberts, and other fine varmint cartridges.

H4350 is the go-to powder for the 6.5 Creedmoor.

H4350

Shooters have known the burning speed of this Extreme Extruded propellant for decades. Over time, Hodgdon has modernized H4350 by shortening the grains for improved metering and insensitivity to temperature swings. H4350 is effective in cartridges such as the .243 Winchester, 6mm Remington, .270 Winchester, .338 Winchester Magnum, and many more. For magnums with light to moderate weight bullets, you can't beat it.

Hybrid 100V

This powder combines the technologies of spherical powders and extruded propellants. A spherical powder's chemistry is combined with an extruded propellant's geometry, creating a smooth-metering, short granule extruded-shaped propellant with high energy. Hybrid 100V has a burn speed between H4350 and H4831, yielding superb performance in such popular calibers as .270 Winchester, .243 WSSM, 7mm Remington Magnum, .300 Winchester Magnum, and dozens more.

H4831

It is safe to say that hunters have probably taken more big game with H4831 than any other powder.

Bruce Hodgdon was the first supplier to introduce this popular slow-burning rate in 1950. Since that time, it has become a favorite for cartridges such as the .270 Winchester, .25-06 Remington, .280 Remington, and .300 Winchester Magnum. As an Extreme Extruded propellant, it shares the fine quality of insensitivity to temperature variation, as well as superb uniformity from lot to lot.

One of the author's favorites is H4831SC in the 6.5-284 Norma.

H4831SC®

Ballistically, this Extreme Extruded powder is the exact copy of H4831. Physically, it has a shorter grain size, therefore, the designation SC, or short cut. The shorter, more compact kernels allow the powder to flow through powder measures more smoothly, helping alleviate the constant cutting of granules. With the smoother flow characteristics comes more uniform charge weights while the individual grains orient more compactly, creating better loading density.

Superformance

Superformance is a spherical powder from Hodgdon Powder Company and Hornady. The companies developed it to provide the powder used in Hornady Superformance factory ammunition to handloaders. Superformance delivers striking velocities in cartridges such as the .22-250 Remington, .243 Winchester, and .300 WSM. Speeds of 100 fps over the best-published handloads and even larger gains over factory ammunition are typical. Because this propellant is tailored for specific applications, the number of cartridges and bullets is limited.

H1000

This slow-burning Extreme Extruded powder is perfect for highly over-bored magnums such as the 7mm Remington Magnum, 7mm STW, and .30-378 Weatherby. With heavy bullets, H1000 gives top velocity and performance in such cartridges as the 6mm-284, .257 Weatherby, .270 Winchester, and .300 Winchester Magnum. In a short time, this powder has achieved considerable notoriety among long-range match shooters.

Retumbo

This magnum powder was designed expressly for the large over-bored cartridges such as the 7mm RUM, .300 RUM, .30-378 Weatherby Magnum, etc. Retumbo adds 40-100 more feet per second velocity to these cartridges than other standard magnum powders. It is also an Extreme Powder, making it perfect for big game hunting under all types of conditions.

US869®

This spherical powder is superb with heavy bullets in big, over-bore, magnum rifle cartridges. Because it is very dense, it allows the shooter to use enough powder to create magnum loads. Handloaders use US869 in the .50 BMG, which yields high velocity and great accuracy with 750- and 800-grain projectiles. It is a genuinely great 1000-yard competition propellant.

IMR

IMR Target

The first powder in this new family is a fast-burning pistol powder. This fine-grained, small flake, pistol powder meters superbly, providing precise loads in the smallest pistol cartridges such as the .25 ACP. Performance in match cartridges, such as the .38 Special and .45 ACP, is noted, and target loads for the popular Cowboy Action game are perfect for this propellant, where reduced loads are necessary.

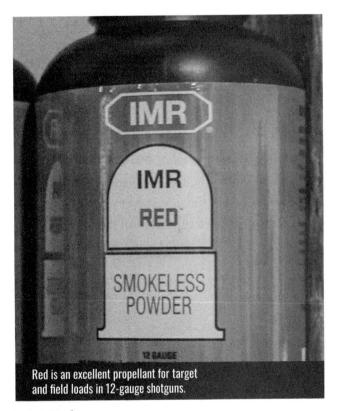

Red is an excellent propellant for target and field loads in 12-gauge shotguns.

IMR Red

IMR developed IMR Red to be an efficient, clean-burning, 12-gauge target powder. This small flake powder delivers top performance in the range of shot weights in 12 gauge, from light 7/8 oz. to 1 1/8 oz. handicap trap loads. Efficient low charge weights, mild muzzle report, and minimal recoil are all attributes of this propellant. Dove and light field loads are other uses for it. IMR Red also performs nicely in various lead pistol target loads, such as match competition and Cowboy reduced loads.

IMR Green

The second of the new IMR Shotshell line is slightly slower burning than IMR Red, making it an ideal Trap Handicap powder and a favorite with sporting clays enthusiasts. It allows the shooter to reach maximum velocity with heavy 1 1/8-oz. target loads, yielding excellent patterns in the process. It's a clean-burning powder and accommodates loads from 7/8 oz. through 1 1/8 oz. 12-gauge loads. It produces some light, 3/4 oz. 20-gauge target loads, especially in Remington STS and Winchester AA HS shells with superb target and light field loads for the discriminating reloader.

IMR Blue

IMR Blue has a slow burn rate and is an excellent choice for heavy 12-gauge 2 3/4-inch field loads, 1 1/4 oz., and 1 3/8 oz. Also, many 3- and 3- 1/2-inch 12-gauge loads are available for the avid turkey hunter. For the "Back Fence" target games, IMR Blue is the ideal burn speed, where 1 1/4 and 1 3/8 oz. loads are the norm. To round out its versatility in hunting loads, data for 10 gauge, 16 gauge, and 20 gauge are also available, providing magnum velocities.

IMR 4227

IMR 4227 is the choice for handgun and rifle magnum velocities and performance. In rifles, this powder delivers excellent velocity and accuracy in such cartridges as the .22 Hornet and .221 Fireball.

IMR 4198

This fast-burning rifle powder gives outstanding performance in cartridges such as the .222 Remington, .221 Fireball, .45-70, and .450 Marlin. It is popular among varmint shooters with small-bore cartridges.

IMR 3031 has been a great choice in both the .308 Winchester and .30-06 Springfield.

IMR 3031

A propellant with many uses, IMR 3031 has long been a favorite of .308 match shooters using 168-grain match bullets. It is equally effective in small-capacity varmint cartridges from .223 Remington to .22-250 Remington, and it's a great .30-30 Winchester powder.

IMR 8208 XBR has been very consistent in the .308 Winchester loaded with match bullets.

IMR 8208 XBR

The latest in the versatile IMR line of fine propellants, this accurate metering, super short-grained rifle powder was designed expressly for the match, varmint, and AR sniper cartridges. Ideally suited for cartridges such as the .223 Remington/5.56mm, .308 Winchester/7.62mm NATO, and the 6mm PPC, shooters will find IMR 8208 XBR insensitive to changes in temperature while yielding max velocities and the potential for tack-driving accuracy.

The author has had outstanding results in the .243 Winchester with IMR 4895.

IMR 4895

Originally a military powder featured in the .30-06, IMR 4895 is extremely versatile. From the .17 Remington to the .243 Winchester to the .375 H&H Magnum, accuracy and performance are excellent. Also, it is a longtime favorite of match shooters.

IMR 4166

This extruded propellant is the first in Hodgdon's Enduron series of powders. The Enduron series's main features are copper fouling reducer, insensitivity to temperature changes, consistent loading density, and

IMR 4166 is insensitive to temperature changes and works exceptionally in the .30-06 and .375 H&H.

environmentally friendly. IMR 4166 is the perfect burn speed for cartridges such as the .308 Winchester/7.62mm NATO, .22-250 Remington, .257 Roberts, and dozens more. Positively, a versatile, match-grade propellant.

IMR 4064

The most versatile propellant in the IMR line, used for .223 Remington, .22-250 Remington, .220 Swift, 6mm Remington, .243 WSSM, .308 Winchester, .338 Winchester Magnum, and the list goes on and on. Versatility with uniformity and accuracy.

IMR 4064 has been a staple in the author's powder supplies for years, being very versatile.

The author likes IMR 4350 for both the .300 Winchester Magnum and .375 H&H.

IMR 4350

The number one choice for the new short magnums, both Remington and Winchester versions. For magnums with light to medium bullet weights, IMR 4350 is the best choice.

IMR 4451 has a burn rate like IMR 4350 and is equally versatile.

IMR 4451

Another new Enduron Technology extruded powder, IMR 4451 gives top performance in the venerable .30-06 and .270 Winchester and .300 WSM, to name just a few. This propellant is ideally suited for many of the mid-range burn speed cartridges. Scroll through the cartridges list on the Hodgdon Reloading Data Center website and see how many of your favorites are covered with this powder.

IMR 4831

Slightly slower in burn speed than IMR 4350, IMR 4831 gives top velocities and performance with heavier bullets in medium-sized magnums.

IMR 4955

IMR 4955 works well with cartridges such as the .270 Winchester, .25-06 Remington, .280 Remington, and .300 Winchester Magnum. It falls directly between IMR 4451 and IMR 7977 in burn speed. As with all Enduron powders, it is temperature insensitive, clean-burning, and minimizes copper fouling.

IMR 7828 SSC

This magnum rifle powder has the same burn rate as standard IMR 7828 and uses the same data. However, due to its short kernels, metering is like spherical powder. This attribute allows up to 4 percent more powder space, and many loads yield higher velocity than standard 7828. Such loads are marked with an asterisk in the data to show where standard 7828 will not fit.

IMR 7977 is a slow-burning powder commonly used for the largest magnum cases.

IMR 7977

The slowest burn rate Enduron extruded powder is a magnum cartridge propellant. IMR 7977 yields outstanding performance in such cartridges as the .300 Winchester Magnum, 7mm Remington Magnum, .338 Lapua Magnum, and a host of other big magnums. Its loading density is perfect for magnums, nicely filling the case at maximum charges, contributing to superb uniformity and accuracy.

IMR 8133

Part of the IMR Legendary Powder line, IMR 8133 is an Enduron Technology powder designed for the large over-bored cartridges. These include the .300 RUM, 6.5mm-300 Weatherby Magnum, 28 Nosler, and a host of other magnums. It provides good loading density, copper fouling reducer, extreme temperature forgiveness, and is environmentally friendly.

WINCHESTER POWDERS

WST

WST is typically used for 12-gauge AA duplicate handloads and standard velocity handgun loads. Ideal for use in .45 Auto match applications. Consistent, clean, low flash, and less smoke are benefits to the shooter.

244

This Winchester pistol powder has all the features for a mid-range burn speed. Winchester 244 Ball Powder Propellant is a Winclean product with a host of attributes, including reduced copper fouling, clean-burning, and precise metering. This powder's versatility is seen in 9mm Luger, .45 ACP, .38 Special, and many more pistol cartridges.

231

One of the most popular reloading propellants, 231 is a pistol powder ideally suited to the .38 Special, .45 Auto, and 9mm standard loads. Consistency, clean-burning, low flash, and a broad range of applications make it a powder of choice for any pistol cartridge reloader.

Super Handicap

Super Handicap is the same propellant used in Winchester's Super Handicap ammunition. This slow-burning, high-energy propellant gives the shooter significant handicap, or long-range sporting clays loads up to 1,250 fps with a 1 1/8-oz. shot charge. It produces fast velocity with excellent patterns.

AutoComp

AutoComp is a high-performance powder optimized for semi-auto pistol competition and self-defense loads. It yields faster split times with improved compensator gas volume in calibers such as 9mm Luger, .40 S&W, .38 Super, and .45 ACP. It creates less muzzle flash and is clean burning.

WSF

This propellant is ideal for Winchester 20-gauge AA Target loads. WSF is an excellent choice to maximize velocities in 12 gauge 1-1/8 oz. and 1-1/4 oz. loads. It also performs well in .38 Super, 9mm, and .40 S&W pistol loads. It's an excellent propellant for action pistol applications.

572

Winchester designed this powder to do a myriad of jobs. First, it has the correct burn rate to create the famous 3-3/4 dram equivalent, 1 1/4 oz., 1,330 fps 12-gauge load, originated by Winchester. And, it does it with any brand case. It powers clay target loads superbly in 20 gauge and 28 gauge, top field loads in both, and outstanding field loads for the 16 gauge. It even is used to duplicate the always popular 28-gauge WAAHS target load. Also, 572 has many pistol applications, ranging from the .25 ACP to the .45 ACP, and all popular calibers in between.

296

Winchester developed this propellant for its factory-loaded ammunition for .357 Magnum, .44 Magnum, and .410 bore. Its high loading density provides optimal velocity. Winchester recommends 296 for .410 bore AA loads.

748

748 is the powder of choice for .223 Remington ammunition. The low flame temperature of 748 extends barrel life compared to other similar speed powders. It is ideal

Winchester's 748 is a superb choice for low-capacity cases, such as the .350 Remington Magnum

for a wide variety of centerfire rifle loads, including .222 Remington, .30-30 Winchester, .308 Winchester, and up to .458 Winchester Magnum

760

Combine Winchester components with 760 to duplicate .30-06 Springfield factory load ballistics. 760 has ideal flow characteristics that give it an advantage over other propellants with similar burn rates. Winchester recommends it as an excellent choice for .22-250 Remington, .300 Winchester Magnum, and .300 WSM.

Winchester's StaBall 6.5 is excellent in the 6.5 Creedmoor, 7mm-08 Remington, and similar cases.

StaBall 6.5

StaBall 6.5 is said to be stable in all conditions, hot or cold. Case fill/loading density is 93-100 percent in all cartridges appropriate for the burn speed, creating the perfect conditions for small standard deviations in velocity and pressure, a key element in achieving benchrest accuracy. Like most spherical powders, it meters precisely. It provides speed that eclipses all powders in its burn speed class (30-200 fps), along with a copper fouling reducing additive. Reloaders achieve top performance in these cartridges: 6mm Creedmoor, 6.5 Creedmoor, .270 Winchester, 7mm-08 Remington, and .375 H&H.

ALLIANT POWDERS

Rifle Powders
AR Comp

Alliant designed its new AR-Comp for fast action, high-volume AR shooters, and those who enjoy shooting traditional rifles. It was developed specifically for AR-style rifles and is ideally suited for heavy .223 and .308 match bullets. It is very consistent across temperature extremes.

Power Pro 1200-R

Alliant Powder's Power Pro 1200-R is for high-volume shooters who burn through .223 ammunition at the range. Formulated for progressive loading, it meters exceptionally well, and its double base provides consistent ignition and performance across a range of temperature and humidity extremes.

Power Pro 2000-MR

Power Pro 2000-MR is geared toward target shooters who need the increased speed and round-to-round consistency. Uniformity creates consistent loads to chase accuracy. Improved velocity and density for more efficient metering and loading are additional features, giving you excellent performance in heavy .223 and .308 loads. Enables reloaders to duplicate specific medium rifle heavy bullet factory loads.

Power Pro 4000-MR

For heavy lifting in hunting cartridges or suitable magnum loads for dangerous or large game. This powder is efficient, consistent, and powerful. It delivers superior performance in the 7mm Remington Magnum and .300 Winchester Magnum and enables reloaders to duplicate specific factory loaded ammunition.

Power Pro 4000-MR is one solution to limited magnum case capacity.

Power Pro Varmint

This unique powder technology delivers on-target performance on varmints and is ideal for standard caliber varmint loads.

Reloder 7

Designed for small-caliber varmint loads, Reloder 7 meters consistently and meets the needs of benchrest shooters. It's also great in .45-70 and .450 Marlin.

Reloder 10x

Reloder 10x is a decent choice for light bullet applications in .222 Remington, .223 Remington .22-250 Remington, and key benchrest calibers. You can also use it in light bullet .308 Winchester loads.

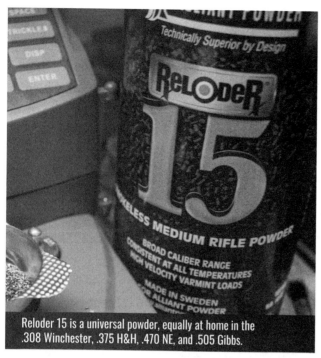

Reloder 15 is a universal powder, equally at home in the .308 Winchester, .375 H&H, .470 NE, and .505 Gibbs.

Reloder 15

This medium speed rifle powder provides excellent .223- and .308-caliber performance. Selected as the powder for the U.S. Military's M118 special ball long-range sniper round.

Reloder 16 is extremely uniform. The author likes it in the .318 Westley Richards.

Reloder 16

Repeatable long-range accuracy requires a propellant that behaves consistently across temperature extremes. Reloder 16 accomplishes this stability using TZ technology, which manipulates the material's response and resists the natural tendency to generate more pressure at higher temperatures and less pressure at lower temperatures. Reloder 16's burn rate is slightly faster than Reloder 17, well within the 4350 burn speed band. These attributes make it ideal for traditional hunting cartridges such as .30-06 Springfield and .270 Winchester, 6.5mm target loads, and tactical applications where temperature stability is required.

Reloder 17

Reloder 17 meters easily and consistently while providing maximum velocity even in extreme weather. It's ideal for short magnum case capacity and has a similar burn speed to IMR 4350.

Reloder 19

Reloder 19 provides superb accuracy in most medium and heavy rifle loads and is the powder of choice for .30-06 and .338 calibers.

Reloder 22

This top-performing powder for big game loads provides excellent metering and is the powder of choice for .270 Winchester, 7mm Remington Magnum, and .300 Winchester Magnum.

Reloder 23

Like its sister product, AR-Comp, the new Reloder 23 from Alliant uses TZ technology to manipulate the material's response and resist the natural tendency to generate more pressure at higher temperatures and less pressure at lower temperatures. Reloder 23 is perfect for long-range target shooters seeking performance like Reloder 22 with temperature stability.

Try Reloder 25 in the Remington Ultra Magnum series and other large cases.

Alliant designed Reloder 33 for the massive .338 Lapua Magnum cartridge.

Reloder 25

This advanced powder for big game hunting features improved, slower-burning, and delivers the high energy that heavy magnum loads need. It's a top choice for over-bore magnums.

Reloder 26

Reloder 26's burn speed falls between Reloder 22 and Reloder 33, and it incorporates EI technology to produce extremely high velocities in magnum cartridges. Reloder 26 has a high bulk density that allows more considerable powder charges, and it provides a consistent, controlled response to temperature changes.

Reloder 33

Specific cartridge loads need specific propellant to perform to their ballistic peak. Reloder 33 is specifically formulated for the long-range .338 Lapua Magnum cartridge, although it is ideal for many other large magnums.

Reloder 50

Alliant designed Reloader 50 for long-range, .50-caliber rifle shooters. With superior velocity and the ability to burn cleaner (with less residue), Reloder 50 delivers lot-to-lot consistency and a density explicitly created for the .50 BMG application.

Sport Pistol

Precision and action shooters need consistent, clean-burning propellant that lets them perform to their peak when a competition is on the line. Alliant's Sport Pistol delivers reliable cycling, excellent charging and case fill, and ballistics that lend themselves to a range of popular loads. Sport Pistol's low-muzzle-flash formulation is also optimized for polymer-coated bullets, whereas comparable powders can dissolve polymer coatings at the bullet base during ignition.

2400

2400 is legendary for its performance in .44 Magnum and other magnum pistol loads. Initially developed for the .22 Hornet, it's also the shooter's choice for .410 bore.

BE-86

The unique extruded flake formulation in BE-86 results in excellent ballistics in a wide array of centerfire pistol loads, with high energy, an ideal burn speed, and less flash. It meters well and is available in 1- and 8-lb. canisters. Like all Alliant Powder offerings, BE-86 provides superior lot-to-lot consistency.

Bullseye

Arguably there have been billions of rounds loaded with Bullseye since Alliant introduced it in 1913. It is a fast-burning, consistent, economical, and accurate propellant. It's popular for loading various competition handgun cartridges.

Power Pistol

Power Pistol is designed for high performance in semi-automatic pistols and is the powder of choice for 9mm, .40 S&W, and .357 SIG.

Power Pro 300-MP

Improved velocity and density for more efficient metering and loading, and maximum velocity and performance in magnum handguns, are among the benefits of trying Power Pro 300-MP.

Unique

Unique is possibly the most versatile shotgun/handgun powder ever made. It's great for 12-, 16-, 20-, and 28-gauge loads. Use with most hulls, primers, and wads.

Shotshell Powders
20/28

Alliant developed 20/28 to deliver competition-grade performance for 20- and 28-gauge clay target shooters. Extremely clean burning with proven lot-to-lot consistency, it's designed for Skeet and Sporting Clays competitors.

410

Alliant Powder's new 410 is the only flake powder designed explicitly for skeet and field loads. A clean-burning .410 powder, it's more efficient with lower powder charge weights, providing optimal loading characteristics.

American Select

Alliant's ultra-clean burning American Select premium powder makes a versatile target load and superior 1-oz. clay target loads. Give it a try for Cowboy Action handgun loads, too.

Blue Dot

Blue Dot is popular for magnum lead shotshell loads 10, 12, 16, and 20 gauge. Consistent and accurate. Doubles as a magnum handgun load.

Clay Dot

Clay Dot is an American-made and extremely clean-burning powder designed for 12-gauge competition shooters. It is engineered to perform like Hodgdon Clays but at an economical price. It's not a bad choice for light and standard 12-gauge target loads with 7/8-, 1- and 1 1/8-oz. payloads. Available in 1-, 4- and 8-lb. containers. Not for use in metallic cartridges.

e3

Alliant Powder's new e3 is a 12-gauge shotshell powder for competitive shooters. It features reduced charge weights, is clean-burning, and has environmental stability. It is a flake powder named after its core qualities of energy, efficiency, and excellence.

Extra-Lite

Extra-Lite is a shotshell propellant that costs less, recoils less, and creates fewer headaches for those 12-gauge shooters transitioning from 1 1/8 to 7/8 and 1-oz. loads. The powder has a density that allows the use of standard components (wads and cases).

Green Dot

Green Dot delivers precise burn rates for uniformly tight patterns, plus lower recoil. It's a versatile shotshell powder for target and field.

Herco

Herco is primarily known as a shotshell powder. Very similar to Green Dot.

Pro Reach

Formulated for long-range 12-gauge clay target shooting, Pro Reach gives shooters the ability to reach out and dust clays at great distances. It's perfect for games such as Back Porch, Protection, Buddy and Annie Oakley and is a solid choice for reloading 12-gauge hunting loads.

Promo

Promo is an economy-priced 12-gauge target powder. It has the same burn speed as Red Dot but is denser, requiring a smaller bushing to obtain the same charge weight.

Red Dot

Red Dot is a popular propellant choice for clay target loads. It's now supposed to run 50 percent cleaner.

Steel

Steel is a new powder for waterfowl shotshells that gives steel shot high velocity within safe pressure limits for 10- and 12-gauge loads. It's consistent at all temperatures and maximizes speed in steel shot loads.

RAMSHOT POWDERS

Rifle Powders
Magnum

Magnum provides outstanding performance from the popular 7mm Remington Magnum and 300 Winchester Magnum through the Remington Ultra Mags and .338 Lapua Magnum. It is a double-base spherical propellant that is right at home in "over-bore" magnum cartridges.

Big Game

Big Game is a good .30-06 Springfield powder. Outstanding velocities and optimal case-fill result in shot-to-shot consistency. These properties allow it to compete in the popular .22-250 Remington and other calibers in this range. It's an extremely clean-burning, double-base spherical powder with outstanding metering properties.

Hunter

Hunter is a double-base, clean-burning, high-performance propellant perfect for elk country cartridges such as the .270 Winchester, .300 WSM, and .338 Winchester Magnum. It's the only spherical powder in the popular 4350 burn range, making it an ideal propellant for a wide range of cartridges. The excellent flow characteristics allow accurate metering and consistent shot-to-shot results.

TAC

TAC is a double-base spherical propellant for extreme accuracy and reliability with heavy bullets in the .223 Remington and match applications in .308 Winchester. It exhibits excellent flow characteristics to ensure consistent metering and charge weights for repeatable results with progressive loading equipment.

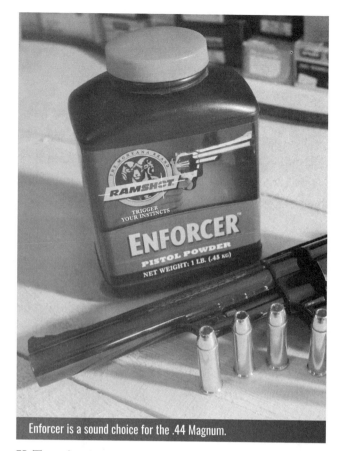
Enforcer is a sound choice for the .44 Magnum.

Handgun Powders

Enforcer

Enforcer is a good choice for high performance, full-power loads in magnum handgun cartridges. It is ideally suited for the .44 Magnum, .454 Casull, .460 S&W, and the .500 S&W. It is a double-base spherical powder with excellent metering qualities that meets the performance expectations for magnum handgun loads.

Silhouette

Silhouette is the choice for competitive shooters in IPSC, IDPA, and USPSA. A double-base high-performance spherical powder, it is an excellent choice for 9mm, .38 Super, .40 S&W, and .45 ACP. It has a low flash signature, high velocity, and clean-burning properties, making it a practical choice for indoor ranges and law enforcement applications.

True Blue

True Blue is the perfect powder for classic handgun calibers such as the .38 Special, .44 Special, and .45 Long Colt. It is a double-base, spherical powder with great metering properties that make it ideal for high volume, progressive reloading equipment. It works well with cast bullets and is also perfect for 9mm law enforcement rounds.

X-Terminator

X-Terminator is a double-base spherical powder designed for the high-volume .223 varmint hunters requiring a clean-burning, accurate propellant. Excellent flow characteristics and small grain size allow trouble-free loading in small diameter case necks. It performs extremely well with light to medium weight bullets in the .223 Remington. It is also an excellent choice for .17 Remington, .20-caliber cartridges, .222 Remington, and the .45-70 Government.

LRT

As one of the slowest spherical powders ever developed, LRT is high performance at extreme ranges. Ramshot designed it specifically for the .338 Lapua Magnum using heavy, high ballistic coefficient bullets. LRT offers high load densities and low standard deviations for superior accuracy. Hunters who prefer the advantages of over-bore magnums such as the .257 Weatherby or .30 Nosler will find that LRT meters easily.

ZIP has given great results in the author's .45 ACP.

ZIP

ZIP is a clean-burning, double-base propellant designed for a wide range of handgun calibers. Low charge weights make it an economical and versatile choice for high-volume shooters with the added benefit of low recoil, low flash, and minimum residue. 9mm, .40 S&W and .45 ACP are just a few of the cartridges that are well-matched with this powder.

Shotshell Powders
Competition

Competition is an extremely clean-burning powder for 12-gauge target shooters. It's a double-base modified (flattened) spherical propellant for the 12-gauge competitive clay target shooter demanding a clean-burning powder with low recoil and consistent performance. It is a low bulk density powder that is also well suited for many low-pressure, low-velocity Cowboy Action loads.

Rifle Powders
Accurate 5744

Accurate 5744 is an extremely fast-burning, double-base, extruded powder. You can use it in a wide range of rifle calibers and magnum handguns. 5744 gives you excellent ignition and consistency over a vast performance range. Low bulk density and superior ignition characteristics make 5744 an excellent choice for reduced loads in many rifle calibers and large-capacity blackpowder cartridges such as the .45-70 through .45-120 and .50-90 through .50-120.

Accurate LT-30

Representing the Light Target line of benchrest-grade powders, Alliant optimized LT-30 for use in the .30 BR cartridge. While still in its development phase, LT-30 was used to win numerous matches, even claiming a world record along the way. With a burn rate like 4198, this single-base fine-grained powder is at home in many smaller capacity cartridges, including the 6.5 Grendel and .222 Remington.

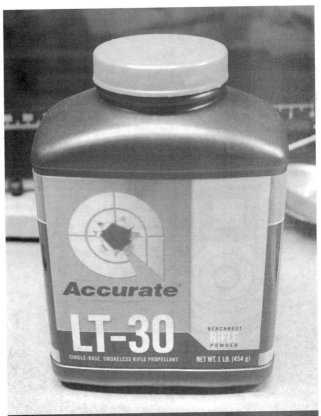

LT-30 is a smart choice for smaller cases, such as the 6.5 Grendel.

Accurate LT-32

LT-32 is a fine-grained extruded powder developed for 6mm PPC benchrest competitors. Already a proven match-winner, LT-32's excellent shot-to-shot consistency, and low standard deviations make it a solid choice for competition use. Due to its small grain size, LT-32 flows like a spherical powder and allows for very precise handloading. It also offers outstanding accuracy in varmint and tactical cartridges, including the .223 Remington and .308 Winchester.

Accurate 2015 is a fantastic choice for the popular varmint cartridges.

Accurate 2015

Accurate 2015 is a fast-burning, single-base, extruded rifle powder that performs very well in small to medium varmint calibers (.223 Rem, .204 Ruger). 2015 is a popular choice for benchrest calibers and recommended for large-bore straight-wall cartridges (.45-70, .458 Winchester Magnum). 2015 offers excellent ignition characteristics and shot-to-shot consistency.

Accurate 2200

Introduced to meet the increasing demand for a high-performance small-bore propellant, Accurate 2200 has become a varmint hunting favorite. It is an excellent choice for many cartridges, including the .223 Remington, 6.5 Grendel, and 6.8 SPC. Spherical granules allow precise metering and easy flow through small cartridge necks, making Accurate 2200 ideal for use in progressive reloading machines.

Accurate 2230

Accurate 2230 is a fast-burning, double-base, spherical rifle propellant. Alliant designed it for the .223 Remington, but you can use it in many small- and medium-caliber cartridges such as the .308 Winchester. 2230 also works well in big-bore straight-wall cartridges such as the .458 Winchester. The excellent flow characteristics and grain size of 2230 make it ideal for progressive loading.

Accurate 2460

Accurate 2460 is a fast-burning, double-base, spherical rifle powder that is a slower derivative of AA2230. It is suitable for small- and medium-sized caliber applications but with slightly higher loading densities than AA2230. It provides an additional option for shooters to fine-tune and optimize loads and combinations with calibers ranging from the .223 Remington, .308 Winchester, and light bullets in the .30-06 Springfield. 2460 is within the threshold limit for M14 systems.

Accurate 2495

Accurate 2495 is a single-base, extruded rifle powder developed for the .308 Winchester. It can be used over a wide range of rifle calibers and is an extremely popular powder for NRA High Power shooting disciplines and heavy bullet .223 Remington target applications. 2495 is a versatile propellant with excellent ignition characteristics that provide shot-to-shot consistency.

Accurate 2520

Accurate 2520 is a medium-burning, double-base, spherical rifle propellant designed around the .308 Winchester 2520 is known as the "Camp Perry" powder and is extremely popular with many service shooters. 2520 also performs exceptionally well in .223 Remington with heavy match bullets (62 to 80 grains). This versatile powder has superb flow characteristics and is well within the threshold limit for the M14 systems.

Accurate 2700

Accurate 2700 is a medium-burning, double-base, spherical rifle powder that is ideally suited for the .30-06 Springfield and other medium-capacity calibers such as the .22-250 Remington, .220 Swift, and the .243 Winchester 2700 provides excellent velocities and performance in the Winchester Super Short Magnum cartridges.

Accurate 4064

Accurate 4064 is an intermediate-burning, single-base, short cut extruded rifle powder developed for the .30-06 Springfield. It works extremely well in calibers such as .22-250 Remington, .220 Swift, .243 WSM, 7x57 Mauser, and the .325 WSM. 4064 is a popular choice for High Power shooters using the M1 Garand.

Accurate 4350

Accurate 4350 is a short cut, single-base, extruded rifle powder in the popular 4350 burn range. A highly versatile powder, 4350 can be used in a wide range of cartridges from the popular .243 Winchester to the .338 Winchester Magnum with excellent results. Accurate 4350 is also an exceptional choice for the 6mm Rem, .270 Winchester, .280 Remington, and .300 WSM. This short cut extruded powder meters accurately, resulting in excellent shot-to-shot consistency.

Accurate 1680

Accurate 1680 is an extremely fast-burning, double-base, spherical rifle powder. It is well suited for large capacity, high-performance handgun cartridges such as the .454 Casull, .460 S&W, and .500 S&W. 1680 is also an excellent choice for the .22 Hornet and 7.62x39mm, as well as other low capacity rifle cartridges.

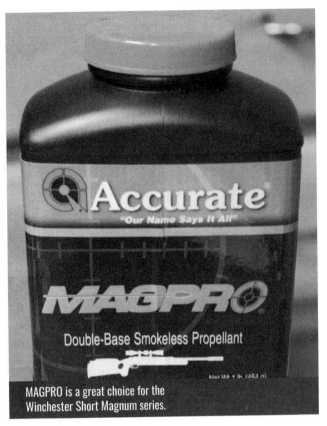

MAGPRO is a great choice for the Winchester Short Magnum series.

Accurate MAGPRO

Accurate MAGPRO is a slow-burning, double-base, spherical rifle powder developed specifically for the Short magnums of both Winchester (WSM) and Remington (SAUM). This powder excels in the 6.5x284, .270 WSM, and the 7mm WSM. It is an excellent choice for belted cartridges such as the .300 Winchester Magnum. You can expect consistent performance from its excellent metering properties.

Handgun Powders
Accurate No. 2

Accurate No. 2 is an extremely fast-burning, double-base, spherical handgun powder suitable for a wide range of handgun calibers. Low recoil and subdued flash make No. 2 well suited for short barrel, concealed carry applications. No. 2 is a non-position-sensitive powder, and low charge weights make it an economical and versatile choice for high-volume handgun shooters.

Accurate No. 5

Accurate No. 5 is a fast-burning, double-base, spherical handgun propellant. This powder is versatile, and you can load it in many handgun calibers. No. 5 offers a wide performance range from target and Cowboy Action applications to full-power defense loads. It meters well and strikes a good balance between ballistics and cost-efficiency.

Accurate No. 7

Accurate No. 7 is an intermediate-burning, double-base, spherical powder suitable for a wide range of handgun calibers. No. 7 is a solid choice for high-performance semi-auto handguns such as the .357 Sig, .38 Super, and .40 S&W. It is also a cost-effective solution in larger magnum handgun calibers.

Accurate No. 9

Accurate No. 9 is a double-base, spherical powder ideal for high power loads in traditional magnums such as the .357 Magnum, .41 Remington Magnum, and .44 Remington Magnum. It is particularly well-suited to the .357 Sig and 10mm Auto, providing high velocities and excellent case-fill. You can use No. 9 with large magnums such as the .460 S&W and .500 S&W for economical target loads.

Accurate 4100

Accurate 4100 is a double-base, slow-burning spherical powder with exceptional metering characteristics. It is a dandy for high-performance, full-power loads in magnum handgun cartridges. It is ideal for the .357 Magnum, .41 Magnum, .44 Magnum, .454 Casull, .460 S&W, and the .500 S&W.

Accurate No. 11FS

No. 11FS is intended for full-power loads in magnum handguns and smaller-capacity rifle cartridges. This double-base spherical propellant was developed with an eye toward personal defense and incorporates a flash-suppressant that substantially reduces muzzle signature in low light conditions. In the .300 Blackout, No. 11FS can generate extremely high velocities with lighter bullets, making it the best propellant choice for shooters looking to maximize downrange performance in that cartridge.

Accurate TCM

In 2017, Western Powders partnered with Armscor International to provide a canister-grade propellant for Armscor's innovative .22 TCM cartridge. This fun little cartridge takes handgun performance to a new level for small game hunting and plinking, producing 2,000 fps at the muzzle with virtually no recoil. Accurate TCM also has a place with old favorites, with data for hunting loads in .357 Magnum, .41 Magnum, and high-pressure .45 Colt cartridges.

Shotshell Powders
Accurate Nitro 100 NF

Nitro 100 New Formulation (NF) is a fast-burning, flattened spherical, double-base shotshell powder that is a clean-burning, cost-effective choice for all 12-gauge target applications. NOTE: The reformulated Nitro 100 has been optimized to improve flow and ignition characteristics.

Accurate Solo 1000

Accurate Solo 1000 is a fast-burning, single-base, flake shotgun powder. Solo 1000 was the pioneer in the clean-burning revolution and is an excellent choice for trap, sporting clays, and skeet shooting. Solo 1000 is an ultra-clean burning powder that is well suited for target handgun loads in .45 ACP and Cowboy Action cartridges.

A lineup of Norma's excellent rifle powders.

NORMA POWDERS

Rifle Powders
Norma 200

Norma 200 is a fast-burning rifle powder intended for small bores such as the .222 and .223 Remington. It's accurate and easy to meter and an excellent choice for low-pressure big bores such as the .45-70 Government.

Norma 201

Norma optimized 201 for the .223 Remington It is proven to be a top performer across a wide spectrum of cartridges. Accuracy in the 6mm BR with lighter bullets is superb, while its versatility in older calibers makes it ideal in service rifles from around the world.

Norma 202

Norma developed 202 for the .308 Winchester. It delivers notable performance in most medium-capacity cartridges, including the .22-250 Remington and .220 Swift.

Norma 203B

Norma 203B is for heavy match bullets in the .308 Winchester. Its versatility brings fine performance to favorites such as the .220 Swift and .30-06 and the powerful .338 Winchester Magnum

Norma 204

Norma 204 is a slow-burning powder that delivers outstanding performance in a wide range of cartridges, including the .243 Winchester, .300 WSM, and 7mm Remington Magnum

Norma 217

Norma 217 is a slow-burning magnum powder that maximizes performance in large magnum cartridges. Created for the .30-.378 Weatherby, .338 Lapua Magnum, and the Remington Ultra Magnums, Norma 217 offers high velocity and match accuracy.

Norma MRP

Norma MRP is a magnum rifle powder created for 1000-yard competitions and long-range hunting rifles. A winner in cartridges such as the 6.5X284, .270 Winchester, and the .300 Winchester Magnum, MRP is an extremely versatile magnum powder.

Norma URP

Norma URP is the "hunter's powder." It covers the range of cartridges hunters typically use in search of deer and elk. Ideal for the .30-06 Springfield, it also works perfectly in cartridges as diverse as the 6.5x55 Swede and the .338 Winchester Magnum

SHOOTER'S WORLD POWDERS

Clean Shot

Ballistic results for this propellant show it to be highly versatile, with low residue in many pistol cartridges. It has a similar burn rate to Winchester 231, Hodgdon Titegroup, and Accurate No. 2. You can use it in virtually all pistol cartridges and 12-gauge shotshell target loads. It is a spherical propellant with fine grains and meters consistently with volumetric chargers.

Due to its gas generation rate, loaders can achieve high velocities with .45 Auto, .38 Special, and .45 Colt, and similar low-pressure cartridges. This propellant achieves nominal velocities in high-pressure semi-automatic firearms chambered in 9mm, .40 S&W, .380 Auto, and others. You can also try it for reduced loads in virtually any revolver cartridge, whether magnum or standard.

Ultimate Pistol

Every manufactured batch of Ultimate Pistol is tested for superior ignition with both lead-free and standard lead styphnate primers. This quality control ensures reliable ignition. It is versatile, and can be used in the .380 Auto, 9mm Luger, .40 S&W, .38 Special, 38 Super, and .45 Automatic cartridges. From a competition standpoint, Ultimate Pistol's burn rate is similar to Winchester Autocomp. However, the burn rate modifier is within the propellant grain. This recipe provides more reliable ignition and consistent velocity.

The grain geometry of Ultimate Pistol promotes highly consistent charging. With a volumetric powder dump, the manufacturer claims a total charge variation of no more than "one-tenth of a grain," or +/- 0.05 grain. Its gas generation rate should enable handgun cartridge reloaders to reach "self-defense" velocities while maintaining reasonable pressure levels.

Auto Pistol

Auto Pistol is a bulk form of the Lovex D036 reloading propellant. For loaders interested in attaining standard or +P velocities in 9mm Luger, or an optimized propellant for the .357 SIG, as well as correct energy levels for cycling carbines with subsonic loads, this propellant is a wise choice. It will also perform well with .380 Auto, .44 Special, .45 Colt, heavy-bullet .40 S&W, and some light-to-moderate bullet .357 Magnum loads. It's an alternative to Longshot, HS-6, and Accurate No 5.

As the name implies, the powder's primary purpose is to enhance virtually all automatic pistols' cycling. From self-defense ammo to competition loads to realistic training ammunition, it can assist the shooter with optimized reliability.

Auto Pistol is a spherical-type propellant. It meters through charge plates consistently and will work with a high-speed loader with good flow. It contains a level of flash suppressant.

Major Pistol

Major Pistol is a canister form of the Lovex D037.1 reloading propellant. It is similar in burn speed to Accurate No. 7, 2400, and Blue Dot. The gas generation rate is appropriate for cartridges such as the 9mm and 10mm Auto, .357 SIG, .45 Colt, .410 shotshell, light-bullet magnum handgun loads, and other high-intensity pistol cartridges. It is perfect for short-barrel magnum revolvers, where you need complete combustion, high-velocity, and low muzzle flash. It is also possible to achieve extremely high velocities in 9mm Luger with Major Pistol. It meters through charge plates consistently and will work with high-speed loaders with good flow. It contains a flash suppressant.

Heavy Pistol

Ballistics results for the Heavy Pistol propellant show it appropriate for magnum pistol applications, .300 Blackout with lightweight projectiles, and some other specialty ammunition. It is similar in burn speed to Accurate No. 9 and has similar applications as Alliant 2400, Hodgdon H110, or Winchester 296. The superior ignition of this propellant permits less-than-full loading density. Therefore, it is unnecessary to load "full-power" loads with this propellant to achieve safe results.

Heavy Pistol runs exceptionally clean, and is accurate with either cast or jacketed projectiles, and exhibits low muzzle flash. This powder meters through charge plates consistently and will flow well in a high-speed loader.

Buffalo Rifle

Buffalo Rifle has a burn rate optimized for straight-walled rifle cartridges and reduced-recoil, reduced-energy loads in virtually all rifle applications. Chambers where the bullet diameter is virtually the same as the internal case diameter, such as .38-55 Winchester, .45-70 Gov't, and numerous Schuetzen calibers, will benefit from Buffalo Rifle.

The propellant's standard test load is .30-06 Springfield, a 168-grain bullet, and 22 grains of propellant — this loading density is less than 50 percent. Yet, it burns extremely well in this condition. It can significantly expand a hunting rifle's utility if the loader desires to shoot cast lead or standard jacketed bullets.

The surface of this propellant's grains holds no deterrent or burn rate modifier. Therefore, it ignites consistently with low loading densities in typical rifle loads. This same ignition characteristic aids accuracy when used with cast lead bullets and long-throated chambers.

Buffalo Rifle is an extruded propellant that exhibits good flow characteristics through a volumetric powder dump. The grain is narrow and cut short.

Tactical Rifle

Tactical Rifle has been a secret of OEM loaders for some time. It is a clean .223 Remington and .308 Winchester propellant and an excellent alternative to H335 and BLC(2). Optimized for 55-grain .223 Remington and 147/150 grain .308 Winchester, it also provides sub-minute accuracy with numerous match loads. It is extremely low in residue, muzzle smoke and is flash suppressed.

The propellant flows well through a volumetric charger. Loaders will see no more than 1/10th of a grain of variation in charge weight from a powder drop. This result has been tested in Dillon, RCBS, Lee, Hornady, Hollywood, and Lyman chargers.

Additionally, it enables reloaders to meet the velocity and pressure specifications of popular rounds for AR and M1A platforms. It provides ample gas pressure and volume for reliable cycling of these operating mechanisms.

Match Rifle

Match Rifle is highly versatile and has shown exceptional accuracy in .223 Remington/5.56mm, and .308 Winchester. It is similar in burn speed to Accurate 2520, CFE223, and IMR 4064. It holds the broadest utility across all moderate rifle propellants.

Its gas generation rate is appropriate for cartridges of the light to heavy sectional density .223 Remington and .308 Winchester It can load the 55-grain, through 77- and 80-grain .223 Remington It loads the 150-, 168- and 175-grain .308 Winchester and all .30-30 combinations. It works in .30-06, in 7mm-08, 6mm BR, 6mm PPC, .204 Ruger, and similar cartridges.

Match Rifle's burn rate and geometry yields low residue and ample port pressure to cycle AR, M1, M1A, G3, and G36 systems.

Precision Rifle

Precision Rifle has a burn rate and temperature sensitivity similar to Hodgdon Varget. Testing has indicated that velocity variation at both ambient and extreme temperatures out-performs that of Varget. This characteristic should benefit those seeking superior accuracy.

Precision Rifle has a burn rate that permits use in a wide range of centerfire rifle cartridges. It is an extruded propellant with good flow characteristics through volumetric powder dumps. The grain is narrow and cut short. Due to its cleanliness of burn and incorporated flash suppressant, there is virtually no muzzle flash.

Long Rifle

Long Rifle has a burn rate optimized for 6.5 Creedmoor, .260 Remington, and .30-06 Springfield. Evaluation in the .300 Winchester Magnum indicates its ability to meet 2,900 fps with a 190-grain bullet.

It yields high loading densities and optimized velocities, whether with lightweight, moderate, or heavy bullets loaded in the 6.5 Creedmoor.

Despite being an extruded propellant, it has good flow characteristics through a volumetric powder dump. The grain is narrow and cut short.

VIHTVOURI POWDERS

Rifle Powders
N100

N110, formerly known as 4N19 and N3SS, is a tubular powder type with grain dimensions of 1.1 mm and a diameter of 0.8 mm. The N110 is a fast-burning powder, making it a versatile product for pistol and rifle loads. The ignition is best with small rifle primers. It is suitable especially for small rifle cases such as .22 Hornet, .30 Carbine, and magnum pistol and revolver cartridges such as .357 S&W Magnum, .41 Magnum, .44 Magnum, .454 Casull, and .500 S&W. This powder is one of the favorites for hunting and varmint loads.

N120

Vihtavuori N120 rifle powder works great in small calibers with light bullets and short barrel rifles, especially in .222 Remington and 7.62x39mm. Formerly known as N 21, the Finnish Army also uses the powder. Its burn rate is fast, slightly slower than that of N110. N120 needs higher pressure than N110 to optimize the burning, and its grain size is the smallest in the company's rifle powder family — only 0.8mm in length and 0.6mm in diameter. This size makes the loadability in powder measures easy.

N130

N130, formerly known as N303, is a multipurpose powder for various rifle calibers and is suitable for small game hunting and target shooting.

The N130 is used in many factory-loaded .22-caliber and 6mm PPC cartridges. It is also an excellent handloading choice for lighter bullets in caliber .223 Remington and straight-wall rifle cases such as the .45-70 Government and the .458 Winchester Magnum

The N130 is a single-base, tubular rifle powder type with grain dimensions of 1.0mm in length and 0.6mm in diameter. Its burn rate is relatively fast. The grain size of N130 is the same as N133 and N135, but due to differences in surface coatings, the burning behavior of these powders is different.

N133

Originally developed for the 5.56 NATO cartridge, Vihtavuori's N133 is a rifle powder for centerfire .22-caliber and PPC cartridges.

N133 is a tubular powder with grain dimensions of 1.1mm in length and 0.8mm in diameter. The burn rate is medium, and it works with .223 Remington. It is also a top choice for 6mm PPC standard rifle and benchrest loads with the Lapua .220 Russian brass. N133 is probably the most popular powder in 100m and 200m benchrest shooting competitions: countless competitors have taken trophies using this reloading powder.

N135

Developed originally for the 7.62x51 NATO M80 Ball, Vihtavuori's N135 is today a universal gun powder used by reloaders for a large range of calibers .222 Remington to .458 Winchester Magnum.

N135 is a tubular powder type with grain dimensions of 1.0mm in length and 0.8mm in diameter. The burn rate is medium. N135, N133, and N130 all have the same grain dimensions, but those powders' burning behavior varies due to the different surface coating. N135 is used primarily by medium game hunters and long-range target shooters.

N140

N140 was initially developed for the 7.62x53R cartridge for the Finnish Army. It is a tubular powder type with grain dimensions of 1.0mm in length and a diameter of 0.9mm. The structure, grain geometry, and graphite coating make it work excellent in all reloading machines. N140 powder burns at a medium speed, making it a versatile handloading option for small game hunting and sport shooting applications.

N140 cannot reach the highest muzzle velocity possible, but it is ideal for achieving the best possible accuracy. This powder is multipurpose. You can load it in a wide range of calibers from .223 Remington to .308 Winchester, .30-06 Springfield, and .375 H&H Magnum, to name a few.

N150

Use Vihtavuori N150 with heavier bullets in accuracy and hunting loads in cartridges with middle case volumes, such as the .30-06 Springfield, .308 Winchester, and 6.5x55 SE.

N150 is a tubular powder type with grain dimensions

of 1.3mm in length and 1.1mm in diameter, and the nearly symmetrical shape makes it a good companion for all kinds of reloading equipment. The burn rate of N150 is medium. It is also one of the most temperature-insensitive powders, with an added decoppering agent, reducing copper fouling in rifle barrels.

N160

Vihtavuori's N160 rifle powder is especially suitable for large and magnum calibers (especially belted Magnums) starting from .30-06 with heavier bullets, .243 Winchester, .260 Remington, 6.5 Creedmoor, 6.5x55 SE, 7mm Weatherby Magnum, .300 Winchester Magnum, .338 Winchester Magnum, and all the Winchester Short Magnums. It also fits large capacity/small-bore cartridges such as the 6.5-284 Norma.

N160 is a tubular powder type with grain dimensions of 1.3mm in length and 1.1mm in diameter. The burn rate is medium to slow. Use N160 for big game hunting ammunition, especially with heavier bullets.

N165

Designed for long-range performance, Vihtavuori N165 is a universal powder for magnum rifle calibers with heavy bullets. It works exceptionally well in .338 Lapua Magnum with 250-grain bullets but can be used for handloading a wide variety of calibers ranging from 6.5x55 SE to .416 Rigby.

The N165 powder grain size (1.3mm in length by 1.0mm in diameter) matches its "big brother" N160, but the surface coating creates the difference in burning characteristics.

N165 is an extremely slow-burning rifle powder, making it a superior choice for the same range of cartridges as N160 when using heavier bullets. You can achieve slightly higher velocities than N165.

N170

Vihtavuori N170 is the slowest-burning rifle powder in the N100 series (not taking 20N29 and 24N41 into account). It is one of the slowest canister-grade powders readily available from any manufacturer on the market. N170 grains are of the cylindrical, single-perforated extruded type. With a length of 1.7mm and a diameter of 1.1mm, the grain size is relatively large.

As a slow-burning reloading powder, N170 is a top choice for large capacity cases such as the .300 Weatherby Magnum and .300 RUM. and offers good performance in most of the belted magnum cartridges. Reloaders use N170 in shooting disciplines such as long-range big game hunting and target competitions.

20N29

Vihtavuori initially developed 20N29 as a rifle powder for .50 BMG and military use, and even the name 20N29 originates from the Finnish Army standards.

20N29 is a single-based, surface-treated powder with grain dimensions of 2.3mm in length and 1.3mm in diameter. The burn rate is slower, and the grain size larger than those of the N100 series powders. Use 20N29 primarily in large-caliber and magnum applications with heavy bullets and long-range target shooting. It is ideally suited for the .50 BMG but has also gained a good reputation when used in the .300 Lapua Magnum and .30-378 Weatherby Magnum.

24N41

Vihtavuori 24N41 is a single-based treated rifle powder similar to 20N29. It has a large grain size (length 2.3mm by diameter 1.3mm) and an extremely slow-burning rate ideally suited to the .50 BMG. You can load it in large capacity cases, such as the .300 Lapua Magnum, .300 RUM, and the .338 Lapua Magnum 24N41 is slightly faster than 20N29.

N555

Vihtavuori designed its new N555 smokeless rifle powder for precision rifle platforms chambered in cartridges such as 6mm Creedmoor, 6.5 Creedmoor, .284 Winchester, .260 Remington, and .30-06 Springfield — and for rifle calibers with large case volume and comparatively small bullet diameters, among others.

Competitive shooters and hunters will benefit

from the powder's insensitivity in extreme weather conditions. N555 performs well in the 6.5 Creedmoor. It includes an anti-fouling agent that minimizes barrel fouling to extend your competitive shooting stages. The unmatched lot-to-lot consistency of N555 eliminates costly range time re-developing your favorite loads. The burn rate of N555 is between N550 and N160.

N530

The N530 is the fastest burning of all Vihtavuori high-energy rifle powders. It's an excellent choice for the reloading hunter when a flat trajectory and reasonable velocity are needed. N530 is also an option for many smaller bottlenecked cases such as the .223 Remington or other 5.56mm loads, or large straight-walled cases such as the .45-70 Springfield. It is a good powder for medium capacity cases like the .308 Winchester when using lighter weight bullets of 155 grains or less.

N530 was initially developed and qualified for 5.56x45mm NATO (.223 Remington) in military use. Still, these days it's used in a wide range of loads in cartridges such as the .308 Winchester, 9.3x62, .45-70 Government, and .458 Winchester Magnum.

N540

Vihtavuori N540 is a universal rifle powder for a wide variety of medium-sized calibers suitable for hunting and target shooting. It is an excellent choice for cartridges running from .223/5.56mm to .308 Winchester and .30-06 Springfield with heavier bullet weights.

N540 delivers outstanding accuracy with exceptionally clean burning. You can get a velocity up to 30-40 m/s higher with the same pressure level compared to the N100 series. It is certainly worth trying when using heavier bullets and when higher loading densities and muzzle velocities are needed.

Thanks to its symmetrical size (1.0mm in length and 1.0mm in diameter), N540 meters well in reloading equipment and makes loading easy.

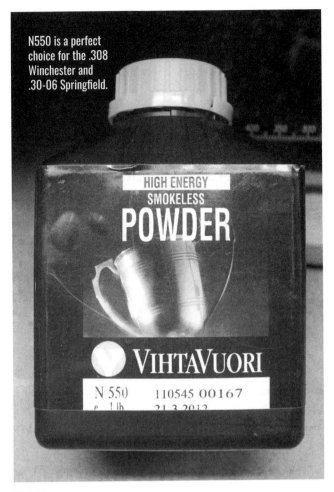

N550 is a perfect choice for the .308 Winchester and .30-06 Springfield.

N560

Load Vihtavuori's N560 rifle powder in large magnum calibers, for example, .270 Winchester, 6.5-284, 7mm Remington Magnum, 7mm Weatherby Magnum, and even the .416 Rigby. It is also an excellent choice for the .338 Lapua Magnum using lighter bullets of 250 grains or less.

It is a tubular type with a large grain and a length of 1.4mm, and a diameter of 1.2mm. The burn rate is slow, between N160 and N165. The N560 is like the N100 series, but nitroglycerine has been added to it to boost velocity. Reloaders use the 500 series powders in rifle cartridges where extra energy is needed to achieve increased loading densities and higher muzzle velocities within maximum pressure limits. So, you get better speed with the same pressure than with, for instance, N165. Common uses for N560 include big game hunting and sniper ammunition, especially for larger-caliber rifles.

N565

Designed to fill the gap between N560 and N570, N565 was created specifically for the .338 Lapua Magnum with 250-grain bullets. In addition to a precisely tailored burn rate, this powder is extremely temperature stable, giving uniform results across a wide range of environments. It uses a decoppering agent to ensure a cleaner barrel when shooting.

Physically, N565 grains are the same size as those of N560. It flows smoothly through powder measures and ensures good loadability and uniformity. The burn rate of the powder is closer to N570, roughly splitting the difference between the two. N565 is a single perforated extruded powder.

While N565 was explicitly developed for military sniping applications, it also has a wide range of sporting uses, particularly long-range shooting and extreme long-range (ELR). It is an ideal choice for calibers such as the 7mm Remington Magnum, .30-06, .300 Winchester Magnum, .300 Norma Magnum, and the .338 Norma Magnum.

N550

Vihtavuori developed its N550 rifle powder for .30-06 Springfield and .308 Winchester calibers in the late 1990s. It is an ideal fit for many of the .30-caliber magnums with lighter bullets but is also useful across a wide range of bore sizes in various shooting disciplines. It is an excellent powder for .30-06 Springfield hunting rounds with heavier bullets and other more powerful loads of 6.5x55 SE.

N550 is a tubular powder type with symmetrical grain dimensions of 1.0mm in length and 1.0mm in diameter. Nitroglycerine has been added to the traditional single-base powder to get better energy. The burn rate of N550 is like N150, and it's on the medium scale of the high energy powders. Higher velocity is acquired with equal pressure compared to the N100 series — without increased wear on the rifle.

N570

Magnum cartridge reloaders requested the development of Vihtavuori's N570 rifle powder. With its large grain size and high bulk density, this high-energy powder's characteristics bring out the maximum velocities of cartridges with large volume cases, such as the 6.5-.284 Norma, .300 Winchester Magnum, .300 RUM, and the .338 Lapua Magnum.

N570 is well suited for long-range target shooting and in military applications with large volume cartridges. It is the slowest of Vihtavuori's high-energy powders and is an extruded, tubular powder type with grain dimensions of 2.3mm in length and 1.3mm in diameter. Due to the large kernel size (like 24N41 and 20N29), you should weigh your N570 charges rather than relying on throws from powder measures, as they do not always deliver consistent charges. This way, you can avoid under- or over-charging cases.

N570 comes with nitro-cellulose grains impregnated with nitroglycerine and non-energetic additives. The result: increased muzzle velocity without increased chamber pressure and wear on the gun.

Handgun/Shotshell Powders
N310

Well-known for its accuracy and extremely clean-burning, N310 is used by pistol shooters reloading calibers from .32 S&W Long Wadcutter up to .45 ACP. N310 is a fast-burning handgun powder and popular with Bullseye pistol shooters.

N310, known as N14 back in the old days, is a single-base, tubular powder type with grain dimensions of 0.7mm in length and 0.6mm in diameter. Thanks to its small, almost symmetrical grain size, the powder flows smoothly and meters well in reloading measures. As with other N300 series powders, N310 is a porous propellant. Porosity is a crucial factor influencing powders' burn characteristics; the more porous the powder, the faster the achieved burning rate.

Use N310 for light target loads, paired with lightweight bullets, but also with heavier bullets. As a very versatile powder, it is also suitable for loading shotshells and is used by shotgun ammunition manufacturers in their premium lines with light 24-gram target loads. Many blank ammunition manufacturers also use N310.

N320

N320, formerly known as 3N22, is a fast-burning, porous handgun powder. You can load N320 in a wide range of pistol calibers from .32 to .45. Sport and hobby shooters such as Cowboy Action competitors like it. The powder type is tubular, with a grain length of 1.1mm and a diameter of 0.8mm. It includes a decoppering agent.

N32C (Tin Star)

N32C (Tin Star) is a specialized powder intended to provide low bulk density for cartridges designed for Cowboy Action Shooters requiring lead bullets for use in single-action revolvers and lever-action rifles. N32C is ideal for many of the older cartridges used in Cowboy Action shooting, such as the .38 Special, .44 Special, and .45 Colt.

The most significant benefit of N32C is its high loading volume. This porous powder fills the case much better than conventional smokeless propellants, providing the loading density needed for those classic blackpowder cartridges. Compared to N320, the case filling ratio can be up to 50 percent higher. This characteristic also makes the powder safer to use — a reloader won't dump double or triple loads in large volume cases by accident. Tin Star gives reliable ignition in all conditions, burns clean, and leaves little fouling or residue. It meters easily, making the task of producing high-quality and uniform loads easier.

N330

N330 handgun powder provides a wide range of latitude for the handgun shooter, serving well for everything from light target to heavy high-velocity loadings. It is a versatile, medium-burning N300-series powder specially designed for 9mm Luger and suitable for .38 Special, .40 S&W, .44 S&W Special, and .45 Colt.

N340

Formerly known as 3N18, N340 is a multipurpose powder developed for 9mm and shotshell loads. It is one of the most popular powders in the N300 series. It can be used for a wide variety of calibers and bullet weights, making it the perfect partner for all kinds of reloading purposes. Handloaders mainly use it for medium- and large-caliber pistols and shotshells with medium and heavy loads.

N340 is a tubular powder type with grain dimensions of 1.0mm in length and 0.8mm in diameter. The same grain size as N320, N330, and N350, only the powder's porosity is different. The burn rate of N340 is medium, and it is extremely clean burning.

N350

As the burn rate of N350 is at the slow end of Vihtavouri's handgun powders, it is ideal for top-end velocities and energies for a broad range of pistol and revolver cartridges. N350 is widely used in pistol shooting and especially in practical shooting. N350 works excellent also in heavy shotgun loads, especially with 36-grain loads or more.

3N37

Vihtavuori's developed its 3N37 handgun powder for .22 rimfire cartridges, but it has since proven to be very versatile for all competitive handgun shooting disciplines. It is a tubular, porous powder type with grain dimensions of 0.6mm in length and a diameter of 0.6mm. The symmetrical grain size makes metering a breeze in powder measures. Its medium burn rate is like N350.

It is an excellent powder for 9mm Major loads for IPSC open competitions, and it's prevalent in USPSA and IPSC practical pistol shooting disciplines. In addition to practical shooting, 3N37 is also widely used as a submachine gun powder. It offers consistent, extreme precision, with clean-burning characteristics.

3N38

Vihtavuori's 3N38 powder is designed especially for competitive handgun shooting with high-velocity loads in 9mm and .40 S&W cartridges. It's a single-based, tubular powder type and a small granule powder (0.6mm length by 0.6mm diameter). 3N38 is popular in practical shooting, especially among IPSC and USPSA competitors. A relatively slow-burning propellant, 3N38 is a good option for making Major loads with decent accuracy potential and clean-burning characteristics.

N105 Super Magnum

N105 Super Magnum is Vihtavuori's slowest-burning pistol powder, intended for the most powerful handgun cartridges in use today, particularly with heavy bullets and large case volume. Many of these specialized rounds operate at rifle pressures. For such powerhouse calibers as the .454 Casull or .500 S&W, N105 is an excellent reloading powder choice. ⦀

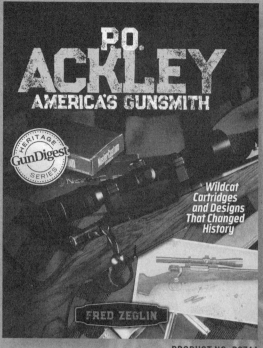